I0049749

PIETRO PARMEGGIANI

BLACK MOVES FIRST

© 2025 Pietro Parmeggiani
Black Moves First
The Science and Art of Successful Negotiation
Foreword by Santiago Lange

Edited by Agenzia Dedalo and First Editing
Editing: David Fivoli
Proofreading: Domenico Russo
Graphics and layout: Giorgia Ragona
Cover design: Sabrina van Hoften

Back cover photo: Roberto Baroncini

Negotiation Academy
www.negoziazione.academy
Negoziazione Academy is a trademark of Pietro Parmeggiani

All rights reserved
First edition April 2025

To respect the privacy of some individuals and companies, names and
identifiers have been changed in various cases.

The author has taken a sensitive and interchangeable approach to the
use of gender pronouns, using male and female pronouns indifferently
and interchangeably.

This book may be purchased in bulk for promotional, educational,
or corporate use.
Please contact **hello@negoziazione.academy**

In memory of my beloved brother Paolo

Index

Foreword

When Pietro asked me to write the foreword to his book, I immediately agreed because he is a dear friend, and I hold him in high esteem.

However, I soon realized I had a problem: his book is about negotiation. I am not a negotiator, and I hold little faith in negotiation as a philosophy of life.

I don't like to impose anything on anyone, and I have always felt that in negotiations, we try to convince the other person that things are different from what they believe.

But then I read *Black Moves First,* and I realized a few things.

First, I suffer from what Pietro identifies in the first chapter of his magnificent book as fear of, or even aversion to, negotiation.

Sometimes this is a problem, I admit. At the time of this writing, I am negotiating with my neighbors in Cabrera de Mar, the beautiful village on the outskirts of Barcelona where I live. I would love to buy their house.

They are an elderly Spanish couple, and I have an excellent relationship with them; they cared for my children when they were kids and are among the most generous and kind people I know.

The house they live in is no longer suitable for their needs, and it would be great for me to buy it because I need more space. The problem is that right now, the amount I can offer them is less than what they would like, and here we get stuck.

I don't want to offend them—they are friends. And I would never want to give the impression that I want to take advantage of them.

Reading Pietro's book, I realized that I should prepare a strategy and begin a respectful negotiation in which both sides "discuss to reach an understanding."

Negotiating skillfully does not mean screwing the other person over or taking advantage of them. It means finding the best solution to the problem (to any situation), a solution that will please everyone.

The point is that I find it challenging to deal with this conversation. That's how I am; I still have much to learn when it comes to negotiations!

I have been, and still am, the head of many sports teams whose decisions and strategies I direct.

A prime example was the period before the Rio 2016 Olympic Games, where I was to compete in the Nacra 17 mixed class of sailing together with Cecilia Carranza.

Less than one year before the Games, I had surgery for lung cancer. My slow recovery kept us out of the water for several months.

I knew we were lagging behind our competitors, so I proposed a drastic plan: to settle in Rio de Janeiro nine months before the beginning of the competition.

The idea was bold and involved much effort, as I had to convince the rest of the team—especially Cecilia, my partner on the Olympic catamaran we were competing with. Ceci hesitated, because she would have to spend a long time away from her family, and the "forced cohabitation" could wear us down.

I, however, insisted. We finally did it, and it worked: we won the gold medal!

I still remember the details of the meeting where I proposed the plan. I did not experience the process as a negotiation, but after reading Pietro's book, I realized that it was. I understood that the success of my "unconscious negotiation" was the preparation: The proposal was masterfully designed, and I was convinced it was good enough!

I firmly believe that in a high-performance team, there are indispensable values, such as preparation, hard work, dedication, commitment, honesty, and respect. All of us have a vision and methodology that we share based on these values and principles.

Of course, reading Pietro's book, I realized I could still improve my negotiations (conscious or unconscious!).

Looking back on that decision-making process (and many others), I see that I often leave little room for other team members and their ideas. I am so convinced of my vision that I tend to impose it on others, assuming all share in it, and in doing so I close myself off from the possibility of enriching it.

That's why *Black Moves First* was a great learning experience for me, as it taught me how to generate constructive and productive dialogue when pursuing a shared goal.

So, I thank Pietro and confirm that his book on negotiation is surprisingly valuable for everyone, from businesspeople to Olympians!

Santiago Lange

Introduction

This book is based on three significant truths.

First, negotiation is an art (and also a science, as we shall see) that is always useful to us. And I'm not just talking about business. We negotiate whenever we want something from someone else. Most of the time, this happens unconsciously; negotiation is not limited to the world of finance, business, or certain thriller movies where the FBI agent on duty has to free hostages held by terrorists. The truth is, we all negotiate every day, in different ways and with various goals.

Second, while each negotiation differs in purpose and importance, they're all identical in essence. Therefore, it is possible to learn how to identify situations and manage the entire process by following a precise methodology that can make every negotiation a success.

Finally, leadership often requires negotiation: good leaders are inevitably effective negotiators.

Yet most people do not negotiate as much as they could and should, and when they do, they fail to prepare properly, ultimately not achieving as much as they deserve.

Negotiating is about satisfying a need, solving a problem, and managing conflict.

Negotiating allows people to achieve what they want while giving others the same opportunity.

I emphasize that this is not a book in which an insider teaches *magic tricks* to become skillful and effective negotiators. That would be impossible, since every negotiation is unique and cannot be replicated.

Instead, this text seeks to present a method and teach a discipline. Through my decades of experience, and using numerous concrete examples, I address the entire negotiation process in depth, exploring both technical and psychological details.

In the following pages, you will not find easy shortcuts, but a method I have named *Incontro*, which will help you turn your negotiations into successes.

It is derived not from theoretical speculation, but from my personal need for growth and change. It is also suitable for any negotiation.

I am certain that if I had not decided to work on my negotiation skills, my life—both professional and personal—would have taken a drastically different course.

My method will help you save time and money, close important deals, negotiate under challenging conditions, improve working relationships, claim (and create) more value, and resolve seemingly unmanageable disputes.

By learning to negotiate, you can ask for what you need and work with others to reach win–win agreements.

You can build stronger connections with others, because negotiation is not just about closing a deal—it's about building lasting relationships.

You will also gain confidence in your ability to defend yourself and your ideas.

Now, all that remains is for me to wish you happy reading!

Pietro

There's nothing wrong with being afraid. It's okay: sometimes fear keeps us safe, sometimes it limits us.

Kerry Washington

CHAPTER 1

NEGOTIATION:
AN ESSENTIAL SKILL

The Grass Is Always Greener on the Other Side

We start with this assumption: life is negotiation.

Most of our daily interactions, whether at work or with family, boil down to expressing a simple primary impulse: *I want to*.

Let me give you some examples.

Last week, I met Giovanni Ramberti, a Swiss friend of mine. He's a real estate agent who lives and works in St. Moritz. While scrolling through his magnificent portfolio, I saw a beautiful penthouse on Dimlej Street, for which the owner *wants* 2 million Swiss francs.

While searching for the general manager of our US subsidiary, I met a candidate named Jim Ward. He made it clear that, to change jobs and lead our company, he wanted a raise in his compensation package of at least 8 percent.

My colleague Kim Raguel *wants* her daughter to complete all her homework right after lunch and before going out with friends.

In negotiation, misusing the term *I want* instead of the more appropriate *I need* is the source of multiple problems.

To uncover the real needs of our negotiating partner beyond their "stated desires," it is helpful to consider all aspects of their situation.

Here's a quick practical tip for distinguishing a negotiator's wants from their *needs*: Desires are what you are asking for—specific and measurable requests that are usually relatively rigid and expressed in black and white. For example, a request to get a product at a particular price or to order only a certain number of units.

On the other hand, a negotiator's needs are more closely related to why they are asking for what they want. These are more general and subjective.

We must never forget that we negotiate to satisfy two distinct and essential needs: influencing others' behavior, but also gathering information. We must also recognize that, in the multiple interactions of negotiation, each party wants something from the other.

Returning to Giovanni, Jim, and Kim: their careers, wealth, fame, emotional wellbeing, and so much more depend on their ability to negotiate.

And this is true not only for them. It's true for everyone.

Fear of Negotiating

The first step in handling the many negotiations one faces in daily life is to recognize and overcome the aversion to negotiation. Many people dislike negotiating; others are afraid because they cannot take the plunge and turn anxiety into confidence.

We are all fearful when it comes to negotiating.

Some people, even if they are brilliant, feel that they are not skilled negotiators, so they look for answers, methods, and pre-packaged tricks on how to negotiate, hoping such formulas will help them.

When I ask my colleagues or clients to help me understand their fears and anxieties, their answers are always fascinating. These responses offer fertile material for study, analysis, and reflection, as well as valuable insights into the topic, and potentially brilliant solutions.

Over the years, this has enabled me to develop a method that can be applied successfully to all negotiations, whatever they may be.

The method works because it was created by a street artist in the real world, where all negotiations occur. It is not the fruit of theoretical conjecture, and was not born in a university seminar room. On the contrary, it results from years of experience, reflection, and study, which have improved it to perfection—or nearly so.

We start with anxiety and fear.

Fear has many facets. There is the fear of not being up to the negotiation and coming out with "broken bones." There is the apprehension of failing to close the deal, perhaps saying or doing something wrong. There is the anxiety that the negotiation will escalate into conflict, with the potential to damage the relationship. There is the concern of paying too high a price to avoid missing out on the value at stake. There is the doubt about not having enough courage to dare and ask for more, or to raise the ante—and so much more.

I will give you an example.

It's a busy time for Matteo, the sales area manager of a leading multinational aluminum laminate processing company. It's the end of the year, Christmas is just a few weeks away, and there are a thousand things to do all at once. Matteo landed in Charlotte, North Carolina, late last night, after missing his connecting flight in New York. He is a little anxious as he eats breakfast—this is an important day. There's heavy traffic as he drives to the company where his business meeting will take place. He arrives, parks, and enters the large meeting room. White coffee with sugar, a muffin, some small talk. He is at the table with his client, a client his company has supplied for years to mutual satisfaction.

It is time to finalize the contract for next year. Customer turnover and profitability are important to Matteo's company, particularly considering the investment in and imminent commencement of the new production line, which will significantly increase production capacity. The market is growing slightly, and Matteo must take advantage of this. It would be a catastrophe if he didn't. Even stable volumes would mean a loss of market share, and a decrease in sales (even a small one) would be severe, because Matteo will not be able to sell those quantities elsewhere on equivalent terms.

On the other side of the table are the heads of various business functions at the corporate level: purchasing, supply chain, quality, and research & development. Instead of talking immediately about the contract for next year, they present some slides showing a deterioration in quality and on-time deliveries. This is nothing new; it has been a make-or-break year, and the customer is unhappy.

Matteo looks for arguments, improvises a defense, and grasps at straws, but numbers are numbers, and they're stacked against him. It's like being down by ten points in the first quarter of a football game — the outcome is still uncertain, but the pressure is on. Matteo's kick-off. Discussion moves to the coming year's business: growth prospects are attractive, and the company even seems intent on significantly increasing purchase volumes. Matteo is fascinated by the opportunities before his eyes. He's already imagining the renovations he can make to his home with the bonus he'll get from his delighted boss. In short, it's tempting to take up the challenge.

The customer, however, points out that they have two other proposals on the table that are better than Matteo's, and asks for a price reduction.

Tones become heated, and Matteo cannot find a way out. It would take a reaction—a series of responses—to get the negotiation back on track and close the deal. The problem is that the probability of failure gives him great uncertainty and generates enormous anxiety. Matteo tries to respond, but he is entirely at the mercy of the client. The client has an in-depth understanding, addresses topics logically, and makes requests in rapid sequence, to which Matteo (because of his anxieties and fears) responds with repeated concessions.

Fear at the negotiating table can happen to novices and experienced professionals alike. It matters little whether the anxiety stems from inexperience or the fear of losing a critical deal: negotiators often let emotions take over and guide their actions and reactions.

Many people are afraid to negotiate because they are insufficiently prepared, don't understand the process in its entirety, or are unfamiliar with the strategies and tactics that can and should be employed during negotiation (or when and why to use them).

It's quite simple: the **negotiation process** is the route the parties take from point A (where they are) to point B (where they want to be). The **substance**, on the other hand, is what the parties want to achieve by negotiating. Moreover, the parties themselves determine the who, where, how, and when to intervene.

As you can see, it's all straightforward—nothing complicated and nothing to fear.

Nevertheless, negotiation instills great fear. If they can, many people avoid it, not realizing that they engage in negotiation on a daily basis.

Your Half Line

Most of us engage in formal negotiations throughout our lives.

We negotiate over personal issues such as where we go on vacation, the school our children attend, and the color of our bathroom tiles. We negotiate over professional issues like the terms of a job offer, the purchase price of a facility, and setting up a contract with a new supplier.

However, there are also informal and less obvious negotiations that we take part in daily, sometimes without even realizing it.

Persuading one's children to eat vegetables and fruit, for example, is a negotiation. (Don't tell me how it turned out—I already know.) So is resolving a conflict with a colleague, or convincing a customer to accept a late delivery.

The point is that we negotiate all the time without even realizing it. We start negotiating from an early age. We negotiate with our parents when we want something they think we shouldn't have, or with a friend or sibling over a toy we covet.

As we grow up, these negotiations become more complicated and sophisticated: negotiations occur with friends, family, schoolmates, and eventually with colleagues, superiors, customers, suppliers, and shareholders.

Although these situations vary greatly throughout our lives (and from person to person), the skills and abilities needed for successful negotiation remain the same.

When asked to define negotiation, I answer, "Negotiation is a discussion aimed at reaching an agreement."

In light of this, negotiation encompasses a wide range of discussions we engage in throughout our lives (both personal and professional) with strangers and acquaintances.

Think of a horror movie. Were you scared while watching it? Did you jump out of your seat several times in the theater? Well, the good news is that negotiation isn't so scary.

Just as the terror of a horror movie fades when the lights come back on, so too must the fears you have about claiming your worth. You must be able to negotiate what you are worth or what you are proposing. And believe me, if you are prepared, it is possible.

Beneath the appearance of an inability or disinclination to negotiate lies a simple lack of self-confidence. But I assure you, becoming a better negotiator is easier than you think. First, you must identify your fears and limitations, then plan to overcome them.

I worked at Charoen Pokphand Group, a Thai conglomerate, for eight years. Whenever the CEO Marss Kuo was planning a negotiation that was in any way out of the ordinary, he'd say, "Pietro, will you help us in this negotiation?"

Marss was a true leader with uncommon skills. He had penetrating understanding, and a vision of the future that guided his decisions to promote collective welfare. His choices and actions were a continuous source of inspiration and motivation for me. I found new challenges and encouragement in his demands, but it was never a foregone conclusion that we would achieve the desired result, especially when dealing with people from unfamiliar cultures.

That experience helped me express myself in new contexts, enhance the qualities I already possessed, and acquire new ones.

Marss never showed me the route, but always suggested ways to discover it. His critical spirit pushed me to question myself and step out of my comfort zone. We negotiated together many times; he appreciated my contributions and my original approach to situations.

This ability was not a given, because no one is born a negotiator. This may not seem like good news. However, I am used to seeing the glass as half full—indeed, always a little more than half full—so I also have a positive spin to put on this.

Over the years, as I have observed and studied my staff, my clients, and the many people I have negotiated with, I have repeatedly concluded that most people can significantly improve their negotiation skills through study, preparation, and practice.

I have followed this path over the years. It has been filled with learning, research, organizational design, preparation, application, and practice. Over time, I have developed a method that I have continued to refine, redefine, and optimize, striving for perfection.

I will never stop working on these three elements because, while the method works excellently today and I am doing well, I believe I can always do even better.

It Is Never Too Late

I have one regret: I embarked on this journey late. Or rather, I realized late how important it was to be a skillful negotiator.

How many opportunities have I left on the table, how many have I missed in negotiation, and how much extra effort have I put in to achieve the same result? How many times could I have achieved more if I had mastered the science and art of negotiation earlier?

I was an inquisitive child: I asked many questions and observed with interest the behavior of people older than me.

As I grew up, my curiosity turned into "professional curiosity."

I began to study and delve deeper into the subject, trying to understand the winning techniques and strategies to get the most out of each negotiation.

At first, I thought I was an experienced negotiator; however, I realized that, while the way I handled negotiations to a T sometimes allowed me to achieve the desired results, I needed more consistency. So I challenged myself, improving my negotiation skills and my ability to actively listen, understand the other party's needs, and identify points of agreement.

My method is now sound and practical. I got great results, learning to negotiate constructively. You, too, can benefit from these techniques and achieve your goals, in both your personal and professional life. Learning to negotiate is a fundamental skill for anyone who wants to succeed: knowing how and when to deal can make the difference between success and failure. So don't hesitate to invest time and resources in improving your negotiation skills.

Mastering negotiation can lead to improvements in every aspect of your life.

Better Not to Sit at the Table

Although you may come to love negotiation immensely and feel increasingly tempted to negotiate at every available opportunity, remember that sometimes it is preferable to walk away, accepting what is offered, rather than spend too much time and effort trying to secure the best deal possible.

Knowing how to negotiate is one thing. Knowing when to negotiate—and more importantly, when *not to*—is an entirely different matter. I value my time, so I assign an hourly rate to remind myself of this, and to avoid the temptation to negotiate unnecessarily.

The global law firm I use charges hourly rates of €900 for the managing partner level, and lower rates for the partner, legal director, and others. They are skilled, professional, and competent—the best among the legal teams I have dealt with.

When my staff members present me with invoices for legal fees for payment approval, I experience a few moments of bewilderment and some perplexity. But even though they are steep, I never even think about negotiating them.

I apply the same logic: if the total cost (time spent negotiating multiplied by the hourly rate) is greater than the expected benefit, I do not negotiate.

Of course, I am not referring to flea markets, tourist souvenir shops, and street vendors, where the price tag is there to be negotiated. In such cases, bargaining is accepted—even expected—and the process often ends in a compromise between the merchant's commercial ambitions and the tourist's goal of making a bargain.

In the real world, modern retail stores, such as those in shopping malls, do not involve negotiation.

I also avoid negotiating when my **leverage** is weak. Leverage refers to the power one party in a negotiation has with which to influence the other party to move closer to their own position.

Let me give you an example.

It is 1990, and I have recently started working at Proxima, a software consulting company.

On the eve of my thesis defense at the University of Bologna, I was traveling to meet an important client on the outskirts of Lyon.

My car breaks down. I call roadside assistance, and my vehicle is towed to the nearest service center. The gruff mechanic informs me that my *bécane* (loosely translated as "banger") is in bad shape and will take at least two days to repair due to the complexity of the issue.

I plead with the mechanic and explain my circumstances, but there is nothing to be done: I must find an alternative. I am in a difficult situation. Tomorrow morning, I need to be in Bologna to graduate, and I am stranded. The garage offers to call a cab, which will charge the equivalent of €250 to take me to the nearest airport—a steep price, but I have no choice.

In this case, I agreed. I needed to return to Italy as soon as possible and had no alternative but to accept the cab. The taxi driver knew I was desperate. In short: I had zero leverage.

Also, remember that it is never worth negotiating when the negotiation sends the wrong signal. For instance, imagine you are early in your career, and your boss—who holds you in high regard—asks you to work on a crucial presentation over the weekend.

If you were to request something in return, you might come across as ungrateful, since your boss has trusted you with an important task.

There are also cases where negotiating is culturally inappropriate. For example, as mentioned earlier, you do not negotiate prices in shopping mall stores. This principle also applies when dealing with people from other countries and cultures, which is why it is crucial to research in advance **whether** and **under what circumstances** negotiation is acceptable.

Always remember that the negotiating norms of other countries and cultures may differ from those of your own. You could embarrass yourself (and them) by attempting to negotiate when it is inappropriate to do so.

Another situation in which negotiating is pointless is when your best alternative far exceeds any possible outcome of a negotiated agreement. When this is the case, it's simply a waste of time to negotiate.

Negotiation Technology

Negotiation is often seen as a game in which two or more participants enter into competition. In negotiation training courses, participants consistently demonstrate a strong desire to learn the "winning trick" that will knock out their counterpart, conclude the negotiation, and close the deal.

Sorry to disappoint you: there are no tricks, only skills. It is best to be clear: mine is a methodical, structured, and precise approach. It is a system for negotiating successfully.

I have called it *Incontro*, and it involves seven steps to arrive at a successful negotiation. It consists of successive related events. In some cases, the time between events is minimal, and in others, more time passes. I have put this system together so that even busy people can easily benefit from it. The method is a result of study, humility, and ethics, as well as constant motivation to improve and grow.

Making this system one's own implies becoming aware of one's weaknesses without devaluing oneself.

The fact that there are seven stages is no accident: in many cultures, the number seven indicates completeness. In the dream world, seven represent success, inner enrichment, personal growth, wisdom, and achievement.

Does *Incontro* always work? If followed precisely, yes. If not, the process does not give the expected result. It works because it is well articulated and includes principles, tools, and recommendations for each step. By following this method, you can get the best results through the power of negotiation.

Incontro is a passion, because it requires from those who want to apply it at least as much love as I put into building it, modifying it, testing it, and perfecting it.

Now it's your turn to make it your own and take full advantage of it, putting that same passion into it.

The seven stages of *Incontro* are:
1. To negotiate or not to negotiate
2. Preparation and planning
3. Discussion, proposal, negotiation
4. Agreement
5. Debrief
6. Follow-up
7. Archiving

The activities of the first stage of the process may seem trivial or obvious. However, it is imperative to be clear about them, if only to avoid wasting time in situations in which it is better not to negotiate. Indeed, such situations may have happened to you, and if they haven't, believe me when I say they could, potentially with painful consequences.

Evaluating whether or not to negotiate can also be connected to the second stage. Let me explain: if you have not taken the time to prepare and plan, or you are dissatisfied with your level of preparation, it is better to assess the situation and consider not negotiating.

Additionally, I refuse to negotiate when the person sitting at the table lacks the authority to close a deal, when the other party is negotiating in bad faith or using unethical tactics, or when I have reached my lower limit on one or more points, and further "downward movement" would put me or my company in a difficult position.

In my experience, 80 percent of the success of a negotiation depends on the second stage (Preparation and Planning). The more complex the negotiation, the more thorough this stage needs to be.

As a sportsman and strong advocate of training, I firmly believe you train before the game, not during it. A good negotiation plan is based on carefully prepared, studied, and chosen strategies, as well as on adapting tactics to new challenges.

Preparation is based on research and intelligence, not guesswork or assumptions. For example, preparing for a negotiation with compatriots is one thing, but it can be completely different when closing a business deal with partners from other cultures or countries. Thorough preparation in advance can help prevent difficulties.

So, **remember**: the earlier you prepare, the more likely you are to anticipate problems that could hinder a successful negotiation.

The third stage (Discussion, Proposal, Negotiation) is "pure negotiation." During the discussion, both sides present their specific situations and cases. Asking the right questions is crucial to understanding the fundamental interests of the other party, just as it is equally important to listen carefully to their responses. This is followed by the presentation of offers and proposals for a possible agreement, which are reviewed and adjusted in search of the most compelling proposition that includes mutual benefits aligned with the parties' common interests.

The next stage (Agreement) occurs when the parties reach an understanding. This stage should not be overlooked, as it is often a source of misunderstanding. I always suggest summarizing the essential elements of the agreement, going into detail if necessary to prevent future disputes that might arise after the meeting.

The fifth phase (Debrief) consists of a post-negotiation evaluation. It is a vital practice to undertake regardless of the outcome—whether positive or negative—and whether you conducted the negotiation alone or as part of a team. This phase allows for revisiting the highlights of the process, analyzing them from various perspectives, capturing nuances of what transpired, and providing a deeper understanding of what went differently than expected and why.

The penultimate stage (Follow-up) is perhaps the most underestimated. Even after completing the negotiation (which is a central and critical part of the process), it is not truly complete without follow-up activities. Failure to perform these steps risks wasting all your negotiation efforts.

In addition to creating a detailed list of follow-up activities, it is important to specify who will carry them out, ensuring tasks are assigned to responsible individuals and given clear deadlines.

The seventh and final stage (Archiving) involves creating an archive to systematically record your negotiations.

I recommend using keywords and organizing the archive into sections that detail the tactics used and which include comments on the negotiations. This archive will prove invaluable for extracting quick insights and serve as a resource for future discussions.

Minimal Errors, Maximum Success

Mistakes in negotiation can have profound financial and strategic consequences, as they can jeopardize the outcome of a deal, impact professional careers, and ruin established relationships.

Before refining my method and **negotiation routine**, how often did I avoid a negotiation? How often did I leave more on the table than I had to? How many times did I feel forced to give in?

Before negotiating became a habit, I thought negotiation was a contest, with winners and losers.

Although I was always meticulous in my approach, I still needed to prepare correctly, spending more time to clarify the goal I wanted to achieve. Even though I was familiar with the subject of the negotiation and the discussion that would take place, my abilities would only come through sporadically. Sometimes I would negotiate so poorly that the negotiating partner would not take me seriously and take advantage of me. I remember that I was often too greedy, because I wanted to overdo it, as if I were playing Hearts. I always wanted all the no-points cards for myself—the ace, king, queen, and jack, and the diamonds and clubs—and, not satisfied, I would "shoot the moon."

I had yet to realize that achieving a good result means finding an agreement with a slight disparity that gives us a small advantage. Too big of a difference never leads to lasting and satisfactory arrangements for all negotiating partners. Sometimes I needed to negotiate more because I did not highlight my needs, interests, and expectations. I did not state my needs well enough when I came to the negotiating table, and as a result, I needed to listen carefully to the needs of the negotiating partner.

I used to focus almost exclusively on price. Price is of course an essential element, but often only one factor that needs to be considered. I used to focus on this variable exclusively, discussing price alone at length, without thinking about the possibility of leveraging other elements as well, especially when I could not achieve what was the correct monetary value for a service or product.

I was rigid. I was inflexible. I was uncreative.

Sometimes I should have considered all possible elements. Sometimes I thought some points were unavoidable, even when they were not.

This rigidity has placed me in many difficult situations. I remember often saying, "This point is off the table, not even up for discussion," when I should have taken a different approach, as everything is negotiable.

So many times, I have been aggressive and overbearing, even resorting to classic phrases like, "This is my best and final offer!"—only to trigger an immediate breakdown in discussions and negotiations. Inevitably, I would contradict myself shortly after with a further price drop or an additional concession.

Had I been a hostage negotiator, their deaths might weigh on my conscience today, as I used to be impatient and made no effort to hide it. I would set deadlines when my negotiating partner stalled, and I would often settle for any agreement—even unfavorable ones for me or my company—just to end the standoff. Sometimes I feared saying the wrong thing; other times, I felt uncomfortable asking for what I needed, bargaining, rejecting offers, or pushing back. I worried that discussions might escalate into arguments or lead to embarrassing situations.

In short, I was afraid to negotiate. My fear of conflict and inability to create optimal conditions for an open discussion meant I struggled to clearly and calmly state the boundaries I was willing to accept and the limits I refused to cross.

Today, I realize that I often approached negotiations with a fixed mindset, focused solely on achieving my goals without considering alternative plans for when things didn't go as expected. I rarely asked myself whether there was a reasonable outcome I could accept if my initial goals failed. What opportunities might I seize if my primary objective couldn't be reached? I didn't ask. My vision was too rigid, and I failed to explore viable alternatives.

Looking back, I see that I should have spent more time building relationships with my negotiating partners. I was too preoccupied with the end goal and didn't make an effort to better understand the people I was dealing with.

Had I invested time in meaningful conversations with them, I would have gained deeper insights into their interests, goals, expectations, and concerns. This could have fostered trust and mutual respect.

I've come to understand that successful negotiation hinges on one critical element: communication. I mistakenly believed that communication was mainly about talking. In reality, I should have prioritized listening and empathy—key tools for uncovering the true interests and motivations of the other party.

Throughout my professional experience and daily life, I've engaged in countless negotiations—whether in union talks, company matters, or dealings with partners, coworkers, customers, and suppliers. Yet, the results often felt unsatisfactory. I struggled and sensed something was missing— something deeper than just the exchange of words or ideas. I realized that to achieve truly successful outcomes, I needed to shift my approach, and that's when the importance of preparation became evident.

Preparing for Ambitious Goals

A project needed to be included in my strategy for success.

In sports, possessing a sense of limits is beneficial—perhaps even healthy. It represents an ongoing commitment to push boundaries, a promise to pursue ambitious projects, victories, and even learn from defeats. Similarly, in negotiation, recognizing our own limits and the limits of the situation is crucial. But once those limits are acknowledged, the real challenge lies in preparing for more ambitious goals—setting objectives that stretch our capabilities and force us to adapt, grow, and collaborate effectively.

Sometimes people confuse competitive activity with training, but as a sportsman, I have always sought the latter. Over time, I realized I needed to apply the same approach to negotiation. I decided to study, prepare, and practice. I learned from the best, and piece by piece, with modesty, humility, and perseverance, I reached a point where I could negotiate with enjoyment.

Now, I prepare carefully for negotiations: I gather all relevant information, set a shared agenda, and devote thought to the venue for the meeting. I establish a positive relationship with my negotiating partner to understand their interests and needs. During negotiations, I focus on both tangible and intangible elements, using creativity while avoiding rigidity or ultimatums. Thanks to this preparation, I can confidently approach bargaining, even when my expectations are ambitious, knowing that conflict can be minimized.

I now handle negotiations calmly, whether in my personal or professional life. Every day, countless negotiations arise: deciding what to buy, how much to pay, where to go, what to do, solving problems, agreeing on requirements, or securing resources. My "toolbox" is equipped with everything I need to achieve the best possible results while continuing to develop my skills and reap the rewards of successful negotiations.

By improving my negotiation skills, I've enhanced the efficiency and effectiveness of the entire process. Today, I can recognize situations clearly and define paths to success, achieving win–win results in both informal peer agreements and more formal negotiations.

I find fulfillment in knowing that each time I prepare for a negotiation, I am working toward success, not failure. I approach it with commitment and passion, applying my methods with the confidence that they can improve my life.

I am certain that you, too, have thought, "I'd like to improve my negotiation skills." I know this because I've heard it from so many people who feel frustrated about their abilities and want to improve but don't know where to start. Many mistakenly believe that negotiation is an innate talent requiring drastic changes to master, when the reality is a different matter entirely.

If you want to become a skilled negotiator, understand that there is a direct relationship between **your actions** and the **results** you achieve.

I recommend following my method. Although it may seem difficult at first, with time, you can elevate your negotiations to an advanced level. You'll need to work on yourself and learn to observe others. This will require effort, but the results will be rewarding and will last a lifetime. What you become in the process is far more important than what you achieve, because it will be yours forever, and no one can take it away.

I often ask myself **Who am I becoming?** rather than **What am I achieving?**

There are days when progress feels small, but the size of the change doesn't matter. What matters is that it happens consistently. Each small change builds on the last and makes future improvements easier. With each step, your confidence grows, bringing you closer to becoming a better negotiator. Each success reinforces your belief in your ability to negotiate effectively and achieve your goals.

You might worry that you're not good enough, especially if past attempts have been unsuccessful, but there's no need for fear. Often, the problem isn't a lack of ability but insufficient training.

Improvement brings awareness, and success is a state of mind. Once you accept this, you'll realize that if you choose a path, you can walk it all the way to your goal.

How often have you thought about improving but done nothing? This can make you feel incapable and helpless. When you desire something but don't work for it, you place your goal on a pedestal, making it seem unreachable.

However, when you decide to change, improve, and take action, you train yourself to trust in your abilities. Even achieving small goals can spark the engine of change. Starting down a new path may be challenging at first, but with persistence, it becomes easier over time.

The best way to do something is simply to do it! Life is a constant negotiation with ourselves and others, and we are surrounded by opportunities to negotiate every day, everywhere. Observing the world around us offers countless lessons, and there is always something new to learn. So, instead of standing still, take that first step toward the change you desire.

If you are willing to listen without prejudice and observe without judgment, opening your mind to the signs around you, you will always learn something. I've embraced this mindset and continue to practice it: always observing my surroundings, the people I'm with, and the situations I encounter. There is no "perfect" time, company, or place to learn, grow, and improve—just do it.

At present, I am observing two people discussing business in the Lufthansa lounge in Frankfurt, adopting the same level of interest as my company's human resources manager during an interview with a potential candidate—or as my architect during a visit to the construction site of a property I am renovating. Daily life itself is a source of learning. Life gives us lessons; it is up to us to recognize and absorb them. I have learned a great deal from others. People should not only be observed and admired but also imitated, for even the most experienced among us was once a beginner.

The fact that you are reading this book demonstrates your desire to change and improve. Together, we will turn words into action. There will be no room for regrets, fears, difficulties, or failures. Like so many others, you want to learn to negotiate because you believe you deserve more or wish to make every negotiation successful. You may not realize it yet, but your learning journey has already begun. To truly improve, however, you must adopt my method and make it a healthy habit.

When asked about the most important factor in successful negotiation, I respond without hesitation: "Having a method." And remember, age does not matter—you can become a skilled negotiator at any stage of life.

Why wait to acquire skills you can use for the rest of your life? By starting now, you can improve steadily over time. Everyone who has embarked on this journey has achieved remarkable results. All you need to do is take the first step. Put aside the fear of not being good enough—lack of courage is the most common excuse for those unable to change their lives. However, missed opportunities, both now and in the future, cannot be justified by lack of courage alone.

I can help you, because what holds you back is not fear but your ambition to succeed.

When you fail to accomplish something within your capabilities, you might think the problem is a lack of desire or motivation. However, in most cases, the real issue lies in not knowing the proper method. Personally, I believe motivation is a false problem; with the right method, you can act consistently and effectively.

Trust me, because this is the only tool that truly works. It is rooted in you and the skills you need to bring about meaningful change in your life. Our goal is to succeed in negotiation, and I will guide you with the right method to facilitate this process.

The Force of Habit

Over the years, I have worked with many people and companies, helping them negotiate. Although they are not celebrities like Roger Federer, Tim Cook, or Elon Musk, I have worked with equally extraordinary people. Regardless of their fame or the size of their companies, I have always given my best to help my clients maximize their potential, and the people and organizations I have worked with have been equally deserving of success. Together, we have navigated wins and losses, building trusting relationships that have grown stronger over time.

The greatest credit for these victories belongs to my clients, who successfully applied the negotiation method I shared with them and tailored it to their unique needs. By doing so, they were able to handle unpredictable negotiation scenarios and achieve their desired outcomes. They followed a method, a structured routine, and a flexible procedure that could adapt to each case—even when unforeseen challenges arose during negotiations.

My method is rooted in preparation—extensive preparation. It is in dealing with unforeseen situations that preparation and technique make the biggest difference. One of the most common topics I discuss is career and salary negotiation. With over two decades of experience conducting job interviews across three continents, I have observed that only three out of five people negotiate their salaries, one out of five does so inconsistently, and one out of five surprisingly never negotiates at all. Additionally, during performance evaluations, nearly half of employees fail to discuss the possibility of a raise. Linda Babcock conducted a study of the starting salaries of master's graduates and found that men earned 7.6 percent more than women, almost $4,000 more on average (Babcock and Laschever 2003). To explain the gap, she looked at negotiation rates and found that 57 percent of men negotiated their salaries, compared to only 7 percent of women, despite advice from the university's career services to negotiate.

Those who did negotiate, mostly men, increased their starting salaries by an average of 7.4 percent ($4,053), suggesting that the gender pay gap could have been closed if more women had negotiated their offers. Even a modest 7 percent raise at the start of a career can lead to significant differences by retirement.

Consider this example: You and a colleague both start with a salary of €100,000 per year. Your colleague negotiates a 7 percent raise, increasing their salary to €107,000. Assuming similar opportunities for promotions and raises, to match your colleague's retirement wealth, you would need to work an additional eight years. While eight years may seem like a small amount of time early in your career—since retirement feels distant and the focus is on immediate goals—by the time you're approaching the later stages of your career, those extra years of work become increasingly significant. At that point, you realize how much those missed opportunities have cost you, but unfortunately, they cannot be reclaimed.

In summary, salary negotiation is a crucial aspect of professional life, particularly for women. Even a small raise can have a lasting impact, contributing to greater financial security in the future.

Fortunately, times are changing, and there is growing awareness among women about the importance of negotiating. While progress is being made, wage increases still tend to favor men. Regardless of your gender or career stage—whether you are starting your first job or navigating your fifth—learning to negotiate is vital.

I am here to guide you with practical tips to prepare effectively. My method applies to all types of negotiations, including job interviews and performance reviews. Fear often holds people back from asking for more, particularly in salary negotiations. However, I firmly believe that salary negotiation should not be intimidating. My clients often share the feeling that *not* negotiating is far scarier than trying to do so.

When facing their first job interview, many young people are understandably concerned about salary discussions. Preparation is key. Even seasoned professionals who have worked for years and changed jobs multiple times can feel anxious when negotiating salary. My advice is to always approach these situations with a clear figure in mind. Without one, you risk being at the mercy of an experienced HR manager who can control the conversation.

I frequently use the term "tare," referring to the adjustment needed to align with realistic expectations. Research the salary range for your role and seniority level, along with other key parameters like industry standards, geographic location, company size, and job responsibilities to understand your market value. Having this benchmark, which also takes into account your education, experience, and the demand for your skillset, is essential for positioning yourself effectively.

Always aim for the upper end of the range—or slightly above. This is important for two reasons: first, there is nothing wrong with asking for a higher salary; second, employers almost always negotiate downward. You need room to maneuver to secure a satisfactory outcome. Avoid being excessive, though. If your demand seems unrealistic, your counterpart may assume you lack basic knowledge of the market

Every number carries psychological significance. For example, numbers ending in zero or five are often seen as placeholders or approximations, inviting negotiation. In contrast, specific numbers suggest seriousness and deliberation. For instance, instead of asking for €55,000, request €56,000. Avoid overly precise figures, like €55,400, as they can seem arbitrary and detract from your credibility. A specific but reasonable figure conveys confidence and determination, making it more likely that you will receive a final offer closer to your expectations.

In salary negotiations, preparation, strategy, and precision are key to achieving success. By following these principles, you can approach negotiations with confidence and secure outcomes that align with your goals.

Having a specific number in mind is not enough. Presenting yourself convincingly and demonstrating your value as an employee are also crucial. When negotiating a pay raise, thorough preparation is essential. I suggest creating a list of your merits and accomplishments, highlighting your skills, and detailing the value you bring to the company. Testimonials from clients or colleagues, as well as strong references, can further support your case. In my experience, negotiating on Thursdays can increase your chances of success. People tend to be more rigid and less accommodating early in the week but become more flexible and open toward the end. Thursday and Friday mornings are particularly favorable, since most people want to wrap up their work before the weekend.

When negotiating salary for a new job, the company or recruiter may ask for your current salary and possibly even a copy of your pay slip for verification. In such cases, it's essential to be honest. Provide your actual salary, including benefits and bonuses, but quickly steer the conversation toward your experience, skills, and market value. This approach allows you to emphasize your potential and desire for professional growth.

In negotiation jargon, the first number mentioned is known as the "anchor." This is the most critical, because it sets the parameters for the rest of the conversation. If the anchor is too low, the final offer will likely fall short of your expectations. For this reason, you should always aim to be the first to mention a number, thereby controlling the anchor. Additionally, always ask for more than you want. Research in psychology shows that your negotiating partner is more likely to feel satisfied if they believe they've successfully negotiated down from your initial request. Don't be afraid to aim high: the worst that can happen is a counteroffer, while the worst outcome of not negotiating is receiving nothing extra at all.

The first offer plays into two fundamental psychological principles: **comparison** and **reciprocity**. When you present an ambitious but reasonable offer, your negotiating partner may feel relieved and more inclined to negotiate or accept it if they see a realistic prospect of agreement. If you later modify your offer by making a concession, they will perceive it as fair in comparison to the original request, leaving them with a sense of satisfaction because they feel they've secured a better deal. This works on the principle of comparison, where people assess outcomes by comparing them to other available alternatives.

By starting with an ambitious offer, you can also leverage the principle of reciprocity. For example, if you initially propose 100 and your negotiating partner refuses, you can make a significant concession to ninety. This act creates a sense of obligation on their part to meet you halfway or reciprocate in some way.

Avoid stating ranges, like, "I would like a salary between 45,000 and 50,000." Doing so signals that you're open to concessions, and your negotiating partner will likely focus on the lower figure. Instead, shift the discussion away from your current earnings and focus on what the market is paying for someone with your skills and experience—your **market value**.

Sharing personal needs during a negotiation, such as increased childcare costs or a partner's job loss, can be a mistake. This information might be used against you. If the other party knows your vulnerabilities, they can exploit them to their advantage. For example, if they know you desperately need a job, they may offer you a lower salary than you could otherwise negotiate. Similarly, if they're aware of your financial struggles, they might propose a deal that pressures you to compromise on other important issues.

To conclude, successful negotiation requires a combination of preparation, strategic anchoring, and maintaining professionalism. Focus on your value, avoid unnecessary disclosures, and leverage the psychological principles of comparison and reciprocity to achieve the best possible outcome.

There Is No One Size Fits All

In general, it is better to keep your personal needs and emotions out of the negotiation; instead, focus your attention on the concrete interests and goals you want to achieve with the agreement.

This way, you can make more rational decisions and secure a beneficial deal without exposing your private life.

When we receive an offer, there's often a strong urge to respond immediately. However, I suggest taking your time and remaining silent. Often, just a few seconds of silence will prompt the negotiating partner to improve their offer. This approach may seem counterintuitive, because it involves resisting instinctive reactions, but negotiation is inherently complex. I have worked to make it easier, and the good news is that the more you practice, the easier it becomes. Even better, applying my method will not only simplify the process but also improve your results.

I have found great satisfaction in various areas of negotiation, particularly in managing family conflicts. These are frequent, inevitable, and something we've all experienced at some point. It is essential to recognize conflicts, learn how to manage them, and approach them as opportunities for growth, collaboration, and resolution, rather than merely as clashes or disputes.

The family serves as a kind of training ground for conflict resolution, as it is a natural arena for relational, generational, and even external conflicts. In the family, we learn from a young age to manage differences, appreciate diverse perspectives, and build stronger relationships. These skills become part of our physical and psychological makeup, shaping how we interact in all areas of life, including the workplace.

At work, I often advocate for a creative approach to negotiation. Creativity can be a game-changer, especially in business deals where economic value alone may not suffice. Creativity involves uncovering hidden opportunities within challenges and reimagining possible solutions.

Humans tend to approach negotiations by focusing solely on their own needs, often ignoring the needs of the other party. However, considering both sides' needs increases the likelihood of reaching mutually beneficial outcomes. Complicating matters further are emotions, which can stifle creativity. Anger, in particular, is a major obstacle. It often stems from fear or a lack of confidence, and is by nature self-centered. Emotional outbursts tend to escalate conflicts rather than resolve them. Improving your ability to manage negative emotions, especially anger, is a decisive step toward more creative and successful negotiation.

Another limitation in negotiation is the inability to fully assess current realities and foresee potential developments. As you gain confidence through practice, you'll find it easier to turn challenges into opportunities. This confidence will allow you to focus on solving problems rather than disputes, negative emotions, or excessively competitive tactics. The next time emotions threaten to derail a negotiation, channel your energy into creative problem-solving—it will help meet both your own needs and those of your negotiating partner.

Over the past twenty-five years, I have regularly negotiated with large multinational companies. I recall Jacques Lalauze of Gemplus (now part of the Thales Group) telling me upon his retirement that he always admired my creativity and ability to generate new ideas during negotiations.

Another area of expertise for me has been mergers and acquisitions. These transactions, involving the union of two or more companies or the acquisition of one by another, may seem daunting due to their complexity and high stakes. My initial involvement in this field came out of necessity in 2003 when a French group acquired the company I was managing. Since then, I have handled acquisitions directly a few times and supported many more as an advisor during preparatory and negotiation stages.

Contrary to popular belief, mergers and acquisitions are not as complicated as they seem. While the financial stakes are high, the principles of negotiation remain the same. The key to success lies in applying a clear method.

Here's a secret: negotiating a child's curfew on a Saturday night can be more challenging than negotiating an acquisition!

In mergers and acquisitions, people often focus solely on the purchase price, overlooking the equally important task of risk-sharing, which is addressed during final contract negotiations. To simplify the process, I recommend drafting key terms early in the negotiation. These should include the purpose of the agreement, timing, performance expectations, price, payment terms, and any other critical elements. This method ensures shared understanding, demonstrates commitment, and establishes ground rules for future discussions.

While some professionals skip this step and proceed directly to due diligence and final contracts, I assure you that investing time in drafting a well-structured negotiating proposal saves both time and money. I learned this firsthand during a negotiation with Dai Nippon in Japan, where we were negotiating a major contract for printing supplies. By carefully outlining the terms in a well-structured proposal, I was able to address key points early on and avoid misunderstandings later. This method proved so effective that it has become an indispensable part of my approach, delivering reliable results ever since.

The way key terms are negotiated has significant consequences for both the seller and the buyer. On one hand, the seller risks leaving substantial economic value on the table and undermining the terms of the strategic agreement. On the other hand, the buyer may find themselves locked into situations that require review during the drafting of the final contract, potentially exposing them to constraints that limit their ability to walk away from the deal.

Using negotiating leverage at different stages of the deal to strengthen one's position is a prime example of how an effective method can make a difference. A critical aspect of negotiating pivotal terms is understanding how leverage shifts as the deal cycle progresses. The seller typically holds the most leverage during the arrangement of the key terms, as they can capitalize on the competitive tension generated by interest from multiple buyers. However, from that point onward, the seller's leverage begins to decrease, while the buyer's leverage tends to increase.

Once the key terms are agreed on, the seller often enters exclusive negotiations with a single buyer (or, in some cases, two). This reduces the competitive tension mentioned earlier, further shifting the balance of leverage toward the buyer.

Going Beyond the Obvious

Is there a way to optimize an already concluded agreement? Is it possible to improve a completed negotiation or even a signed contract?

It's common to assume that the answer to these questions is, "No."

I used to think this way too, until I learned otherwise. Negotiation is often viewed as mere bargaining or haggling, but it is actually a creative problem-solving process.

I firmly believe the goal of negotiation is not just to reach an agreement but to find a solution that best satisfies both your own needs and those of your negotiating partner. For example, in 2014, I helped a client negotiate the purchase of an industrial property exceeding 10 hectares.[1]

After a long and exhausting legal dispute, the buyer and seller—both stubborn entrepreneurs—set aside their lawyers, appraisers, and the court to reach an agreement. On a Friday morning, I met with the CEO and CFO, who were thrilled about the deal they had just finalized. They had purchased the property from the owner (who was also a neighbor) at a reasonable price, and secured a discount on some services the owner provided.

Although the agreement was formalized and all parties were satisfied, I asked them if they had considered exploring the possibility of improving it. My question left them stunned. They were happy with the outcome and didn't see why further improvement was necessary. I then challenged them with open-ended questions that required creative thinking:

"What options haven't been discussed yet?"

"How much value could we generate if we added them?"

"What would we be missing if we failed to become if we found a mistake?"

---

1   10 hectares is approximately 24.7 acres.

These questions hit the mark, sparking their imagination and creativity. I could see from their expressions that new ideas were taking shape. Intentionally, I refrained from providing solutions.

The following Monday, they called to request a meeting, having spent the weekend brainstorming. During our meeting, they shared their ideas, and together we developed and refined additional proposals to maximize the deal's value. These included a larger initial payment to address the seller's treasury needs, improved property boundaries, and an adjusted allocation of energy usage based on time slots—benefiting both parties significantly. By focusing on maximizing value, they transformed a good deal into a great one.

This opportunity for optimization is often overlooked. Many people miss the chance to elevate an agreement to its full potential. When I suggest renegotiating an existing deal, I often encounter skepticism, as people assume it's too complex. But it's not. The hardest part—reaching the initial agreement—has already been accomplished. By this stage, the pressure has eased, and new opportunities can emerge.

So, what's the secret? Ask simple, thought-provoking questions to unlock complex problems.

What's the risk? There's virtually none. If you discover no additional value, you still have a solid agreement in place.

Whenever I advise clients to renegotiate, I stress the importance of reassuring their negotiating partner that this is not about reneging on previous agreements. On the contrary, the goal is to enhance the deal for the benefit of both parties. It's crucial to convey that the existing agreement is satisfactory in its current form, and the intent is to explore opportunities for mutual improvement. The key is to emphasize that any new agreement will only move forward if it benefits both sides equally.

Preparation is critical. I always recommend coming to the table with a few preliminary ideas, even if they aren't perfect. Initial suggestions can serve as a springboard for generating better ones, turning the renegotiation into a collaborative process—a "ping-pong match" of problem-solving.

To succeed, you need to encourage everyone involved to think differently. Many people don't realize there's a more creative and fulfilling way to negotiate—one that can yield better results for everyone involved!

Your Power to Choose

My mother had the privilege of knowing the fascinating American businesswoman Mary Kay Ash. She had a powerful impact on my mother, as evidenced in her frequent quotation of one of Ash's ideas: "There are three kinds of people in this world: those who make things happen, those who watch things happen, and those who wonder what happened. We all have a choice. You can decide which type you want to be."

Like Mary Kay Ash, I have always chosen to be in the first group. I want to invite you to join it as well—and to feel the same regret I once felt: realizing too late how important it is to become a skilled negotiator, both in personal and professional life.

How many opportunities have I let slip through my fingers? How many times have I failed to maximize the potential of a negotiation? How much energy have I wasted to achieve the same results, over and over again? And how often has this happened to you?

It's happened to me—and likely to you as well.

In those moments of indecision, when we're stuck at an impasse, we often postpone action to what I call an "infinite tomorrow." This happens every time we face a critical decision— one that feels difficult or impossible to undo. In such moments, what exactly are you focusing on? The potential gain? Or the possible loss?

It's not entirely your fault. The human mind—still a mystery in many ways—is wired to be more sensitive to loss than to gain. This perceptual distortion, known as **loss aversion**,[2] can unconsciously influence our decisions if we don't understand and manage it properly.

2　　The concept of loss aversion in behavioral economics has been studied extensively by psychologists Daniel Kahneman and Amos Tversky (1982).

When you're in a negotiation and focus solely on what you might lose, you remain trapped in a present that's already part of the past. You do nothing to create your future.

Objectively, risk exposes us to fear. Yet, it also triggers an emotional wave that facilitates learning and growth. Taking risks makes life far less tedious and is a remarkable source of growth. Remember, we are biologically designed to take risks, learn, and evolve. Think about how much you've learned each time you made a choice and risked losing something. The emotions tied to those moments etched valuable lessons within you—lessons no one can take away.

This doesn't mean you should pursue every wild idea without adequate information or an understanding of the consequences. Doing so might leave you dreading your boss's reaction—or worse, facing a "friendly" dismissal letter.

Do you think it's time to learn how to recognize and manage risks, fears, and emotions? You could delay addressing the problem, but doing so acknowledges its existence. That makes you a worried procrastinator who avoids action—someone who will have to face the issue eventually.

In our fast-paced, ever-changing world, clinging to the status quo is harmful. No matter what you say or tell yourself, actions speak louder than words. Unfortunately, many people are content with the status quo and overlook incredible opportunities because they fail to recognize them.

When I understood the importance of being a skillful negotiator, I assigned this goal a sense of **urgency**. Using the logic of emergency room triage, I labeled it Level 2 urgency. It wasn't a Level 1 emergency—a situation threatening immediate harm to vital functions. But it was more pressing than a Level 3 deferable emergency, something less severe with no immediate developmental risk. Instead, it was an urgency, defined as a matter **of urgent importance**.

When people truly feel a sense of urgency, they recognize the need for immediate action—not something to schedule for later when it's convenient. Urgency means acting now and making real progress every day. Significant challenges require urgent action because they are pivotal to success, survival, winning, or losing.

A sense of urgency is like a project team meeting convened unexpectedly, where participants instinctively know the meeting's purpose is critical. It's not driven by a belief that everything is fine—or that everything is a disaster—but by the understanding that the work ahead holds immense opportunity and risk.

Urgent action arises not from complacency, anxiety, frustration, or anger but from a visceral determination to move forward—and to act now.

Final Call: The Train Is About to Depart

Once you decide to act, you are ready to follow my method, which can be applied to any negotiation or situation. It's a process where two or more negotiating partners, often with competing motivations and goals, come together to find a solution that satisfies everyone. I will help you enhance your ability to handle all kinds of scenarios, sharpening skills essential for reaching mutually beneficial agreements, such as conflict management and creative thinking. In short, I will teach you a method that enables consistent negotiation success.

Remember, meeting halfway does not necessarily mean conducting a successful negotiation, nor does reaching a compromise. Avoiding confrontation or uncomfortable situations doesn't equate to success, just as obtaining more concessions than you grant to your negotiating partner isn't a true measure of achievement.

A successful negotiation is one in which the interests of all parties are satisfied. With *Incontro*, my method, your negotiations will consistently succeed because you will achieve that satisfaction. By interests, I mean the needs, wants, goals, fears, and concerns that shape what each party hopes to achieve. Too often, we confuse demands with the reasons underlying them. For example, if you are negotiating a lease for a commercial property and request a 6+6 year term,[3] your demand is legitimized by the fact that you plan to modernize the premises, incurring significant expenses that require amortization over several fiscal years. Using my method, you will explore multiple options to meet your own interests and those of your negotiating partner.

---

3   In Italy, the 6+6 year lease is primarily used for commercial leases and is structured to provide long-term stability for both tenants and landlords in the commercial sector.

Although the negotiation may be complex, challenging, lengthy, and exhausting, you will ultimately feel satisfied. From the moment you sit down to the moment you reach an agreement, you will have created real value. You will also understand the importance of coming prepared—having developed a range of options and identifying your best alternative to a negotiated agreement (BATNA), the course of action you'll pursue if a deal cannot be reached.

This preparation enables you to achieve more satisfying outcomes than the agreement itself.

I hope you consistently reach agreements where all parties' interests align. However, when this isn't possible, you must have a strong alternative. If the best option offered by your negotiating partner is worth less than your BATNA, it's better to walk away. You'll leave the table knowing you made the right decision, as your alternative better meets your needs.

Moreover, you will learn to identify whom to negotiate with, avoiding the frustration of lengthy discussions with someone who lacks the authority to close the deal.

You will develop the ability to structure realistic agreements, understanding that a good deal is one in which each party commits to specific actions (or inactions) in a defined manner, within a set timeframe. These commitments—provide a service, pay a fee, deliver a product—must be operational, meaning they are detailed, practical, and achievable.

You'll avoid the temptation to enter seemingly advantageous yet unrealistic deals, such as agreements with a supplier who later proves unable to fulfill their obligations. These experiences often lead to regret over having negotiated under unfavorable terms.

Instead, you will recognize that a successful deal is always one in which all parties can fulfill their commitments.

You will also avoid communication mistakes, understanding that improving your communication skills will directly enhance your negotiation abilities. Discussion doesn't mean arguing or shouting—it means exchanging ideas, thoughts, and opinions. Communication is an art, one that you, too, can master to excel in any negotiation.

Your negotiating partner will only understand your thoughts and ideas if you choose to share them clearly and effectively.

You will become adept at managing relationships—an essential factor in successful negotiation. Strong relationship management will also enable you to develop new, positive relationships and even repair damaged ones. This will be possible through the deliberate use of respect, transparency, and trust—the "tools" you'll leverage to collaboratively resolve problems and build enduring partnerships.

And last but not least, you will soon get to negotiate while having fun, and have fun while negotiating!

- Negotiation is an integral part of your life, not just about the Wall Street way of business.
- In negotiation, needs are essential, and wants are optional: it is helpful to distinguish between the two.
- Negotiation is a skill you can acquire, and everyone can become a better negotiator.
- In negotiation, preparation and method overcome fear, ensuring effective handling of situations.
- Following an easy and universal method for every negotiation will lead to better results.
- Don't live with regrets: act now to improve in negotiation and not miss more opportunities.
- There is a method that is easy to follow, and applicable to every negotiation.
- Negotiation is fun and continuous learning; you will never stop learning.
- Build good habits to improve your approach consistently, every day.
- By following my advice, you will become adept at successfully structuring all kinds of negotiations.

*Of course, everything I told Rustichello
is not even half of what I saw and what happened to me.*

Marco Polo

CHAPTER 2

MY STORY

A New Adventure

"Mr. Pietro Parmeggiani, the Commission, having examined the curriculum you have completed and having evaluated your thesis, awards you a final grade of 100 out of 110.[4] By the authority vested in me by the Magnifico Rettore[5] of the University of Bologna, I proclaim you Dottore[6] in economics and business administration."

The committee chair shakes my hand as the committee members stand. I hastily say my goodbyes, starting with the customary greetings from the female professors and moving on to the co-chair.

With the seven points I received for the thesis, I had reached my final grade goal.

Finally, I greet Sandro Sandri, the professor of corporate finance, who believed in me and in the challenging and innovative thesis I had proposed to him.

I remember the sound of my footsteps on the wooden stairs

---

4   In the Italian university system, final grades are assigned on a scale of 66 to 110. The score reflects the weighted average of the exam results and the evaluation of the final paper. A score of 100 out of 110 indicates a high level of academic achievement.

5   The title *Rector Magnificus* is a Latin term used in European universities, particularly in countries such as Italy and the Netherlands, to refer to the head or president of a university. The Rector Magnificus is responsible for the academic and administrative leadership of the institution and often serves as the public face of the university during formal ceremonies and events.

6   In Italy, the title "Dottore" is formally awarded upon completion of a master's degree and is often used informally for those with that degree. This differs from the US, where "Doctor" typically refers to someone with a PhD or professional doctorate (e.g., MD).

as I left classroom five on Via Zamboni; then nothing—no party, no dinner, no bottles. Nothing. I walked home. The satisfaction of my accomplishment shielding me from the cold December wind that whistled under the porches of Via Belle Arti.

I immediately returned to the office of the company that had hired me as a management consultant a few months before graduation. I had a lot of work to do before the Christmas break, managing extremely demanding projects for some printing and publishing companies, with deadlines approaching.

Reorganization projects allowed me to immerse myself in many different realities: from small family-owned businesses to multisite conglomerates of bewildering complexity. In the initial stages, my interlocutors were the sponsors of the organizational intervention, such as owners and general managers. Working with them was an excellent opportunity to learn and grow, because I had access to numbers, market analyses, strategies, organizational models, layouts, organizational charts, job descriptions, budgets, costs, procedures, and instructions. All I had to do was ask, and I was immediately provided with numbers, details, and explanations. I was the one who decided when to shut off the flow of information that fed my curiosity and my desire to grow, to do better, and to know. I felt essential even though I was not.

Months passed quickly; projects were completed, others were assigned. I was doing well in the company because I was valued, and my work was fun. I got to travel, buy new technology that interested me, and eat in good restaurants with friends.

The companies I served were able to implement the solutions I proposed, improving their competitiveness and margins. I worked hard, and when I was assigned new project management resources, my financial situation improved.

During the week, in the long hours behind the wheel of my slightly battered white Volvo 240 SW, I had only one thought: to work in the best Italian companies in the graphic arts industry. Being in close contact with successful entrepreneurs and managers on a daily basis strengthened my desire and determination to become one of them.

"When I'm 40, I want to be the head of a good company," I used to say to myself. "I've studied what it takes to run a business, specialized in corporate finance, speak and write three languages—Italian, Spanish, and French—and I'm not bad at English either. I'm ambitious and so much more! What am I missing?"

I asked myself this same question every morning in front of the mirror, and every day I gave myself the same answer: "Nothing. I'm not missing anything."

But I was wrong, and on some level, I was aware that I was missing something. I was also aware of what I was and what I did not want to be. I had great self-awareness and an excessive tendency to focus on my inner world of thoughts, emotions, and behaviors, to which I attached great importance. I spoke little because I only listened. I impressed my interlocutors with my insight and incisiveness. But when I was encouraged to continue, I would become self-conscious and clam up.

This trait sometimes made me uncomfortable. I realized that being in the company of a taciturn individual can be unsettling for those who enjoy a chat. I often found myself lost in my own thoughts, carrying on an internal dialogue throughout the day. This introspective nature led me to withdraw from engaging with others and to limit my interactions as much as possible.

Talking about myself, my feelings, and personal matters was out of the question. I was shy and absorbed in listening to myself and the world. I preferred to be in the company of nature, especially the sea, mainly because I don't like crowds and chatter, especially when it comes from those who are unable to keep quiet.

I believed that I had no difficulty relating to others, that I was just sensitive and disinclined to making small talk. I preferred to stay in the center of my peace and let in only those who could respect my world, only those who could see the wonder of it and did not have any desire to change it.

I realized, however, that I needed to improve the "missing piece." I thought the best way to do that was to leave the gilded world of consulting, with its high salary and security of working in a well-structured company. I needed the adrenaline rush of front-line experience and selling a product—perhaps a complex one—to real-life clients, perhaps even in foreign countries!

Coincidentally, Sergio, a friend of my then-girlfriend, was looking for an export area manager to develop the digital musical instrument division. It was the perfect position. I was looking for a front-line sales role, and the technology side of the business would allow me to combine my various interests and skills. The opportunity to work with innovative products and build a division from the ground up was exciting. For the second time in my career (but sadly, not the last), I took the job without negotiating salary and began my adventure in the world of music.

No offense to music lovers, musicians, and instrument dealers, but my relationship with active music-making (i.e., creating music, not just listening to it) has always been terrible; I might even call it a "hate relationship," and it's been that way ever since middle school, when a recorder was put in my hands. Playing never appealed to me! But this time, I didn't have to play the instruments—just sell them. We weren't competing directly with high-end brands like Yamaha or Roland, nor were we targeting entry-level brands like Casio or Kawai. While Casio and Kawai offer reliable, affordable instruments, they often lack the advanced features, superior sound quality, and craftsmanship musicians seek in top-tier brands. Our products aimed to fill a clear gap in the mid-range market, offering a blend of quality and innovation positioned between the basics and the best.

Our pianos were beautiful. One of my greatest assets was the aesthetic appeal of the instruments, which was highly appreciated by buyers—so much so that some saw them as decorative pieces. Our customers, however, were not architects or interior designers but mainly distributors of musical instruments, chain stores (both Italian and international), or private buyers. I managed markets in France, the United Kingdom, Benelux, and the Iberian Peninsula.

As good as the pianos looked, the quality of the product left something to be desired; not even the famous tightrope walker

Philippe Petit[7] would have been able to balance the numerous complaints that came in. We even shipped a 2.75-meter-long[8] concert grand piano to Japan, black with white legs and pedal board. The months I spent at the company were the best free MBA I could have had: I quickly learned everything you should not do. I left the company two years later, on my own terms, satisfied because my intuition had been confirmed: it was the right decision to invest time in sales. Sales is indeed a ruthless environment where only those with a wide range of skills can succeed. I became a skilled salesman, making our piano seem like the right choice to customers, the one that would best meet their potential buyers' needs. I created value for the solution I proposed and sold by building trust with the customer. At that point, I was ready to move on to something more challenging, perhaps in a more structured and competitive environment.

Tiziano Terzani,[9] whom I had the honor and privilege to meet, used to say that in life, "a good opportunity always presents itself; the problem, if any, is knowing how to recognize it." Sometimes it is not easy, but at least twice during this period, good opportunities came my way.

In 1995, I was in a favorable situation: I was offered a job as export area manager by two companies, Technogym[10] and

7   Philippe Petit (born 1949) is a French high-wire artist best known for his daring and unauthorized walk between the Twin Towers of the World Trade Center in New York City on August 7, 1974. This act, which took place 1,350 feet above the ground, is considered one of the greatest high-wire feats in history. Petit's remarkable achievement was later chronicled in his book *To Reach the Clouds,* which inspired the Academy Award-winning documentary *Man on Wire* and the feature film *The Walk.*

8   A length of 2.75 meters is approximately 9 feet and 0.25 inches.

9   Tiziano Terzani (1938–2004) was an Italian journalist, writer, and war correspondent, known for his insightful and evocative reporting on Asia. For more than thirty years, he worked for the German news magazine *Der Spiegel* and authored several acclaimed books, including *A Fortune-Teller Told Me* and *Goodnight, Mister Lenin*. Terzani's work often blended journalism with personal reflection, offering deep cultural and historical perspectives on the places he covered.

10   Technogym is a global leader in fitness and wellness solutions, founded in 1983 by Nerio Alessandri in Cesena, Italy. The company designs and manu-

Lucchesi, both attractive, dynamic, and with potential for growth. In Technogym, I was part of the selection process for an area sales manager position.

Technogym made me an exciting offer, both in terms of the remuneration package and intangible perks. However, I turned it down because, during the selection process, I sensed that the corporate environment was permeated by rivalry for rivalry's sake, which I felt would be of little benefit to the company. I liked to run harder than others; I was as comfortable in the relay as in the 400-meter hurdles, and didn't mind running the marathon when necessary. I was equally happy working with others as I was on my own: the main thing was to make progress toward a goal. The last thing I wanted was the distraction of one-upmanship.

I found these qualities at the second firm, Lucchesi. The first interviews were held at their headquarters, housed in a pastel-colored early-twentieth-century villa in a suburb of Bologna. It had marble floors polished like mirrors, exposed wooden beams, a lawn with centuries-old oaks, and a beautiful magnolia tree. The modern factory, on the other hand, was located twenty kilometers[11] outside Bologna, in Minerbio.[12] I liked everything: the company's style, the warmth of the Lucchesi family, and the quality of life in Bologna.

Founded in 1977 on an entrepreneur's hunch, the company had become Europe's leading manufacturer of plastic films for packaging, credit cards, and graphic arts. Over the years, Lucchesi had grown to a saturation point, and the family decided to leverage market growth by making further investments.

---

factures high-end fitness equipment and digital technologies for professional and home use. Technogym has been the official supplier of numerous Olympic Games and is recognized for its innovative approach to integrating wellness into everyday life. Its products are used by elite athletes and fitness enthusiasts around the world.

11   Twenty kilometers is approximately 12.4 miles.

12   Minerbio is a small village located just outside of Bologna, in the Emilia-Romagna region of Italy. Known for its charming rural landscapes and historic architecture, it offers a glimpse into the quieter, more traditional side of Italian life.

In 1994, sales had reached 56 billion lire,[13] and the owner had invested 48 billion lire in new plants, scheduled to come online in June 1996. The European market was well managed, and the decision to increase production capacity was driven by the need to expand into non-European countries. My role was to lead this expansion, supported by two account managers and the sales manager. This team formed the core of the company's export structure. The challenge was to penetrate markets dominated by competitors such as Ineos, VKW-Staufen, and Klöckner Pentaplast—industrial giants and established leaders outside of Europe.

I met with the sales manager twice, which was followed by a meeting with the CEO and then another meeting with the person to whom I would report. "Where do you see yourself in ten years?" the owner asked me during my fifth interview.

"In the chair you're currently sitting in," I responded, unable to hide my ambition.

My answer was met with an exchange of glances and a long silence. For a moment, I thought I'd gone too far, but then Franco Lucchesi smiled at me: "All right, Pietro. See you Monday, September 4, at eight o'clock."

I had sold myself well. I knew, however, that I needed to brush up my professional skills for this job, and my knowledge of English was insufficient. To improve it, I spent August in Freshwater, on the Isle of Wight, at the summer residence of the George family, who hosted students. My French and Spanish needed no improvement; I was already capable of carrying on conversations and business correspondence in those languages.

I showed up on September 4 as excited and energized as if it were my first day of school, and I was immediately assigned to a training program set up by my boss, Andrea.[14]

---

13   The Italian lira (ITL) was the official currency of Italy before it adopted the euro (€) in 2002. Introduced in 1861 during the unification of Italy, the lira was used for over 140 years. At 1994 exchange rates, sales were approximately $34.7 million (€28.9 million) and investments were approximately $29.8 million (€24.8 million).
14   In Italian, Andrea is traditionally a male name. Although it is commonly used as a female name in English-speaking countries, Germany, and some

Monday: Production process
Tuesday: Product catalog
Wednesday: Applications
Thursday: Industrial costs, transport, pricing, and strategy
Friday: Markets, customers, and international groups

I'd arrive at eight in the morning and spend ten hours in the classroom, where the sales manager meticulously explained everything I needed to know to work with the team. He wanted me to be his backup, imparting his knowledge with a sense of urgency, as if he wanted me to absorb everything quickly. The pace was relentless, almost as if there were a deadline looming that no one had shared with me. Why would Andrea, a seasoned manager, push so hard to transfer such a vast amount of information in such a short time? Was he preparing me for a sudden shift in responsibilities, or was there an impending crisis he hadn't disclosed? Either way, I couldn't shake the feeling that something unusual was happening beneath the surface—something that demanded my full attention, even if I didn't yet understand why. During that first week, I met Mr. and Mrs. Lucchesi only once; I saw them with the plant manager but didn't have the opportunity to speak with them. On the following Monday and Tuesday, my manager explained how to handle foreign markets, and by Wednesday, I was already finding customers and agents in non-European countries.

Two weeks later, Andrea came to my office and asked me to prepare a proposal for a French customer with two plants in Angoulême. It was a meticulously developed and highly sophi-

European countries, in Italy Andrea is equivalent to the English name Andrew. The character in this book is my former boss, an Italian man. Of course, while I now permit myself to call my boss by his first name, back then, he required *lei*. In Italian, "lei" is the formal and polite form of "you," used to address someone deferentially, especially in professional or formal contexts. It is equivalent to using "sir" or "madam" in English or referring to someone as "Mr." or "Mrs." Surname. The use of "lei" reflects the speaker's recognition of the other person's status or position, and is generally expected in interactions with superiors or in situations where politeness and formality are required.

sticated proposal, and I put all my effort into it, consulting with colleagues. To my great surprise, when I presented it to the sales director, he said it was perfect and that I could send it to the customer myself.

At around 7 p.m. that same day, Andrea came into my office again, asking me to prepare our proposal for the annual tender for Datacard by noon the next day. Datacard was the company's largest customer, with five plants on different continents. After requesting a spot offer for Thames in the UK, he closed my office door behind him and went home. I had a standing commitment to play soccer with friends every week, so it was unusual for me to miss a game. This week, however, I had to call and explain that I couldn't make it to our usual midweek match.

As I drove through the congested streets of Bologna, I wondered what was going on: is it normal to transform, in less than ten days, from a simple seller of mid-range digital pianos to an expert PVC salesman? The urgency of the situation puzzled me.

Before long, I was traveling the world at least two weeks each month, delivering the expected results: creating a solid and powerful distribution network and generating volume for the imminent launch of the new production line. The sales activity was similar to my previous work, though the product was different. Sales is sales, after all, and it remained a highly technical endeavor. The customers I was dealing with were however more aligned with my background and culture, as I was now dealing with large organizations and interacting with C-level executives—a perfect match for my education and experience.

In addition to managing the non-European market, I was suddenly assigned oversight of France and the United Kingdom starting in November! I couldn't understand why I was being given so much responsibility, especially without any clear explanation or prior notice. My workload increased exponentially, and I began to question the rationale behind these new assignments.

My activities outside Europe were beginning to bear fruit. Although available production capacity was limited (the new plant was not yet operational), we were able to fill small trial orders to give new customers a chance to evaluate, test, and qualify products. Many wanted to visit the plant, to see for themselves the new factory under construction. The company was remarkably welcoming and generous, and we often took clients to dinner in the Jewish Quarter. Established in 1556, a papal decree had once dictated that it was the only part of the city where Jewish residents were permitted to live. I loved it, located in the historic center and characterized by narrow, crowded streets. We enjoyed bringing clients to this area of Bologna to let them experience the city's unique charm and beauty.

Often, the restaurant of choice was Benso's, located in an alley behind the Acquaderni Gallery, under the two iconic medieval towers, Asinelli and Garisenda.[15] At lunchtime, however, a regular destination was Dandy, in Tintoria, near the plant. I still remember the first time I went there with Andrea. We had a delegation from Singapore and a French guest who spoke no English.

"*Dottore*,[16] translate the menu for our guests!" Andrea instructed.

That day, Daniele, the chef-owner, recommended a guinea fowl timbale with turmeric cream, Chianina tartare (from an Italian breed of large white cattle) with pear angys, pecorino cheese, quail eggs, and a tart of dark chocolate, carrot, sea buckthorn, and orange, along with other items on the menu.

"*Arancia*? Easy: orange. But...*olivello spinoso*?" I racked my brains, unable to find a feasible translation. As it turns out,

---

15   The Asinelli and Garisenda Towers are iconic medieval structures in Bologna, Italy. Built in the twelfth century, they are among the city's most famous landmarks. The Asinelli Tower, at approximately 318 feet (97 meters), is one of the tallest leaning medieval towers in the world. The Garisenda Tower, originally much taller, now stands at about 48 meters (157 feet) due to a significant lean that developed early in its history. Both towers were built by prominent families as symbols of their wealth and power, and they remain important architectural and historical monuments in Bologna.

16   In more colloquial Italian usage than the academic area, "Dottore" is often used as an honorific title to refer to people who have a university degree, especially in fields such as law, medicine, or science. Outside of these professions, the title may be used as a sign of respect, especially in formal or professional contexts. In Italy, the use of "Dottore" reflects a degree of formality and recognition of the person's education and status.

not many native English speakers would even know what "sea buckthorn" is!

From that day, I made it a point to learn the translation of every ingredient (and its preparation) in the three languages I knew. When "*salmerini alpini alla brace su vellutata di pastinaca*" appeared on Dandy's à la carte menu, I impressed everyone: "The chef's suggestion is grilled arctic char on parsnip cream!"

Scent of Promotion

Christmas 1995 arrived. I had only been at Lucchesi for four months, and we were still six months away from the start-up of the new production line. I was putting my heart and soul into the work, and I was beginning to feel the strain. There were nearly 150 employees at the company luncheon, and I sat next to Margherita from accounting. I had met her only a few times before, during the monthly credit meetings where we analyzed the debt positions of various customers and their credit limits.

"Pietro, you're lucky," she said at the end of lunch, "and I don't just mean because you spent the whole day next to me— you're not even my type."

I smiled at her joke and asked her to elaborate.

"You should know a couple of things," she continued. "At the end of the selection process, you were the preferred candidate of Mr. and Mrs. Lucchesi and the CEO, but you were Andrea's second choice. Since the new hire would need to work closely with him, his opinion was crucial. Unfortunately—or maybe fortunately, as time will tell—the successful candidate didn't accept the offer, because the salary was too low and the challenge too demanding. In short, you were next in line.

"At the end of July, the general manager and Andrea had a fight, and both resigned. The former has already left, and Andrea will be leaving soon, with you most likely taking his place. They're looking for a new general manager, you know—staff are burning out quickly, with high turnover among managers and executives. The owners like you, but be careful: Soon, you'll be responsible for the commercial fate of a company carrying substantial debt. You need sales, but more importantly, you need profits and cash flow. If things don't go well or you make a mistake, you're out."

I remember sleeping poorly that night and not having a good Christmas holiday. At least now, I understood the urgency in getting me up to speed with clients and markets, as well as the somewhat chilly attitude toward me.

The year-end break allowed me to take a breather and reflect on my professional growth over the past few months. I had gained in-depth product knowledge, created practical sales proposals, developed the ability to respond to customer queries, and incorporated new options into proposal development.

My previous experience as a consultant had taught me how to manage planning timelines for complex projects and meet associated administrative deadlines.

I had become skilled at managing time and maximizing productivity; I generated revenue and profit by prioritizing major tasks, delegating minor ones, and automating others where possible.

I also convinced customers of the merits of our products and presented them in ways that clarified how their needs could best be met—similar to what I had learned to do with musical instruments.

In the spring of 1996, I turned 30, and none of Margherita's predictions from Christmas Eve had come true or even seemed in the offing. But I didn't mind. I already felt enough psychological pressure to expand our sales area and capture market share from competitors. I was ambitious, but my feelings were mixed: I couldn't decide whether to be glad Andrea was still with the company or to hope for his departure.

Meanwhile, I spent two to three weeks abroad each month. As I met all kinds of people, it became increasingly clear that negotiation wasn't part of every sale. I focused on two distinct stages: first, accurately identifying the customer's real priorities and needs, and then helping them achieve those results to avoid having to negotiate price or value later.

My counterparts were older and more experienced, and I tried to learn from each one as I secured key orders for the new production line. These interactions provided valuable lessons in negotiation, communication, and industry insights that I eagerly absorbed to improve my own skills. Observing their techniques and strategies helped me refine my approach and better understand the nuances of successful dealmaking. Each meeting was unique, and in addition to doing my job, I used the opportunity to analyze different situations and develop new behaviors.

In Sydney, for example, I met Ian Neville, owner of Cardcorp, a pioneering company in the industry. He was looking for a 680-micron film with specific physical and mechanical properties that differed from those offered by competitors. Ian explained his needs, and I was able to sell him on my company's solutions, working closely with colleagues in new product development to meet his requirements.

I also remember a meeting in Red Bank, New Jersey, with Juan Meija of Protec, who later became a close friend. He raised so many objections that I almost faltered, but I managed to sell him material that dispelled his doubts and backed up everything I had said. In short, when customers showed direct interest in our products, I could close the sale and bring the order home.

The road was steeper with Asian customers, especially the Chinese ones. They often rejected proposals outright and made challenging demands. Here, I had to negotiate, taking my time if necessary. Based on my objectives, negotiable and nonnegotiable points, and added or equivalent value, I analyzed possible offers from both the customer's and competitor's perspectives.

One instance still stands out in my mind. A Chinese client I'd been courting for months dismissed my pricing model as "unrealistic" and demanded a 10 percent discount, threatening to walk away. Initially, I approached the situation as I would any sale—emphasizing our product's value and quality. But this time, it didn't work. The client wasn't interested in being convinced; they wanted a deal. I realized this was about negotiating, not presenting solutions. I asked for a day to regroup and analyzed my costs, mapping out a strategy. The next day, I countered with a 3.5 percent discount, contingent on a quarterly blanket order and thirty days net payment terms. I emphasized the added value of our superior quality and service. The client didn't immediately agree, but didn't reject it either. Over the next two weeks, we bartered over details like minimum order quantities and logistics. By defending my position while staying flexible, we reached a deal that worked for both sides.

I fared better in the Philippines, where Evelyn Tan, the charming wife of local tycoon Lucio, seriously considered my proposal with her team. Here, it was up to me to negotiate, present the best options, and position my offer effectively in terms of value and functionality.

Then there were cases I would consider lucky, where the client immediately accepted the best proposed option, allowing me to simply close the sale and call it a day. But sometimes things didn't go so smoothly; often, the client would reject the best proposal, and I'd have to negotiate by presenting a second proposal and working to secure the sale once it was accepted.

I encountered a radically diverse range of clients, each with distinctive expectations and assumptions. Since I spent many hours in the air, I often used the time to reflect on my meetings rather than watching movies. Those lost hours of sleep became a valuable investment: it was then that I began to see the difference between selling and negotiating.

My job was what today would be called B2B—business to business. Unlike my previous work, this role involved significant negotiation, and I soon realized that I was not a natural negotiator. There are, in fact, differences between the skills needed to be a great negotiator, and those required to be a great influencer, business partner, and brand ambassador.

I could sell, and I could match a solution to a problem, but I began to understand that proposing a solution was different from negotiating. I was skilled at explaining and presenting the value of my product or service, and was persuasive in illustrating the benefits to the customer of choosing us over the competition. But even this was different from negotiating.

It became clear that negotiating involved bartering, discussing, acceptable haggling or hard bargaining, securing concessions, and defending one's position.

Since I was better at selling than negotiating, my primary focus was on maximizing value in the selling phase before entering negotiations. However, I realized that I often blurred the lines between selling and negotiating, which sent clear and unmistakable signals of weakness to my negotiating partner. For example, during a negotiation, I might continue to extol the product's benefits, which could be interpreted as a lack of confidence in the value I had already presented, making me seem overly eager to close the deal. On other occasions, I would begin negotiating terms before I had fully established the product's value, thereby weakening my position and reducing the potential value I could secure. This premature shift to negotiation suggested that I was willing to make concessions, undermining my leverage and ultimately impacting the outcome. At that time, I concluded that a productive negotiation could not begin until the sales phase was complete, and both parties were ready and motivated to reach a mutually attractive agreement.

When I returned to the company after a trip, the first thing I'd do was to check to see if Andrea was still there. With Margherita having confided to me that he was expected to leave at any moment, I would look for his car, trying to pick up any clue of his presence. I was torn between asking for an explanation and remaining silent.

In the end, I always chose silence.

Had I become a sales manager, my responsibilities would have extended beyond negotiating with customers. For example, I would have to work with team members like Milena from customer service, who had a passion for theater and yoga and enjoyed taking tourists around Bologna, to arrange more flexible hours—requiring careful negotiation and coordination. I would also have to manage conflicts with the production team in cases of quality issues or late deliveries, as well as setting the annual budget with top management, which would involve rigorous negotiations over volumes, prices, and margins. The scope of negotiations I would need to engage in would expand significantly, encompassing a range of issues I hadn't fully grasped. I would need to strengthen my negotiation skills to communicate effectively with team members and clearly define goals with management. I would be faced with the opportunity to negotiate my salary, benefits package, and other details for my new role. On three previous occasions, I'd accepted an employer's offer without discussion. This time, I promised myself, I would be prepared. I needed to learn how to negotiate in the workplace, understand the personalities I was dealing with, and adopt the most effective steps and techniques to secure the best possible result.

If Andrea were to depart, I would need to interact more extensively with colleagues and employees, delegate specific tasks, create work schedules, agree on project deadlines, and resolve interpersonal conflicts. I needed to develop my charisma and improve my communication and organizational skills. For the former, I had to focus on being genuinely interested in others, actively listening, and showing empathy. I had to work on maintaining eye contact, using open body language, and speaking with confidence and enthusiasm. I also needed to practice storytelling to make my conversations more engaging and relatable. By refining these aspects, I aimed to create a more magnetic presence that could inspire and connect with others on a deeper level.

I knew that I could not yet craft a truly customer-centric sales strategy, and that this limited my business skills.

However, I could still provide sound advice and solutions, build solid relationships, and engage in relevant and insightful conversations. I no longer interrupted unnecessarily, though there remained room for improvement in my listening skills. I focused more on the client's problems, weaknesses, and ideas, and I responded thoughtfully. Yet, I felt the need to form deeper emotional connections and inspire greater trust. I needed to be more disciplined. Sometimes I lacked focus and missed verbal and nonverbal cues from my interviewees. Sure, I could understand a client's feelings, interests, concerns, and desires, but I knew I could do more by picking up on certain subtle signals, understanding things on the fly—even if they weren't spelled out.

It was important to find common interests and topics of conversation unrelated to work. So, I began to memorize personal details about my clients, which helped me build strong relationships with them. Soon, instead of consulting a competitor, they turned to me for advice. I realized that cultivating more genuine relationships improved my credibility, and that human connection, rapport, and mutual trust transformed simple conversations into lasting business relationships. There was still room for improvement: my communication needed to be more engaging, authentic, and narrative, weaving in more personal anecdotes and vivid descriptions to create a more compelling and relatable experience for my audience.

I would address the customer's pain points and needs by using my emotions and understanding those of others. For example, when a client expressed frustration over a delayed project, I empathized with their concerns and shared a similar experience I had. By acknowledging their feelings and offering a solution based on my own understanding, I was able to build trust and demonstrate my commitment to resolving their issues effectively.

I worked hard every day with the sole purpose of achieving the volumes of business the company needed to fill the plants, pay off the enormous debt it had incurred, and satisfy a visionary entrepreneur. At the same time, I worked to overcome my own shortcomings.

Overseas travel continued relentlessly, as 40 percent of the additional capacity was allocated primarily to Asia, the Middle East, Africa, Australia, and New Zealand. We had increased volumes in Canada, the United States, and Mexico thanks to excellent, well-established relationships with global customers. However, this success was largely due to the valuable legacy of Andrea's work over recent years.

My relationship with the two girls in customer service was excellent. Whenever I returned from a trip, they greeted me warmly, as if I were an explorer returning from a great adventure. I was well liked, and not just for the thoughtful souvenirs I brought back: handmade jewelry from local artisans, unique spices from bustling markets, or traditional textiles from far-flung villages. These gifts reflected my genuine appreciation for other cultures and my desire to share a piece of my journey with my colleagues in Italy. But our connection went beyond souvenirs; it was built on mutual respect, kindness, and the joy of sharing stories.

At the end of May, I went to France for five days. By then, Margherita's words at the company lunch had faded from my mind, as nothing she'd said had come to pass. I was focused on the exciting event about to take place: the start-up of the new production line and the installation of all the auxiliary systems. I'd even stopped checking if Andrea's car was still there when I returned to the main office, as I had fully assumed the role of area manager, a position I found fulfilling. As soon as I arrived at headquarters, I would pause to admire the imposing, rounded leaves of the flowering magnolia tree. In those dark-green oval leaves, I found comfort and serenity.

Upon returning from my trip to France, however, I couldn't help but notice that there was now a shiny Mercedes in Andrea's reserved parking space, rather than his own Alfa Romeo. In a split second, my mind analyzed all the possibilities. I walked in. Andrea was sitting at his long desk, and I noticed a key ring with the classic three-pointed star surrounded by the Mercedes laurel wreath. I breathed a sigh of relief: Even though I aspired to an illustrious career, and deep inside felt like I was burning through time and milestones, I still didn't feel ready to take his place. I would have been responsible for a turnover of more than 60 billion lire,[17] a sales team, and numerous agents worldwide. To bring the company to full capacity in the new plants, I would have needed to hire people to whom I could delegate specific markets and clients.

But this wasn't the source of my hesitation and insecurity at the thought of picking up his baton. As I reflected on the responsibilities I would be taking on, it became clear that I still needed to improve certain skills, the most important of which was the discipline to adequately plan and prepare for negotiations.

I admit that I lacked the emotional intelligence needed to manage many aspects of my life, which spilled over into negotiations. I also underestimated one essential factor: I would need to maintain an ongoing relationship with the other party even after talks concluded and an agreement was reached. Finally, I often left too much on the table because I wasn't creative enough in my thinking. Now I know that the lack of an immediate solution doesn't mean that a mutually beneficial outcome is impossible,

---

17   At average 1997 exchange rates, sales were approximately US$35.2 million or €31 million.

it just means that you need to be more creative in finding one. I didn't fully appreciate this at the time.

I spent the following week in my office at Lucchesi's head-quarters in Bologna. I received confirmation that the Mercedes was Andrea's new company car. This was a clear sign that the resignation (which had been a done deal six months earlier, at least according to Margherita) wasn't happening: Andrea had even received a reward. My career trajectory would remain the same—no flash promotion. Despite my initial relief at seeing Andrea continue in his role, I soon realized I was deeply disappointed. I felt even less comfortable than before, partly because I knew I had invested a great deal of effort in anticipation of a promotion that, consciously or unconsciously, I already felt was mine.

Managing expectations at work was becoming more complicated, and recognizing this difficulty was challenging for me. I was going through a tough period, filled with frustration and disappointment, and I was in danger of losing motivation and drive in this complex situation. I was also tempted to let go of my expectations and ambitions and settle into a professional life without particular excitement. However, after a few days, I realized this would be the wrong approach, so I tried to assess my professional achievements. I attempted to reframe my mindset, focusing on successes and the value of social acknowledgment. I aimed to gain more self-knowledge and awareness. The first step was to identify my talents, potential, and values. Once identified, I would try to align them with my true needs.

It was neither easy nor enjoyable, but it was a necessary process that allowed me to define my desires and goals more clearly. My adaptability and resilience during times of crisis came to the fore, and I learned how to deal more effectively with professional disappointments. After all, I'd been at Lucchesi for less than a year and had done excellent work. I had grown and matured, and my prospects were promising. My morale soon recovered, thanks in part to the start of operations of the new calender line and the opportunity to compete in one of the most prestigious offshore regattas in the Mediterranean, the Giraglia, and the Copa del

Rey in Palma de Mallorca. These events offered a much-needed distraction from my professional life, allowing me to disconnect from work and immerse myself in one of my greatest passions: competitive sailing.

Summer passed, and with the arrival of fall, the change of weather seemed to mirror Andrea's behavior: just as the weather cooled, he had become more irritable and pricklier than ever.

The Mentor

In contrast to the growing tension with Andrea, my relationship with Gianfranco, the technical director who also managed purchasing, was a welcome change. He was competitive, a great sportsman—horseback riding, sailing, diving, skiing—and at work, he was disciplined and methodical. His calm, structured approach provided a refreshing balance to the rest of the team's dynamics. He was a pleasure to listen to. One day, while I was at the plant, I asked him if I could sit in on a meeting with Tronox, our supplier of titanium dioxide, a critical raw material in our production process.

Gianfranco was going to discuss volumes and prices for the second half of the year and lay the groundwork for the following year's agreement. He readily agreed, and as we walked to his office, he told me, "Pietro, preparation is the first and perhaps most important part of any negotiation. It doesn't matter what you're negotiating—it could be a contract or just a spot supply of materials or services—but research and preparation are essential. Knowledge can help you make informed decisions and proceed confidently. But it's not enough. One of the most important aspects of negotiation is knowing how to listen. It's easy for negotiators to focus on what they want to achieve, but neglecting to give space to the other party can be counterproductive. Remember, for a negotiation to be successful, both parties need to feel heard."

He then shared some details about the vendor we would be meeting with and explained, in broad terms, his approach and objectives for the negotiation. Curious and impressed by his preparation, I asked him how he managed to stay calm in certain situations.

"Well, negotiations require a lot of patience," he replied. "Negotiations can take a long time, so it's essential to approach them with the understanding that things may go differently than you planned. Negotiations can be stressful, but it's important to stay calm and focused, even when you're frustrated or anxious. Your negotiating partner can pick up on your tension, making the negotiation more difficult. Losing emotional control can be perceived as a sign of weakness, allowing the other party to take advantage. Getting caught up in your own emotions can also interfere with your ability to listen. And, always, you must have integrity! Building a reputation as a fair, honest, and trustworthy negotiator is essential. When companies see you this way, they also trust the company you represent. In short, your integrity enhances the reputation of your organization, making it easier to negotiate future contracts and agreements."

The supplier meeting was exciting and constructive. When it was over, I thanked Gianfranco for allowing me to attend and mentioned how much I'd enjoyed watching the supplier search for solutions to our issues and the passion with which they both negotiated.

Smiling, Gianfranco replied, "You need to develop your problem-solving skills. It's relatively easy for parties to agree on what they have in common, and that's always a good starting point for negotiation. However, thinking creatively and finding various solutions to issues is essential for resolving disagreements. Finally, you must have passion and confidence. Passion for what you're negotiating is the key to getting the best deal possible. When you sincerely believe in your organization and its products and services, you can convey this information positively and confidently. Your genuine passion instills a sense of trust in your counterpart, which can lead to successful negotiations and new business opportunities. I understand that negotiation can seem like one of the most intimidating parts of your job, but it doesn't have to be. With dedication, time, and patience, anyone can master this art."

Driving back from Minerbio to Bologna, I reflected on the meeting. I concluded that some people are simply better negotiators than others, almost as if they are genetically predisposed! Gianfranco was one of those people. I was certainly not at his level, but that didn't make me want to give up and leave negotiation to the experts who had honed their skills through experience and practice. Sure, some people have natural talent, but I was confident anyone can become a better, more skilled negotiator, myself included.

I had taken twenty-five exams during my university career, but none of them covered negotiation. This was probably because the courses in my field didn't emphasize or even include negotiation skills in their curricula. When I was hired as an area manager, I received no training in either company. And it wasn't just me; none of my friends and acquaintances had taken specific courses on negotiation. Yet improving this particular skill could have made a difference—and would have contributed to my professional growth.

I became increasingly convinced that negotiation was not a mysterious art but a practical skill anyone could learn and improve. Although that afternoon opened my eyes to the possibility of significantly enhancing my negotiation abilities, several months passed before I decided what to do and how to do it. Whenever I tried to focus on a training program for negotiation, pressing daily tasks prevented me from pursuing my intentions. Although improving this skill was critical, market development and sales remained my priorities.

My travel schedule was always intense. The new line was producing well, but it wasn't operating on a continuous cycle—a suboptimal situation for a calender line, which, like machinery in a paper mill or blast furnace, should ideally operate around the clock, seven days a week. Customers from China, Hong Kong, Korea, Japan, Thailand, Singapore, the Philippines, Malaysia, the United States, Canada, Mexico, Australia, and New Zealand were waiting for their orders, along with European clients. Achieving a continuous cycle was essential to ensure continuity in production processes and optimize fixed costs. To strengthen our position in these markets, the company hired an additional area sales manager, who would oversee the German-speaking countries (previously managed by Andrea) and some Asian countries, where I had already secured good contracts and where we only needed to consolidate results. I would focus on developing the North and South American markets.

The first year, with three calender lines in operation, ended exceptionally well—sales brought good profitability, and the owners were pleased with the results. Everything seemed to be going smoothly. The company climate was perfect, and I was happy to work for a company that allowed me to learn from others, travel the world, improve my knowledge, and expand my network. I wouldn't say I enjoyed office work, so traveling a couple of weeks a month was more than welcome. Sure, I was constantly under pressure and had to manage significant mental and physical stress. However, I found that traveling, visiting clients, and getting away from the office helped me feel more productive and focused when I returned. My creativity increased. Being exposed to new cultures, meeting people from other countries, trying new types of food, and listening to international music were all positive experiences, introducing interest and inspiration into my life. Travel broadened my perspective and helped me appreciate the world's diversity. This new outlook improved my problem-solving skills, encouraging me to think more creatively and adapt to different situations. My HR manager, who was always attentive to employee performance, noticed this change. She mentioned she had seen a significant improvement in my problem-solving skills, which reassured me of my personal and professional growth.

Early 1997 brought two more organizational improvements, aimed at further structuring the foreign sales office: Alessandra was hired to customer service, replacing Fabrizia, who was entrusted with the entire European packaging market.

The new structure reduced my workload (and therefore my stress), allowing me to finally create a program to improve my negotiation skills with key stakeholders both inside and outside the company. I wanted to be able to conduct a business negotiation calmly and rationally, even in complex situations. I wanted to acquire the techniques and tools needed to transform conflict into understanding. I wanted to learn about different negotiation styles so I could choose the most appropriate one for each situation. I started reading books, and taking specific courses was an excellent place to start. My journey began with *Getting Past No: Negotiating in Difficult Situations* by William Ury (1993), followed by *Getting to Yes: Negotiating Agreement Without Giving*

In, also by Ury (with Roger Fisher, 2011), and finally, *Influence: The Psychology of Persuasion* by Robert Cialdini (2021).

These early texts were followed by many others, and I attended some good programs in Bologna and Milan. I was satisfied because I had moved from planning to action, but it wasn't enough. Although I improved my negotiation skills, I felt I needed to devote even more time to my personal growth.

It was the right time to take the leap, because things were improving at the company: the office was well structured, sales were growing, and orders were coming in steadily. I could take some time for myself, which I did by becoming more involved in studying negotiation. I was passionate about the subject and explored it in depth, reading as much as I could. I took the texts with me even on weekends.

One Saturday, while reading in the mountains at the Hotel Ansitz Rungghof in Appiano, my peace was interrupted by the ringing of my cell phone. It was Mr. Lucchesi. He had never before called me on a weekend.

"Good morning, Pietro. How are you? I need to see you."

"Good morning, Mr. Lucchesi. I'm fine, thank you; just relaxing a bit," I replied promptly. "I'm in Trentino; I'll be back tomorrow night, and if you'd like, we can meet Monday morning at eight; I'll be in the office by then, and…"

"Pietro, I expect you at the villa tomorrow morning," he interrupted, not giving me time to finish. "Would you prefer ten or eleven?"

I quickly realized there was no room for negotiation; despite my growing skills, perhaps I still needed more experience. I immediately called Franz Haas's winery to cancel a tasting I had booked. Despite the cancellation, I decided to stop by anyway. Visiting his winery felt like attending school; winemaking is a constant quest for perfection. Science and calculation are essential to making great wines, but love, passion, and determination define their character and depth. Even in that brief visit, I breathed in the art that Franz had in his blood. I thought that perhaps spending time with him and absorbing his loving creative genius might positively influence the outcome of my meeting with Mr. Lucchesi the next day.

I had no idea why there was such urgency, nor did I know what to expect. I thought a lot during the three-hour drive along the Brenner highway, starting with the worst-case scenarios and working my way to the positive ones. Had I perhaps done (or not done) or said (or not said) something that displeased the boss? Or, conversely, was it something he approved of? I considered every possibility, along with its opposite.

I arrived in Bologna for dinner and decided to relax at Battibecco, a charming local restaurant known for its excellent cuisine and cozy atmosphere. Nico Costa, the owner, and his daughter, Erica, always greeted me with genuine warmth, making me feel like part of their family. The rustic decor, combined with their attentive service, created a comforting environment that provided the familiarity and reassurance I needed. Dining at Battibecco wasn't just about the food; it was about the sense of belonging and warm connections that made it a refuge during my visits to Bologna. I was tense because Margherita's words echoed in my head: "If things don't go well or you make a mistake, you're out." Although I was worried and tired from the trip, I managed to fall asleep quickly and get some rest.

The following morning, I arrived at the villa at ten o'clock sharp. The boss's gray BMW 750 was parked in his reserved space. I went upstairs and found Mr. Lucchesi sitting at his large wooden desk. I immediately noticed that he was alone—odd, as his wife usually accompanied him.

"Hello, Pietro. Thanks for coming today. Are you ready to be sales director?" he began, straight to the point.

"Sure," I replied after a brief silence, more out of astonishment at the directness of the question than any doubt about the position being offered.

"Perfect. Then I'll see you tomorrow. Have a nice Sunday," he said, standing to shake my hand and dismissing me. The meeting lasted less than thirty seconds. I spent the rest of the day thinking about the best internal organizational structure for the company, how to reorganize workflows, and considering each team member's role in various sales activities. Not all structures work the same way, and I wanted to avoid trial and error in finding the right solution. I was still debating between a centralized system and a model with faster communication and decision-making.

In a centralized system, where key team decisions are delegated to a single point of contact, all organizational levels are aligned toward a common vision or purpose. My management style, however, leaned more toward a decentralized structure, allowing more opportunities for delegation. This system empowered employees to make decisions, with both the responsibilities and rewards that come with them. Such a setup would increase the company's impact in the field, support our ambitious growth plans, and give my team the freedom to be creative in their tactics. My new role wasn't that of a "pure" sales manager, as I retained all the responsibilities of an area manager. This didn't bother me, as it kept a direct line to the market without having to go through agents or other area managers. Also, having responsibility for the major markets and the two largest credit card manufacturers in the world (Gemplus and Schlumberger) allowed me to maintain an overview of the situation. In such a position, I always felt like a dwarf on the shoulders of giants: I could see more and farther than they could, not because of my vision or insight, but simply because I sat higher. I was elevated precisely because of the greatness of Lucchesi's clients!

The 1997 fiscal year ended on a positive note, with sales exceeding 68 billion lire.[18] Volumes had increased proportionately, reaching over 16,000 metric tons.[19] To manage these significant increases in volume and revenue (up 17 percent and 13 percent, respectively), the headcount rose from 170 to 188. The company hired three key individuals with whom I would interact frequently: another general manager, an experienced plant manager, and a director of integrated logistics.

I was excited because the company was structuring itself to support geographic expansion, sales growth, and product and process innovation. Although a new general manager had been

---

18   At the average exchange rate for 1997, sales were approximately US$ 39.9 million or €35.1 million.
19   A weight of 16,000 tons are approximately 35.2 million pounds.

hired, Mr. Lucchesi often consulted me on issues beyond my role as sales director. I appreciated this trust, as it allowed me to broaden my horizons. However, it also created some relational challenges within the organization, even though I never overstepped my assigned boundaries and responsibilities. I interpreted Lucchesi's behavior as a response to the high turnover among senior managers and the fact that many new leaders, except for the CFO and the technical director, had recently been hired. This likely led him to rely on someone he trusted completely.

Work of Persuasion

The situation became explosive when I learned from Mr. Lucchesi that the plant manager, Michele, had resigned after a heated argument with the general manager over handling some union issues.

"Pietro," the boss said to me, "you have to convince Michele to stay; we can't lose him! You're the only one who can do it. Do whatever it takes, but do it quickly. If you need any information about his job, his contract, his salary, or benefits, get it from administration."

"Mr. Lucchesi, give me some time," I replied.

Michele's resignation would have had a detrimental effect on the production team and, consequently, the company as a whole. It would likely result in a drop in performance in terms of volume, quality, and service. Michele also had a unique charisma, and losing him would almost certainly lead to a decline in morale and productivity.

I spent the entire morning gathering as much information as I could about Michele—his position, career, family, and passions. I tried to understand what had motivated him to leave Umbria[20] and join us after a distinguished career in several multinational companies.

The good news was that Michele hadn't resigned because of a better opportunity elsewhere. Rather, he had decided to leave following a heated exchange with the CEO, who had pressured him to resign. Since Michele had already made the decision to leave, there was a chance I could persuade him to stay. I liked the

---

20   Umbria is a region in central Italy, often referred to as the "Green Heart of Italy" due to its lush landscapes and rolling hills. Unlike its more famous neighbors, Tuscany and Lazio (where Rome is located), Umbria is less frequented by tourists, offering a more authentic and tranquil experience of Italian culture and history. The region is known for its medieval towns, such as Perugia and Assisi, and its rich artistic and culinary traditions.

challenge and found it stimulating, even though I felt the weight of the task. Mr. Lucchesi had delegated this problem to me, and I knew I'd also have to handle the general manager's reaction, regardless of whether I succeeded or failed. But I decided to worry about that later.

In other situations, apologizing and admitting a mistake might have worked, but in this case, I wasn't the one who had argued with Michele or caused his decision. I began considering how I could convince him. I could appeal to his ambition by highlighting the great opportunities within the company, especially for him, and by offering appropriate recognition—not necessarily monetary. At the same time, I needed to avoid sounding insincere with excessive praise. I spent the afternoon planning a possible discussion and proposal, examining potential obstacles and objections. I thought about it all the way home and even during dinner. Finally, I mustered the courage to send him a message.

Hi Michele, I'm coming to Minerbio tomorrow morning. Would you be able to spare me half an hour? I want to talk to you about the bright future of this company!

He replied immediately.

Come to the production meeting at eight o'clock; I'd like to share production figures and ideas with you. Then we'll have coffee together.

Production meetings were always exciting, even when production problems or red (negative) numbers outweighed green (positive) ones. In that room, amid numerous indicators, the team would join forces to find practical solutions to improve and do more, better.

Michele was a leader, a facilitator. He never imposed his opinion, instead encouraging his team to come up with suitable solutions. After the meeting, we took a tour of the plant together.

"We just installed a new thickness gauge system on the 1900mm calender line," he said enthusiastically. "We're testing it, and if it works as expected, we could increase hourly throughput and produce all the overlay you need to bring on new customers!" Then, as we entered the new raw materials warehouse, Michele continued, "We've modified the titanium dioxide pneumatic system; now it doesn't clog anymore."

"Michele," I replied as we walked to the shipping area, "I'm happy to see that your ideas have already become a reality. We're full of orders; the market appreciates our just-in-time system. I foresee strong growth in the foreign market and an increase in orders from both existing customers and those we've recently approached. Our competitors have long and variable lead times."

I then laid a large sheet of paper on a table and showed him graphs with KPIs (key performance indicators) for quality, volume, and margins, along with some ideas for improving scrap utilization in our formulations.

"Wow, Pietro, your idea doesn't seem so far-fetched; it's inspiring. I should have thought of it myself! Working with you is a pleasure; we get along well. You're clear, direct, and transparent. And also extraordinarily creative."

"The same goes for me, Michele. We're similar—everyone says so. Even Mr. and Mrs. Lucchesi think the world of you. I know you decided to leave after a discussion with the general manager," I said without showing surprise, shock, or frustration. "Stay with us. There are excellent opportunities here for both the company and for you. The owners strongly embrace innovation and have great faith in you. Think about it: you and I can help put the company on a continuous cycle with less strain on equipment and maintenance.

"The market is growing, you know that. My projections suggest we could add another 20 billion[21] in sales next year with a 20 percent increase in volume. We've made good progress with volume since I arrived, up 40 percent. We can run year-round on the current shift, and next year we can go to 24/7. At that point,

21   At 1998 exchange rates, the incremental sales were approximately US$11.6 million (€10.3 million).

we could take the company to nearly 110 billion[22] in sales and over 23,000 metric tons[23] in volume."

Michele didn't seem surprised by my attempt to convince him to stay. What I said piqued his interest, and he followed my reasoning and vision for the company's future.

"Once we reach this level, we need to diversify," I continued. "We need to invest in a solvent-based coating and laminating line and open up new horizons and markets with higher-margin products. When we hit those numbers, we'll be attractive enough to be bought by a competitor, or perhaps even enter the orbit of a private equity firm. As you know, top management plays a critical role in these transactions. If our competitors aren't interested in buying us, we could approach investors or venture capitalists. You and I could buy shares in the company, then look for organic growth to explore new projects and technologies. We'll develop new processes and products using your vast experience."

Michele listened carefully. "Pietro, what you're telling me is extremely interesting and thought-provoking. The current organizational structure feels a bit restrictive, and until yesterday I was sure I wanted to leave. Now I'm not so sure. Let me think about it. In the meantime, come to the office, and we'll have a cup of coffee."

I breathed a sigh of relief. I hadn't convinced him yet, but I had broken through his doubts. Maybe I'd convinced him to return across the bridge—or maybe he hadn't crossed it fully to begin with.

Upon my return to headquarters, I joined Mr. Lucchesi in his attic office and informed him, "I spoke with Michele. He'll think about it."

"So you didn't convince him or solve the problem. I thought I made it clear that you had a blank check to do whatever it took to get him to stay," the boss replied roughly and sharply.

---

22   At 1998 exchange rates, projected sales would have been approximately US$56.8 million (€63.6 million).
23   23,000 tons is approximately 50.7 million pounds.

"Mr. Lucchesi, this is a delicate matter. Be confident, and everything will work out for the best," I replied in an equally direct and firm manner.

The relationship with Franco Lucchesi worked because I never offered an opinion without having a sound reason. He was a true entrepreneur, a self-made man. What he said was usually right—but other times, if we had followed his lead, we'd have ended up off course. He also respected my precision and straightforwardness—respectful, of course, but without fear or obsequiousness.

I've never been able to stand people who agree just because of someone's role or rank. When someone says "yes" purely out of deference, it often leads to poor outcomes. Disagreements, con-trasts, and differing opinions are positive and constructive, both at work and in everyday life. It's not necessary to get along with everyone; one must have courage and not be intimidated by fear.

Mr. Lucchesi liked to make decisions quickly. Sometimes I had a hard time following him because his choices weren't always based on a rational process but were influenced by biases and assumptions developed out of previous experiences.

He was quickfire, instinctive, and emotional, while I was more methodical, thoughtful, and logical. Our approaches com-plemented each other. Having nothing more to add, I left him to his thoughts and, since it was Friday, wished him a good weekend. I needed Saturday and Sunday to recharge, partly because the week had been busy. I'd never really been able to disconnect, except when racing on sailing boats. However, due to company dynamics in recent months, I'd slowed down with my sailing commitments. I was happy to be called up for the last regattas of the season: the Swan Cup in Porto Cervo, the Nioularge in Saint Tropez, and the Barcolana in Trieste. These events gave me the opportunity to relax and enjoy my favorite sport. That weekend, I sailed in a regatta less important than those I usually competed in, but it was just as relaxing, and I managed to forget about the issue with Michele.

When it came, Michele's reply was brief: He asked if he could speak to Mr. Lucchesi on Tuesday, with me present.

"Thank you, Michele, that's great to hear. I'll arrange a meeting with him after the weekly quality meeting. I want to say now that I'll respect whatever decision you make."

The quality meeting, focused on analyzing major customer complaints, was shorter than usual. Since Michele's arrival, the number of complaints had dropped, as had the financial repercussions of them. He had succeeded in transferring his passion to the production manager, department heads, and all the employees.

Mr. Lucchesi was visibly tense, as indicated by some of his facial expressions. His anxiety stemmed from his deep concern about Michele's potential departure. The company's success under Michele's leadership had been significant, and Mr. Lucchesi didn't hide his emotions, clearly worried about the impact of losing such a valuable team member.

"I think the decision to resign, while painful, was the right one," Michele stated. "I believe certain tones should not be used. People who constantly criticize others have, in my opinion, significant inner issues. Often, criticism is used to hide one's own flaws and frustrations; it's an action meant to inflate one's ego and diminish others. In view of the accusations made against me, I had no choice but to resign."

My eyes met Mr. Lucchesi's. All I saw was disappointment and disillusionment.

"When I came to the company, the situation wasn't good, and I showed what I could do. Generally, a good professional, given optimal conditions, can add value to the organization. If that happens, they'll be even more motivated to achieve the desired results. When I submitted my resignation, I told myself, 'No doubt they'll find a suitable replacement.'"

Unfortunately, his words left little room for ambiguity: Michele was speaking as a former employee and was already thinking about his replacement. He had had a chance to reconsider his decision, perhaps made in the heat of the moment—an instinctive choice he might not have made under normal circumstances. At least that's what Mr. Lucchesi and I hoped, but Michele's words weighed heavily on us.

Then something shifted. "I appreciated what Pietro told me on Friday. I especially appreciated his clarity and ingenuity. It's inspiring for any director. The plans and prospects are extremely ambitious, and the conditions here are set to achieve those results." Michele continued, "I want to emphasize my loyalty to the company. I don't want my actions to call that loyalty into question or undermine your confidence in me. In light of what Pietro has told me, I'll retrace my steps if the door is still open, because I see a bright future here, full of potential and promise. Therefore, I believe it's wise to remain in my role. I wish to withdraw my resignation."

These words brought smiles back to our faces, especially to Mr. Lucchesi, who was usually a man of few words. "Thank you, Michele! Great decision," he said, and embraced him.[24] Then, with the same emotion and sincerity, he hugged me as well.

While no one is indispensable, the loss of someone like Michele, with essential skills and years of knowledge and experience, could have been extremely damaging. I was pleased the rift had been mended—something I had a part in, though I felt I had done far less than Michele and Mr. Lucchesi credited me for.

The outcome led me to wonder how long this newfound calm would last. Who would inform the general manager that Michele's resignation had been withdrawn and, more importantly, explain the reasons for his change of heart? How would he react? What would happen when he learned of my involvement? What would be the consequences for the relationships among the general manager, Mr. Lucchesi, Michele, and me?

In my words, Michele had found reassurance and convinced himself to stay rather than seek new paths. He just needed to be seen and judged as consistent, to feel his commitment aligned with the image he had of himself.

---

24   In Italian culture, expressions of warmth and affection, such as hugs, are common even in professional settings, especially when celebrating success or showing appreciation. This may differ from the norms in some other cultures, where workplace interactions tend to be more formal and reserved. In Italy, these gestures reflect a strong sense of camaraderie, mutual respect, and shared accomplishment.

We are often insecure about ourselves, and we recognize those insecurities in others. Michele felt comfortable with me and was naturally drawn to me. I had always seen him behave as a seasoned professional, willing to listen to those he saw as authoritative or knowledgeable. Our conversations were warm and friendly. He liked me, and that influenced him.

I had also deliberately included persuasive elements in the speech I gave him, although I imagine he would have easily found another good job, as he was a skilled professional.

The point is that I wanted Michele to feel that staying with us was a unique growth opportunity and, as such, more appealing than any alternative. The idea of missing this opportunity was a powerful motivator to encourage him to act quickly.

I See New Horizons

The case was closed, and I could leave for a ten-day trip to the United States to increase our market share with peace of mind. The US market, the largest in the world, offered huge volumes but at low price levels. We had to deal with both local and foreign competitors, manage logistics and delivery times, and ensure top-tier service levels. Most customers were concentrated on the East Coast, with significant clusters in Illinois, New Jersey, and Pennsylvania. We had a large customer in Boston that was almost exclusively supplied by our Italian competitor, Ineos, as well as clients in California, Colorado, Indiana, and Nevada.

After each trip, I would send a visit report to the owners, management, and relevant colleagues on the distribution list—prepared during the long flight or while waiting at the airport to send promptly upon my return. I did that this time, and on Monday morning, I received a Mail Delivery Failure message from the general manager's address. I should have been more attentive. I spent the first few hours with the area managers, catching up on their activities. Then I focused on the customer service representatives, analyzing various indicators, order intake trends, and delivery times for our product lines. One of the company's strengths and unique selling points was our service: fast, efficient, and consistent. Thanks to new investments and cutting-edge technical solutions, we operated with remarkable agility. Any order received by Tuesday would be shipped by the following Friday, and for lacquered overlay alone, the lead time was four weeks. My meeting with the customer service team was interrupted when Mr. Lucchesi burst in.

"Pietro, I need to talk to you. Can you come up to the attic? Right away."

He often had urgent requests and struggled to distinguish between truly important matters and those that could wait. To me, "urgent" meant something that had to be done immediately, but the word itself doesn't necessarily indicate the importance of the event it refers to: something urgent isn't necessarily important, and something important doesn't necessarily have to be urgent. "Important" refers to something of great value or significance that demands due and serious consideration. The main difference between important and urgent is time. But he was the boss, so I dropped everything and joined Mr. Lucchesi in his office.

"Pietro, things aren't going well here, and I've already decided that I want you to be the new general manager. It's a real powder keg—will you take it?" he asked, following his usual style: straight to the point, no frills, no hedging.

"Well, that's an excellent question! It's not the first time you've asked me something like that," I replied, using a filler phrase to buy time—a common tactic. I was unprepared for the situation and needed a moment to think. I was in a quandary: should I accept, accept with conditions, or decline the offer? Too many options, and I didn't have time!

"I understand that you're at a loss for words to thank me," Lucchesi continued. "I'll take your silence to indicate acceptance. You certainly meet my expectations—you're the right man to run this company! I'll adjust your contract, and you'll be happy."

At this point, he looked at me. I was still silent.

"Pietro, you exude extraordinary passion. You can handle the pressure and responsibility of a high-profile position, especially at this critical time for our company," Lucchesi said. "You have a clear vision that allows you to develop a business strategy, and we must always stay ahead of our competitors by anticipating market trends. But passion alone isn't enough. This company won't last if we make the wrong choices. Enough is enough! I can no longer afford mistakes! They're expensive and disruptive. My company has the potential to go far, but only with the right leadership. It's crucial to attract talented human capital that aligns with and supports the company's mission and vision."

I continued to listen, without saying anything.

"You communicate, and you communicate effectively. You handled Michele's case brilliantly, proving you're on top of things. I listen to you when you address the organization and see that you're comfortable with customers. I was especially impressed when I saw you confidently interact with new people in a social setting."

While the boss spoke, my mind was racing. Formally, I would report to the board of directors, but in reality, I'd report to Mr. Lucchesi. I knew that my specific responsibilities might differ slightly from what I'd envisioned and from what I'd seen throughout my career, but I would be responsible for the company's ultimate success or failure.

"You'll retain responsibility for sales management," Lucchesi said, "because I don't want to delegate large accounts to anyone else—they're too important. You'll need to manage relationships with them carefully, keeping a close watch and ensuring they're satisfied with our company. You'll also have to train an assistant, because no one else has your knowledge. Although I've never seen you negotiate with Gemplus, Schlumberger, Selp, McNaughton, and Antalis, the results you bring home speak for themselves. In your new role, you'll negotiate more frequently, not only with customers but also across multiple tasks and projects. You'll need to stay organized and ensure tasks are completed on time—you can't afford to overlook details. Of course, you can delegate."

Finally, I decided to reply.

"Thank you for your confidence, Mr. Lucchesi. I will not disappoint you," I said. Although my voice was confident, I felt nervous about taking the proverbial leap.

As I descended the attic stair, my heart was smiling. I was happy, feeling a moment of great excitement, personal satisfaction, and gratitude. My first thoughts were of my mother and father, with gratitude to them for teaching me the value of hard work and perseverance. With their support, I had made it this far. I felt proud of my work, grateful for the company's confidence in me, and energized by the opportunities on the horizon. My job as commercial director would remain the same, with finance, administration, and controlling added to my responsibilities. Still, I felt confident that I would manage everything to the best of my ability, thanks to my academic background and skills. I knew I would need to devote significant energy to working with banks to support growth projects in the future. I would also be working on new product lines, creating and maintaining competitive advantages, expanding into potential new markets, mitigating risks, capitalizing on opportunities, and countless other tasks.

It was a big challenge, no doubt. I would have to learn how to make better use of input from other employees. I felt it was essential to create a new role from scratch: the Chief People Officer (CPO), who would focus on building and sustaining the company's culture and oversee all aspects of human resources, from hiring new employees to developing training programs and improving retention rates.

I was inheriting an important legacy: leading a company with a strongly family-oriented culture. I knew that my vision and values would take this deeply rooted corporate identity in multiple and diverse directions. I also knew that the organization would observe my behavior closely, analyzing every action I took or didn't take. I would be judged even on the most mundane decisions, such as what I wore and how I presented myself. As general manager I bore significant responsibility, because how I interacted with others would set the tone for the organization. Although the company had an owner whose last name wasn't mine, I was becoming the face of the organization to an even greater extent. I would represent the company to employees, customers, suppliers, and a range of other parties, conveying key elements of the company's identity.

From that moment, I realized I would never really be "out of office," because someone would always be watching or listening. I understood that while I could create an out-of-office message, no one would truly respect it. Everyone would assume I read every message, even those copied merely to keep me informed, and that I would answer the phone at any hour.

For the fourth time in my life—and thankfully the last—I accepted a job without negotiating the terms. I never regretted it, as Lucchesi was extraordinarily generous with me. In this contract, which he prepared unilaterally, he included safeguards and guarantees that I should have requested but didn't think to.

These clauses offered greater benefits and protections, such as provisions for change of ownership, dismissal without just cause, and severance pay. These provisions would later prove to be invaluable. Since then, in all my subsequent employment contracts, I've had the confidence to insist on similar protections and have had them accepted. Today, I recommend to everyone, if they have the leverage, to ensure these clauses are included for their own protection.

Dismissal without just cause is a critical clause in employment contracts, ensuring that employees are entitled to specific protections if they are terminated without a valid reason. Typically, this clause stipulates that an employer cannot terminate an employee arbitrarily without providing compensation or following due process. When paired with severance pay provisions, it offers a safety net for employees who lose their job unexpectedly, granting them financial stability during the transition. Severance pay is compensation provided to employees upon termination, calculated based on their tenure, salary, or other factors. It not only supports the employee's financial needs but also acknowledges their contributions to the organization. Together, these clauses empower employees by offering security in uncertain situations, fostering a sense of fairness, and encouraging professional risk-taking without fear of sudden financial destabilization.

The following year, I was managing a company with almost two hundred employees. While subsequent developments in my career have dwarfed that, at the time, it felt significant. The years that followed were intense. Many of the things I had discussed with Michele came to pass, thanks to Mr. Lucchesi's intelligence and entrepreneurial spirit and the responsiveness of the markets, which were particularly dynamic in those years.

We moved to continuous production, as otherwise, we wouldn't have been able to meet the volumes the market demanded. Growth continued steadily until 2001, when we invested in an innovative coating and laminating line, opening up new prospects in the market for higher-margin products. This pace continued until 2002, with sales reaching €58 million,[25] 23,500 metric tons in volume,[26] and 285 employees.

Unfortunately, private equity interest never materialized, and in June 2003, Lucchesi sold his shares to a French group. The new owner wanted to enter markets where we were leaders, and rather than invest in new equipment, they opted to acquire a fully operational company. I immediately realized there would be no place for me and that the new owners would want to manage everything themselves—I knew my time at the company would be short. I didn't want to end up like the salmon that swims upstream against all odds only to become sashimi at an all-you-can-eat restaurant. So, when I was asked to step down and make way for the new shareholder's son as general manager, I seized the opportunity to negotiate my exit package. I decided to accept the new terms, and although it was my first time, I was thoroughly prepared. I still remember meticulously preparing, designing, and planning the meeting with the son of the new owner in my office at the end of July 2003.

That was a long time ago. When I think about it, I smile. I smile because I came prepared, determined to achieve two results: a significant salary increase and a bonus tied to improved business performance. From my perspective, there was no need to soften my demands to maintain a good relationship, because the primary goal was to maximize the salary increase. Sooner or later, one of two conditions would arise: dismissal or resignation. I went to the meeting confident that the company would leverage group synergies in various ways: renegotiating debt with banks, increasing purchasing power with suppliers, optimizing production among the different sites, and reducing the workforce by merging certain group functions.

My interviewer began by saying, "I want to take over as general manager; you will be the sales manager."

As soon as he said that, I knew I would have an advantage. I understood the difference between wanting and needing, and saw that he would do anything to secure the position. I made it

---

25   At average exchange rates for 2002, sales were approximately $61.3 million.
26   A weight of 23,500 tons is approximately 51.8 million pounds.

clear that the role was mine and that I saw no reason to step back. At the same time, however, I left the door open and asked what he could offer me to relinquish my position.

"Pietro, I can raise your salary by 20 percent," he replied.

"Honestly, 20 percent seems a little low; I was expecting much more," I replied, then remained silent.

He was struggling. "All right, Pietro, I can go up to 30 percent, but no more," he said.

"We're still far from what I had in mind, but if you agree, let's put that aside for a moment and discuss a performance-related bonus. I was thinking of a bonus tied to EBITDA."

"Well, I was thinking of giving you a 1 percent bonus on profit. What do you think?"

I found it strange to tie the bonus to gross profit. At that time, the company had positive EBITDA due to depreciation from large investments, but gross profit was low.

So I proposed a mechanism I had already worked out before the meeting: "Starting with fiscal 2004 and for each year thereafter, I will receive a bonus of 2 percent calculated on whichever is greater: the gross profit at the end of the fiscal year; or the increase in gross profit compared to 2003."

"Mon dieu, c'est trop!"[27] he replied. "I can give one percentage point, but two is too much! We don't have much money right now. Maybe later we'll see."

"Well, I'm willing to accept your proposal of a 1 percent bonus, a one-time bonus equivalent to five months' salary to be paid in August, and a 35 percent salary increase. Alternatively, I'd also accept a 1.5 percent bonus, a one-time bonus of four months' salary, and a 30 percent salary increase." I was prepared to trade a larger bonus (which I wouldn't see, as I'd be dismissed or resign before the end of 2004) for a combination of a meaningful one-time payment and a more significant salary increase, which was my real priority.

---

27   "Mon dieu, c'est trop!" is a French expression that translates to "My God, that's too much!" It's often used to express being overwhelmed or surprised by something excessive or disproportionate.

"All right, Pietro. I want to be the general manager, as I told you. So you'll be the director of sales, marketing, and research and development. Let's settle on a 1 percent bonus on profits, a one-time bonus of four months' salary, and a 35 percent salary increase."

"I accept this proposal. You're the general manager!"

The title was important to him, and stepping back in exchange for the new package was no problem for me—quite the opposite. I was fired on December 19 of the same year, citing the elimination of the position as the reason. It was one of the best Christmas gifts I ever received. I spent the holidays with my family, and after a brief but persuasive courtship by the Charoen Pokphand Group, the Thai conglomerate that now employs more than 350,000 people, I moved to Asia, where I stayed for eight years.

I sued my former company for additional benefits (the grounds of "elimination of position" were weak) and severance pay. I won in the first instance in 2006 and in the Supreme Court in 2010, after losing in the Court of Appeals. In addition to the satisfaction of my court victory, I received in the first instance what Mr. Lucchesi had wisely and generously included in my employment contract, modifying it in my favor.

To my dismay, Lucchesi S.p.A. closed its doors for good in November 2012, and its parent company, burdened by over €100 million of debt, changed hands a few years later.

But that is another story.

- It is essential to know how to relate to others in all circumstances.
- Learn from negative experiences.
- A good opportunity will always present itself; the problem is knowing how to recognize it.
- If you travel a lot, use your downtime to study and prepare.
- Knowing how to sell does not automatically mean knowing how to negotiate.
- A truly productive negotiation can only begin after the selling phase is complete.
- Building more genuine relationships improves your credibility.
- Preparation is the first and most important activity in a negotiation.
- A reputation as a fair, honest, and reliable negotiator is essential: work on establishing one.
- Negotiation is not a mysterious art but a practical skill that anyone can learn and improve.
- Be aware of your weaknesses and work hard to overcome them.
- Learn from your skilled superior, colleagues and rivals.

I am what I am today because of the choices I made yesterday. What I do today will determine who I will be tomorrow.

Eleanor Roosevelt

CHAPTER 3

WHEN NOT NEGOTIATING
IS THE RIGHT CHOICE

Don't Assume Anything

In every company I have worked for, I have sought to create organizational structures that value employees. I am fascinated by the idea of seeing people motivated and committed to giving their best on every project. My focus has always been on fostering a strong connection between team members and the goals they aim to achieve. Every team member should be accountable for results, working together to devise and apply the best strategies to complete a project successfully.

I have also been fortunate to work with individuals who possess excellent practical competences, relational skills and aptitudes. These people, when valued and entrusted with ambitious projects, often exceed expectations. At times, I have been criticized for delegating too much and favoring an excessively horizontal structure, but I have never felt that I lost control. On the contrary, I have consistently achieved results within the established timelines. This success stems from selecting the most suitable people to lead teams—those who understand the critical dynamics within the organization.

In the organizational model I find most effective, authority gives way to negotiation. Authority can be understood as the forceful imposition of decisions on others. Negotiation, in contrast, is subtler, but an equally powerful influence, and becomes the primary modus operandi for advancing projects and activities. Negotiation is both an art and a science—the art of achieving what you want!

But let's take a step back: should one always negotiate? The answer is no.

Sometimes, not negotiating is the better option. However, the decision not to negotiate, to accept an offer outright, or to walk away must be a conscious and deliberate choice—not an act of avoidance driven by fear, self-doubt, or reluctance to engage. Whatever decision you make, you take responsibility for its consequences. Even if the decision turns out to be a mistake, you gain valuable experience and learn what to do differently in the future.

On the other hand, when you choose not to decide at all (and yes, inaction is a decision), you leave the resolution of the problem to chance, hoping it will solve itself. Taking an active role means managing your emotions, especially fear. Life constantly demands choices and decisions, many of which lead to negotiations—often fraught with mixed feelings and complex emotions. Deciding not to negotiate is a multifaceted issue requiring as much analysis and preparation as a decision to engage in negotiation.

Even in simple negotiations, it is essential to examine the core concerns, interests, needs, desires, and motivations of all parties—both your own and your negotiating partner's, whether explicit or implicit. From there, you can explore options: the choices each party might consider to meet their interests. Finally, you must analyze your best alternative to a negotiated agreement (BATNA), which represents the course of action you'll take if no agreement is reached.

This comprehensive approach enables you to determine whether an agreement can be legitimate and fair. It also lays the groundwork for potential future collaborations with your negotiating partner. If you believe the current deal will be the last interaction with the other party, your considerations may shift, as you have fewer implications to consider post-agreement.

There's no such thing as an "improvised negotiation"—the phrase is a contradiction in terms. Negotiation requires thorough preparation, while improvisation is better suited for casual discussions. Even in such cases, you're not truly improvising; you're drawing on a deep understanding of the subject matter and relying on accumulated experience. Unfortunately, all too often, individuals and organizations rush into negotiations unprepared.

They fail to allocate sufficient time to preparation or overlook critical elements entirely.

For example:

"Pietro, tomorrow morning, I have to negotiate a supply contract with Leonardo S.p.A. It's a commission worth €17 million over three years. What do you recommend?"

Failing to prepare means preparing to fail. If negotiation is unavoidable, lack of preparation will impact the outcome—not just in terms of monetary value but also in the quality of the deal or the relationship itself. If you find yourself in a negotiation without adequate preparation, you must at least define your interests, options, and BATNA. Using practical and expedited logic can help mitigate risks, though it isn't without pitfalls.

For instance, if you unexpectedly find yourself in a negotiation, should you stall, or seize the moment and capitalize on the opportunity? Consider whether your negotiating partner is deliberately trying to catch you off guard to gain an advantage. Knowing when to act—and how to act—is critical to navigating these situations effectively.

Informal bargaining situations arise frequently. Consider a business lunch, a chance meeting with a friend in a bookstore, or a conversation with the person seated next to you on an airplane. Learning to improvise in such scenarios becomes a fundamental skill for any negotiator.

However, in reality, improvisation is often a misnomer, as what appears to be spontaneous decision-making is actually the result of accumulated experience and knowledge. Skilled negotiators may seem to improvise, but what they are actually doing is drawing on years of practice, intuition, and a deep understanding of negotiation dynamics. They are able to quickly adapt to unforeseen circumstances because they have developed a flexible mindset, allowing them to respond effectively to changing situations. This ability to improvise is, in fact, a reflection of their prior preparation, strategic thinking, and experience in similar contexts.

A few years ago, I found myself in just such a situation while traveling by train from Rome to Milan.

"Sorry to bother you," said the distinguished gentleman seated in front of me. "My name is Silvio Alessandrini. I'm a lawyer from Siena. I couldn't help overhearing your phone call, and since you're selling it, I'd be interested in the land in Monteriggioni you mentioned. I'm offering you 35 percent more than your asking price. I know the property well: it's poor in nutrients and well drained, with excellent composition and exposure to the sun."

I took a deep breath, consciously remaining calm.

"It's a pleasure to meet you," I replied. "Don't worry, it wasn't a confidential conversation. And, by the way, I commend you on your expertise in land and vineyards."[28]

With this opening, I aimed to show respect and begin building a relationship. I then asked a series of questions to shift the interaction from straightforward haggling to an exchange of information. As we spoke, I jotted down notes about his responses to gather useful insights. The train had just passed Bologna, leaving me less than an hour before arriving in Milan. To buy time, I deliberately wrote and repeated things slowly, stalling the process.

"Mr. Alessandrini, I'm fascinated by your knowledge of enology. I mean no disrespect, but I need to join a video call now. It won't take long. Do you mind if we continue our discussion afterward?"

Using the analogy of a game of poker, I was choosing neither to **call** nor **fold**.[29] Instead, I was delaying the negotiation, and the need to make any such decision. This gave me time to prepare, even with the limited window I had. Using the meeting as an excuse, I focused on the essentials: I clarified my interests,

---

28   In Italy, it is generally more culturally acceptable to casually join in a conversation after overhearing it, especially in public places, and may not be considered rude. This is in contrast to some other cultures where this behavior may be considered intrusive or rude. The context and manner of engagement play an important role in determining the appropriateness of such interactions.
29   In poker, a *call* is when a player decides to match the current bet made by another player in order to remain in that hand. On the other hand, to *fold* is when a player decides to forfeit their hand by not matching the bet. This player forfeits any chance of winning the current round and discards their cards, effectively ending the hand.

analyzed what I had learned about my counterpart, and messaged friends who were land experts for a better understanding of the property's value. I also reached out to a lawyer in Colle di Val d'Elsa for background on Mr. Alessandrini, and reassessed my alternatives to the proposed deal.

Just before the train reached Lodi,[30] we scheduled a follow-up meeting for the next day to discuss the transaction in detail and finalize a preliminary sale contract.

While this was an extreme case, there are many situations in which circumstances might force you to avoid negotiation altogether.

When is it not worth negotiating?

Negotiation is not worthwhile if there is little or no value to be gained or if the risks outweigh the potential rewards. This includes scenarios where the emotional toll outweighs the benefits, or where engaging in negotiation could escalate a minor issue into a major problem—for example, arguing over a small contractual clause could lead to a breakdown in an otherwise positive business relationship. Additionally, you should avoid negotiating if the people involved lack the authority to make binding decisions or agreements.

Our minds often jump to conclusions to save time and cognitive energy, which can lead to errors in judgment.

A principle that applies perfectly here is drawn from *The Four Agreements* by Don Miguel Ruiz (1997), a spiritual teacher and author who studied the wisdom of the Toltecs, a pre-Columbian culture of central Mexico. Among his teachings, the third agreement—assume nothing—is particularly illuminating for negotiation.

If you have doubts, ask questions rather than make assumptions. We often misunderstand situations because we lack sufficient knowledge about others. Never assume that the person you're negotiating with has full authority just because they're at the table. If you do, you might find yourself in a bad situation.

---

30   Lodi is a town about thirty kilometers (about 18.64 miles) southeast of Milan, with a train journey time of about twenty-five minutes between the two.

Always gather the necessary information, and remember that it's perfectly legitimate to ask for clarification.

It's better to avoid negotiating than to discover later that what you thought was a final agreement was merely the starting point for further discussions with another party. Be cautious, and ensure that all aspects of the agreement are clear and agreed upon before considering the matter resolved.

People and Problems

In negotiations, it is crucial to separate people from problems. People are not the problem, and if you approach a negotiation as if they are, you will probably get nowhere. If you don't separate the person from the problem, you may feel offended (or risk offending someone else) rather than finding mutually beneficial solutions.

We often confuse problems and people without realizing it. You must always handle people respectfully, and one of the prerequisites for a successful negotiation is to continually ask yourself whether you are separating the person from the problem, and whether you are prepared to deal effectively with both. There are also situations where people you would prefer to avoid may be at the negotiating table.

Imagine you are invited to negotiate next year's deal by the purchasing director of one of your major global customers. In the list of attendees, however, you see the name of the site manager of the Spanish plant, who has clearly expressed his dislike for your products and has shown reluctance to work with your company. This could add a layer of complexity to the negotiation, especially if his views influence the decision-making process. In such a case, it might seem tempting to avoid the negotiation, but that may not always be possible. Instead, focus on managing the situation effectively by preparing thoroughly. Take the time to understand the root of the plant manager's dissatisfaction and address those concerns proactively, perhaps through a pre-meeting conversation or by ensuring your team is aligned on addressing his concerns. During the negotiation, remain calm and professional, focusing on common goals and shared interests. Keep the discussion constructive and avoid personal conflicts. If necessary, offer to have a separate discussion with the plant manager after the main meeting to address any specific issues that may arise, ensuring that his concerns are heard without derailing the broader negotiations.

In situations like these (or even more complex ones), if you care about maintaining a good relationship with the negotiating partner, express your appreciation for them. Clearly state that you prefer to avoid negotiating, without going into detail or explaining the real reason for your decision, especially if it might offend the other party. In general, remember that when you report a problem (for example, "The warehouse is a mess!"), someone on the other side of the table may take your words as a personal attack or blame. When people hear comments about substance, they may infer something negative about the speaker's attitude.

Another case where negotiation makes little sense is when the best alternative to a negotiated agreement far outweighs the best possible outcome of any negotiation scenario. Given these premises, engaging in negotiation is unnecessary and dangerous. I always approach negotiations optimistically, believing I can contribute, because I am convinced that I bring valuable opportunities for my interests and those of the negotiating partner. However, I prefer to refrain from negotiating if, after thorough preparation, I realize that the only possible outcome is a **distributive** negotiation where, as in sports, there is a clear winner and loser. There is no opportunity to turn the negotiation into an **integrative** one, where the two parties work together to find the best solution by sharing information and resources.

I also avoid negotiating when I lack power and leverage. Otherwise, I risk giving in indiscriminately (resulting in a purely distributive negotiation, which will only benefit my negotiating partner, to my own detriment). Once again, preparation is crucial, particularly in accurately assessing negotiating power. If I fail to assess it correctly or overlook the need for an updated evaluation, I face a double risk: underestimating or overestimating my bargaining power might lead me to give up negotiating prematurely. This could force me into less productive alternatives, such as imposing my position or yielding unnecessarily.

To negotiate effectively, each party must know (not just *assume*) the levers in play and understand how and when to use them, considering both their own leverage and that of their negotiating partner. But what do I mean by levers? Leverage can be an actionable **incentive** or **sanction** that encourages the negotiating partner to find our position compelling enough to join the table. Timing, such as a deadline or looming date, can also provide tactical advantage, as it may pressure one side to compromise and weaken their position, especially if they are already weaker. There are also cases where a request to negotiate can send the wrong signal, so it is better not to negotiate at all. For example, imagine you've won a major contract, successfully added a customer to your roster after years of effort, and both sides are happy. A few months later, however, your customer asks for a price reduction on a specific order where their margin is slim. In this case, you could politely decline, explaining your reasons (perhaps your margin is also slim), or offer the discount in the hope that the gesture will be remembered favorably in the future. However, this should generally be avoided, as negotiating in exchange for a "favor" can create an unhealthy dynamic.

The principle of reciprocity may apply, meaning that the customer may expect something in return for the "favor" (such as a discount). This can be problematic as it creates a situation where both parties feel they owe each other something, potentially leading to further requests that can strain the relationship. Also, asking directly for something in return can make you seem ungrateful, as if you do not appreciate the value of the original agreement. Instead, it is better to keep gestures of goodwill implicit and not linked to explicit requests for future concessions, ensuring that the relationship remains professional and based on mutual benefit rather than transactional expectations.

Relationships are built over time on the basis of trust, understanding, respect, and friendship. Such a foundation can make each new negotiation smoother and more efficient. People's desire to feel good about themselves and their concern for others' perceptions can often make them more sensitive to another negotiator's interests, as they seek to maintain positive relationships and avoid conflict. This sensitivity can lead to a greater willingness to accommodate or find mutually beneficial solutions during negotiations. Building a relationship based on trust and communication takes time, but it can be shattered in an instant. Be wise when deciding whether and what to negotiate.

Don't negotiate something trivial today if it might lead to more significant consequences tomorrow. Always adopt a broader perspective, focusing less on short-term gains and more on medium- or long-term advantages. Sometimes, giving up something now can provide a better position later—like sacrificing a pawn in chess to gain a strategic advantage.

Having lived abroad for many years, I've had the opportunity to interact with negotiators from various cultures. This experience has taught me that there is no universal consensus on the purpose of negotiation. For some, the primary goal is to secure a signed contract; for others, it is about fostering a relationship between the two parties. While a signed contract implies the existence of a relationship, its essence often lies in the connection itself.

This cultural difference explains why, in Asia—where relationship-building is emphasized—negotiators invest more time and effort in preliminary discussions. In contrast, North Americans tend to be more direct and hurried, minimizing the initial phase. Cultural context is vital when approaching negotiations: different cultures are based on different interpretations of the world, and they therefore give rise to different negotiation styles. Some see negotiation as a battle to be won, while others strive for a win–win outcome. To succeed in global markets, it is essential to understand how to adapt your negotiating style to fit cross-cultural contexts. Proper preparation is critical when negotiating with someone from a different culture. If you're not adequately prepared, it's often better not to negotiate at all, as the process could become difficult, unpleasant, and counterproductive.

There are also contexts where negotiation is inappropriate. Imagine buying a handbag at Louis Vuitton or shopping at a luxury brand store. None of the following statements would be effective:

"I have a maximum budget of N euros."
"What's the cash price?"
"How far can you come down to meet me?"

"Is that the best you can do?"
"I'll pay N euros if you let me take it now."
"Throw in a gift, and I'll agree to the price."
"I saw this cheaper at another store."

Similarly, these phrases wouldn't work at a shopping mall checkout counter if you were buying everyday items like a toothbrush, cookies, or toilet paper. Negotiating in these situations would be inappropriate and a waste of time.

So why is it acceptable to negotiate with jewelers or farmers? The difference lies not in the value of the purchase or the type of product but in the authority of the person selling it. The Louis Vuitton salesperson or supermarket cashier doesn't have the authority to negotiate, while the owner of a trusted jewelry or grocery store often does. For example, you might comfortably say to your jeweler, "How much for two pairs of earrings if I buy them for Giulia and Alessia?" Similarly, you could ask your grocer, "If I buy the whole Scottish smoked salmon instead of two hundred grams,[31] can you give me a deal?"[32]

Then there's the issue of dealing with unfair negotiators who use unethical tactics. In such cases, caution is paramount. Unfortunately, unethical negotiators often conceal their true intentions, and their tactics may only become apparent after they've already been put into practice. Watch for changes in negotiating style or behavior, as these are often signs of deception.

By "unethical behaviors," I'm referring to those such as bluffing, deception, alteration, falsification, misrepresentation, distortion, selective use of information, and outright lying. These actions erode trust in both personal and professional relationships, create uncertainty, and foster mistrust. They can also lead

31   Two hundred grams of smoked salmon is approximately 7.05 ounces.
32   This type of negotiation is common in Italy, especially in small, locally owned businesses. Italian shoppers often have the opportunity to discuss prices directly with the business owner, a practice that is less common in larger retail environments or more urbanized settings in other countries. While this may occasionally happen in small towns or unique, independent shops elsewhere, it is a more ingrained aspect of everyday transactions in Italy.

to legal or financial consequences and damage the reputations of individuals and companies alike. My advice is simple: always act ethically and transparently. Promoting honesty and personal responsibility will ultimately pay off.

Unethical behavior can manipulate key factors such as interests, options, alternatives, BATNA (best alternative to a negotiated agreement), and reserve value (RV, which we'll discuss further in Chapter 4). Dishonest negotiators often have no qualms about their actions, treating deceit as second nature. If, during preparation, you uncover evidence of dishonesty, consider whether you want to do business with such people. If negotiations take a turn for the worse, be ready to make a smooth exit.

The same caution applies to negotiations initiated in bad faith, where the other party pretends to work toward an agreement but conceals their true motives. These individuals often stall the process with unreasonable last-minute demands or send someone without decision-making authority to the table. Such behaviors are often habitual, so with proper preparation, you should be able to recognize them before entering into negotiations.

Finally, I would avoid negotiating with an unprepared partner who lacks familiarity with negotiation techniques (although exceptions may surprise you). For instance, individuals at different life stages—whether in early youth or advanced age—may have unique approaches. Older people, for example, often share less about their priorities and may be less adept at utilizing available information.

"Do you mind if my grandson comes too?" asked an elderly gentleman who wanted to sell his store.

This was a shrewd move. I appreciated the idea of involving someone younger in the negotiation, as it ensured neither party missed opportunities. However, it also introduced a destabilizing element. While I had often focused on bridging gaps related to differing styles, backgrounds, and goals, this was the first time I had paid attention to overcoming generational barriers in negotiation.

After all, the first people I negotiated with were my parents, born in 1929 and 1931—members of the Silent Generation.

Most of my subsequent negotiations were with Gen Xers and baby boomers. Today, however, I increasingly find myself dealing with millennials, and as a father, I am also negotiating with Gen Z. I don't fixate on these arbitrary generational categorizations, preferring instead to see people as individuals rather than as representatives of their age group.

Depending on the context, you might find yourself negotiating with representatives from three or even four generations at the same table. It is essential to understand, empathize with, and connect with people of different ages, as they may have mindsets vastly different from your own. If you decide to negotiate, prepare thoroughly—this is where the real opportunities begin.

After addressing generational differences, a final note on gender: negotiation is a vital skill for both men and women and applies to countless situations, from salary discussions to contract agreements and even resolving family disagreements. Gender can influence negotiation outcomes, often due to differences in how men and women approach problems.

You may have noticed that men are generally more likely to initiate negotiations than women. They also tend to be more assertive, often securing better deals. However, this gap is narrowing. When women gain negotiation experience, they excel—especially in negotiations involving third parties. Women are often more cooperative, personable, and pleasant during negotiations, and they frequently make more concessions.

These qualities can be assets, but the key takeaway is that negotiation is a skill everyone can and should develop, regardless of gender or generation. My advice to women is to work, to prepare extensively, and to negotiate more often than they might spontaneously be inclined to, because this will be of great help in closing the gender gap bias, such as that a woman who sits at a negotiating table is greedy, or desperate. These outdated perceptions are often rooted in societal expectations about gender roles and can unfairly color how a woman's behavior is interpreted during negotiations. However, by consistently negotiating and building confidence, women can challenge these stereotypes and reshape how they are viewed in professional settings.

- You don't have to negotiate at every opportunity that presents itself.
- It's not worth negotiating when the negotiation is not convenient, beneficial, or worth the effort and commitment required.
- Don't negotiate if you risk turning a small problem into a big problem.
- It is only possible to negotiate if the people around the table have the authority to decide or accept an agreement.
- It does not pay to negotiate when the best alternative to a negotiated agreement exceeds the best possible outcome of the agreement itself.
- Properly assess negotiating power and identify the applicable levers.
- Building a relationship based on trust and communication takes time, but it can be shattered in an instant.
- Cultural context is relevant when approaching negotiations and contracts.
- Always promote honesty and personal responsibility: this behavior will pay off in the long term.

Improvisation is the child of incompetence,
and the mother of fear.
His brother's name is mistake.

mauro_jfp, Twitter

CHAPTER 4

BE PREPARED,
ALWAYS!

Interests, Options, Alternatives

Negotiators usually express two regrets, one before the negotiation and one after.

"We didn't have time to prepare better," is the first.

"We could have negotiated better if we had prepared more thoroughly," is the second.

Over the years, I've found that negotiators often do not follow a suitable method, even when they appreciate the importance of preparation. Often, the mistake is more severe: preparation is lacking altogether. It doesn't matter what the substance of the negotiation is: managing internal conflicts in a company, a multimillion-dollar contract, annual salary reviews, acquisitions, labor union agreements, or even an international peace treaty. Every negotiation requires thoughtful preparation, and failure to prepare properly affects the outcome, no matter what's at stake or how skilled you are.

I'm often asked by executives, managers, and friends how much time I spend preparing for a negotiation.

My answer is always the same: "Never enough."

Two main reasons explain why even experienced negotiators arrive unprepared: they lack a structured preparation method, and they lack a routine for learning from past negotiations. This stems from the mistaken belief that negotiation is purely an art and not also a science. Another common misconception is that preparation is only necessary for extensive, formal negotiations, as if the real action begins at the negotiating table.

In reality, preparation is the most critical stage of any negotiation. The 80/20 rule applies here too: most negotiation success or failure depends on the quality of preparation. Eighty percent of success comes from preparation, while only 20 percent is the actual negotiation. The more prepared you are, the more creative and constructive you will be, and the more options you will bring to the table.

Having more tools allows you to solve problems better. The better the quality of your tools, the more effective and innovative the solutions.

A proactive, unbiased approach is critical to identifying variables of value and understanding their significance to the other party. Such an approach prepares you for circumstances and situations that might otherwise seem to be beyond your control. Systematic, nearly obsessive preparation ensures you won't be caught off guard or at the mercy of the other party's initiatives. Proper preparation sharpens your ability to develop good ideas and persuasive arguments, enabling you to solve problems efficiently to the satisfaction of both you and your negotiating partner.

By operating this way, I've noticed improvements in my competence and self-confidence. Preparing thoroughly from both my perspective and that of my negotiating partner has motivated me to continually refine my approach.

Preparation takes time, and one reason we don't prepare well is that we are too busy with other activities. However, preparation should be viewed as an investment. Time spent preparing saves far more time during the actual negotiation. Preparation also requires commitment and sacrifice, as it means prioritizing future gains over immediate tasks.

I am often criticized for being repetitive, monotonous, or even boring in my emphasis on preparation. I hear these criticisms, but I have no intention of changing.

"Pietro, are you happy with the results I got? We closed a good deal; I managed to maintain last year's prices while increasing quantity."

"Giuseppe, do you think it went well with 3M? I'd like you to answer that after doing the debriefing I taught you. But since you're asking now, I'll say this: you could have done much better if you had followed my suggestion two weeks ago and prepared more thoroughly. You could have pinpointed the problem, been more creative, asked open-ended questions, explored more options, presented elegant and original proposals, and evaluated alternative offers more effectively."

"You're right, Pietro. I just didn't have time."

"Giuseppe, there's no such thing as 'no time.' It's about willpower. If you truly want something, sunset becomes sunrise, Friday becomes Wednesday, and every moment becomes an opportunity."

Here are the three most frequent reasons people give for not preparing adequately:

1. I don't have enough time.
2. I've already done enough.
3. I know how to handle it.

These excuses undermine methodical and thorough preparation. Remember, the principles of proper preparation keep you humble and hungry. Following a disciplined method keeps your feet on the ground. Those who prepare systematically achieve their goals, perform better, and develop greater self-confidence and higher self-esteem.

Many negotiators limit their preparation by focusing solely on what they want to achieve. When observing negotiations, I've noticed that preparation often consists of listing desires and, at most, creating a backup plan for emergencies. The result is limited, reducing the negotiation to a series of demands and concessions.

Preparation is much more than that. It involves consulting resources like my negotiation archive, where I record elements systematically. For me, the archive is like a cookbook—a catalog of comparable situations and time-tested solutions. It provides guidance and serves as a persuasive tool during negotiations.

As discussed in the previous chapter, there are a range of situations in which it's not worth negotiating. Unfortunately, some decisions to avoid negotiation are made superficially, without sufficient analysis of the context. At other times, negotiations occur simply because the matter at hand seems trivial.

Proper preparation helps you navigate these challenges effectively, ensuring every negotiation becomes a well-considered and productive process.

Never underestimate the psychological and social aspects that influence a negotiation, even when the substance of the agreement seems insignificant. Sometimes, achieving the best possible outcome requires focusing not only on the issue at hand but also on personal relationships, power dynamics, and mutual expectations.

That said, I don't want to dissuade you from negotiating as often as you should out of fear of being unprepared. Not all negotiations require extensive preparation, in-depth analysis, or significant resources. For many situations, a few minutes of focused attention on key elements can dramatically improve your effectiveness. Based on my experience at top negotiation schools, observing skilled negotiators, and learning from them, I've identified a few essential points to help you arrive prepared for even simple negotiations.

In just a few minutes, you can create a "map"—a visual or mental representation of the negotiation. While this map may not perfectly match the reality of the situation (as it reflects your perspective, your vision, your representation of the "territory"), it becomes a vital tool for navigating and achieving your desired outcome.

When preparing for a negotiation, it is essential to start by addressing the questions on your checklist. If clarity seems elusive, consulting someone familiar with the situation can provide valuable insights and a fresh perspective. Begin by defining **your interests**. This involves asking yourself key questions such as:

What do I desire?
What am I looking for?
What are my needs, hopes, and fears?

By carefully considering these aspects, you can develop a prioritized list of interests, taking into account the reasons behind each one. Reflect on simple but profound questions like, "Do I care about this?" or "Is this truly my desire?" This process may feel daunting at first, but with practice, articulating your interests will become more intuitive. Aim to identify at least five key points—a challenging but rewarding exercise that will guide your preparation.

With your own interests clearly defined, the next step is to turn your attention to understanding your **negotiating partner's interests**. Apply the same analytical framework:

What might they desire?
What are their needs, hopes, and fears?

Empathy is crucial here, as it enables you to step into their shoes and see the situation from their perspective. This may seem complex initially, but with practice, it will become second nature. Over time, this empathetic approach will evolve into a core skill, allowing you to better anticipate their priorities and concerns. This deeper understanding lays the foundation for constructive dialogue.

Once you have two lists—your own interests and your negotiating partner's—cross-reference them. Comparing these two perspectives is an invaluable exercise that helps identify **options**, potential areas of alignment and mutual benefit. This step may also involve gathering external information, such as market data, historical precedents, or industry norms, to better contextualize the negotiation. By grounding your approach in reliable information, you can ensure the proposed agreement feels equitable and legitimate to both parties.

One common pitfall to avoid in negotiations is the fixation on a single acceptable outcome. Entering a discussion with only one desired resolution in mind can limit your flexibility and hinder progress. Instead, embrace the possibility of multiple outcomes that could satisfy the interests of both parties. The strength of a negotiation often lies in the differences between the parties' priorities. Reflect on how you can enhance the proposal to make it more appealing to the other party. Ask yourself:

What could I add to the arrangement to make it more acceptable (e.g., offering terms or conditions that are in line with their needs or values)?

What could I do to make it more appealing? (e.g., presenting it in a way that highlights the benefits or value to them)?

Consider adding terms or conditions that align with their values or presenting the arrangement in a way that emphasizes mutual benefits. Asymmetrical concessions can also be valuable tools. These are elements that hold little cost or importance to you but are perceived as highly desirable by your counterpart. Similarly, think about what they could provide that would be relatively easy for them but meaningful to you.

Allow yourself to brainstorm freely. Let thoughts and ideas flow without judgment, jotting down even the most unconventional ones. Once you've compiled a list, review and eliminate impractical or impossible ideas. What remains will be a set of viable solutions.

This process can be done alone, with your negotiating team, or with an uninvolved third party who can offer fresh perspectives. An outsider can often identify things you might have missed due to emotional involvement.

Another cornerstone of effective negotiation is having viable alternatives ready. These alternatives act as both practical tools and psychological assets, answering the critical question: "What if I don't close the deal?" A solid alternative provides confidence, empowering you to negotiate without feeling pressured to settle. It's wise to prepare multiple alternatives, organized in order of importance. This approach offers flexibility and increases the likelihood of finding a satisfactory resolution. Remember, not every negotiation needs to conclude with an agreement; sometimes, walking away is the best choice.

Integrity and honesty are nonnegotiable principles throughout this process. Although you might occasionally feel tempted to exploit an advantage, unethical behavior undermines trust and erodes long-term success. Strive to be transparent and fair with both yourself and your counterpart. While there may be moments when you feel mistreated, maintaining ethical standards strengthens relationships and enhances your reputation as a reliable negotiator. Building trust requires effort and consistency, as it is cultivated through fulfilled commitments and demonstrated dependability. Trust not only supports the current negotiation but also establishes a solid foundation for future collaboration.

To safeguard against potential conflicts or misunderstandings, consider external **standards** during your preparation. These could include historical precedents, standard industry practices, independent expert opinions, or relevant market data. External benchmarks serve a dual purpose: they help convince your counterpart that you are being fair and reasonable while protecting you from being subjected to unwarranted demands. Moreover, **evaluate the specific commitment** associated with any proposed agreement. For example, accepting a job offer entails adhering to schedules, following safety regulations, and performing assigned duties. In return, the employer agrees to provide timely compensation, necessary equipment, and opportunities for professional development. Understanding these commitments ensures clarity and prevents future disputes.

Flexibility is another critical aspect of negotiation. While it may be tempting to bind your negotiating partner as tightly as possible, leaving some room for discretion can be advantageous, especially as circumstances evolve. Successful agreements often rest on the confidence that both parties will honor their promises. This confidence grows as each party demonstrates reliability, fulfilling their commitments and reinforcing mutual trust. Conversely, attempting to present yourself as completely inflexible—unable or unwilling to make any concessions—can damage the relationship and undermine the negotiation's success.

By preparing thoroughly, maintaining ethical standards, and focusing on mutually beneficial outcomes, you can navigate negotiations with confidence and poise. This approach not only improves your immediate results but also fosters stronger, more enduring relationships that pave the way for future success.

MY INTERESTS

What are my interests?
Why do I need it?
What are my needs, desires,
expectations and fears?

1 _____

2 _____

3 _____

THEIR INTERESTS

What are their interests?
Why do they need it?
What are their needs, desires,
expectations and fears?

1 _____

2 _____

3 _____

OPTIONS

Possible points of agreement

1 _____

2 _____

3 _____

LEGITIMATE

Useful external standards to
persuade the other party or justify
my position

1 _____

2 _____

3 _____

MY BEST ALTERNATIVE TO THE NEGOTIATED AGREEMENT

If I don't close the deal, what am I going to do?
What is the best alternative?

1 _____

2 _____

3 _____

COMMITMENT

If I close the deal, what are the obligations that come with it?

1 _____

2 _____

3 _____

Everyday Life Is
an Endless Source of Examples

Some negotiations involve minimal stakes but still require a degree of preparation. These are the simple negotiations that occur daily, often without much thought. However, beyond these everyday interactions lies a complex negotiating world—one that involves resolving multiple issues and managing the interests of various parties, sometimes acting on behalf of others. These are complex negotiations.

When transitioning from simple to complex negotiations, additional factors such as **communication**, **relationships**, and **core concerns** come into play.

Let's illustrate this with an example:

Giuseppe, an executive chef I have had the privilege of knowing and advising for many years, plays a pivotal role in one of Milan's most prestigious Michelin-starred restaurants. This establishment is part of a distinguished group of restaurants owned by a client I also know well and with whom I have collaborated closely over the years. Despite my professional connection with the owner, my role in this case is as an independent advisor to Giuseppe, ensuring there is no conflict of interest.

Recently, this client acquired a historic restaurant in Portofino, Liguria, and entrusted Giuseppe with an exciting new challenge: collaborating with the newly hired executive chef to design and implement a comprehensive one-year training program for the Portofino location. Following this period, Giuseppe is set to return to his full responsibilities at the Milan restaurant.

While Giuseppe is genuinely enthusiastic about this opportunity and sees its potential to enhance his career and contribute to the group's success, he is also aware of the increased demands it entails. The new role requires him to take on additional workloads, shoulder greater responsibilities, and travel frequently between

Milan and Portofino.[33] Given these considerations, Giuseppe feels that a 20 percent salary increase is a fair adjustment to reflect these expanded duties. However, he is cautious about how to approach this conversation, concerned that being too firm in his request might lead the owner to assign the task to Franco, a younger and equally talented colleague eager to take on such responsibilities.

As his consultant, I am working with Giuseppe to develop a strategy for presenting his case in a way that underscores his value to the group while maintaining a collaborative and flexible approach. My goal is to ensure that Giuseppe's contributions are recognized and compensated fairly.

To avoid unnecessary concessions, Giuseppe should focus on his **interests** rather than fixating on a rigid position. By preparing alternative **options**, he can create flexibility in the negotiation and increase his chances of achieving a satisfactory outcome.

When negotiating exclusively on the basis of price, options may seem minimal or nonexistent. For example, when purchasing a property, price is often the primary element. However, with creativity and imagination, additional factors can be negotiated, such as the amount of the down payment, the transfer date, or the inclusion of certain extras, like custom kitchen fittings.

The different interests and preferences of the parties can make the negotiation more appealing. Creativity in identifying multiple options allows negotiators to invent trade-offs and discover mutual gains.

It's always helpful to prepare a list of non-monetary offers or requests in advance. Even if the list isn't complete or entirely accurate, it can help you stay focused on other aspects of the negotiation. For instance, in salary negotiations, non-monetary items might include better travel conditions, reimbursements, moving expenses, discounts on company products, or remote work opportunities.

---

33   The distance between Milan and Portofino is approximately 150 kilometers (93 miles), which typically takes about two to two and a half hours by car, depending on traffic and weather conditions. This commute involves driving along scenic roads through the Ligurian countryside, but can be time consuming and tiring, especially if done frequently.

This principle also applies to other types of negotiations, from real estate deals to complex M&A agreements. Examples include extending non-compete clauses, prolonging the use of data centers, including carve-out elements, arranging for cumulative purchases, or structuring contract manufacturing agreements.

This creative approach reminds me of conversations with Anna Maria Testa[34] (creator of the famous Perlana commercials) and Gavino Sanna[35] (known for his Fiat and Barilla commercials, including the creation of Mulino Bianco). They described the synergy between art directors (responsible for visuals) and copywriters (responsible for text) in creating impactful advertising slogans. The collaborative and creative energy they described is equally applicable to negotiations, where creativity and collaboration can lead to innovative solutions.

Negotiation can sometimes resemble a game of ping-pong, with offers and counteroffers bouncing back and forth between buyer and seller. For example, the seller of a property on Lake Como might start at €2,500,000, as listed by the real estate agent. The buyer offers 2,300,000, prompting the seller to counter with €2,390,000. The buyer then counters with 2,350,000, and the seller responds with €2,370,000, which the buyer accepts.

This, however, is not true negotiation.

It is merely haggling: an exchange of offers and counteroffers until the parties meet somewhere in the middle. While understanding this approach can help structure your counteroffer, it is not

---

34   Anna Maria Testa (born 1953) is a pioneering figure in Italian advertising, known for her influential work as a creative consultant and communications expert. With a career spanning several decades, she has contributed significantly to the evolution of advertising in Italy, combining creativity with strategic insight. Beyond her work in advertising, Testa is also recognized for her contributions to the public discourse on creativity and communication, writing and speaking frequently on these topics.

35   Gavino Sanna (born 1940) is one of Italy's most influential advertising executives, renowned for his ability to create memorable and effective campaigns. In addition to his acclaimed work for Fiat and Barilla, Sanna is credited with creating the brand identity for Mulino Bianco, which made the brand a cultural icon in Italy. His campaigns are known for their emotional resonance and storytelling, which have left a lasting impact on Italian advertising.

a strategy I recommend if you aim to secure fair market value or better—unless you are negotiating for a unique property.

Negotiation based on logic is entirely different.

After determining the "range of the right value," you must develop a strategy to close the deal within that range.

Francesco has always been a Porsche enthusiast, a passion he shares with his wife, Giorgia. They are seriously considering buying a 911 Turbo S Convertible from their trusted dealer in Pesaro. The car has less than 3,000 km on the clock and is practically new, having come from a customer who can no longer drive due to a serious health issue. The car perfectly meets their needs (**interests**), and they are ready to negotiate. Francesco has already visited the showroom, tested the car twice, and driven it on the highway and the scenic byways of Pesaro. He has fallen in love with it, but is concerned that the dealer might not accept his financial terms, or might undervalue his used 911 Carrera GTS Convertible, which he intends to trade in as part of the deal.

To prepare for the negotiation, Giorgia helped him compile a list of **alternatives** in case they fail to reach an agreement. She identified similar cars available from official Porsche dealers in Stuttgart, Vienna, and Milan, and secured binding offers from each. This preparation is invaluable, because it equips them to anticipate the dealer's moves if the terms are unreasonable, ensuring they are not at his mercy when discussing price. They also gathered sufficient evidence to assess the fairness of the deal. Additionally, Giorgia analyzed the used car market and identified alternative channels to sell their Porsche Carrera in case the dealer's valuation is too low.

Giulia faces a different scenario. She loves horseback riding and stables her three horses at the Horse Center in Arezzo. The equestrian center, founded over 20 years ago, is showing its age, with stalls in need of maintenance that Paolo, the longtime owner, has neglected. Giulia is unhappy with the situation and is considering moving her horses to another stable. However, the increased driving distance poses a significant inconvenience, so she decides to speak openly with Paolo.

During their first meeting, Giulia is direct, blunt, and firm in demanding full restoration of the three stalls. Paolo reacts angrily and aggressively. Both realize afterward that they should have better managed their emotions, improved their **communication**, and considered the value of their long-standing **relationship**. For Giulia, moving to a new stable would mean driving an extra fifty miles daily to visit her horses. For Paolo, losing an important client like Giulia—who is the only one stabling three horses at his premises—would not only result in lost revenue but could also lead to staff reductions and the departure of several young trainees who admire Giulia for her expertise and willingness to mentor them.

Meanwhile, Mr. Anderson, the Chief Executive Officer of PRO Group, is grappling with a dire financial situation. The performance of the Indian multinational is deteriorating sharply, and the group is struggling to repay its debts. While the first covenant (a clause in the loan agreement) has been met, there is a real risk that subsequent covenants will be breached during the upcoming audit at the end of the year. The CFO has been in talks with three lenders for months, negotiating a debt refinancing deal, and hopes to finalize the agreement within weeks. However, he is concerned that the agreement will demand an even greater **commitment** along with numerous post-signing activities.

In all these cases, the weight of interests, options, alternatives, legitimacy, communication, relationships, and commitment differs. If the issue is significant, as much time as possible should be devoted to each element. Interests—the needs, wants, and fears driving negotiations—are distinct from positions, which represent explicit demands, statements, and offers made during negotiations. Positions are the means, while interests are the ends.

The orange, a juicy fruit, has been the subject of many negotiation exercises. My favorite version is one presented in an introductory negotiation class at the Massachusetts Institute of Technology, which I've slightly modified.

In a high-end restaurant, two highly skilled *chefs de partie* were preparing elaborate recipes, both of which called for one orange/required one orange. Everything was going smoothly until they discovered there was only one orange left in the pantry. The two began to argue over who should get the fruit, and even the *commis* stepped in, siding with one or the other. The *chef pâtissier* needed the orange to create chocolate zest flavored with rosemary and Maldon salt, while the *chef saucier* wanted it to marinate dolphinfish fillet with fresh wild fennel, dill, thyme, and anise seeds.

After much arguing, they decided to cut the orange in half. Yet, neither chef had considered why the other needed the orange. If they had taken the time to discuss their interests—perhaps by sharing their recipes—they would have quickly realized that one needed only the juice for a sauce, while the other required the zest for dessert. There was no need to split the orange in half; they could have simply separated the peel and the flesh, fully satisfying both parties.

Remember that constructing your negotiation style is a flexible process. I suggest avoiding discussions centered solely on solutions, or compromising with yourself and your negotiating partner by seeking middle ground or giving something up. Instead, step back and assess your needs and interests, and those of the other party—not just your solutions. This shift in perspective can reduce conflicts over competing answers and open up more options, increasing the likelihood of getting what you need. As with everything in life, knowing exactly what you want, and communicating it cordially but confidently, greatly increases the likelihood of achieving your goals.

Focusing on interests instead of positions is critical. Often, we make the mistake of centering negotiations on positions, which stifles creativity and risks damaging relationships with negotiating partners. Over the years, I have become more creative by exploring and listing the possible interests of my negotiating partners, rather than focusing solely on my own. This approach has consistently fostered a greater sense of collaboration.

In his book *In Questions, Is the Answer,* Hal Gregersen offers an insightful perspective: he writes that questions have a remarkable ability to unlock new insights and promote positive behavioral changes in all aspects of life. Questions can open up people and reveal new paths for progress, no matter what challenges they face.

Reframed questions, particularly in a negotiation context, share certain essential elements. To explore interests effectively, it is helpful to ask "Why?" and "For what purpose?"

A great way to dig into your interests is by asking yourself "why" multiple times—up to five—starting with the outcome you want from a particular negotiation. Then, delve deeper by continuing to ask "why" until you identify the root of the issue. If you get into the habit of using this method, you will enhance your problem-solving skills and avoid misunderstandings that might derail your negotiation. It's simpler than it sounds and surprisingly effective. The key is to ensure you can provide multiple answers to your questions; otherwise, you're likely dealing with a position rather than an interest.

For instance, if you say, "I will ask for a 5 percent price increase," and your only answer to "why" is a single response, such as "because we need higher margins," then you're dealing with a position. However, if you provide multiple answers—such as "because our margins will decrease with rising raw material costs," "because we need to cool demand," or "because we are market leaders and must be the first to raise prices to set a signal for competitors"—then you are uncovering interests. Once interests are identified, it is helpful to rank them in order of importance.

#	WHY?	WEIGHT
1	Because our margins will decline with the announced increase in raw material costs	50
2	Because we are the market leader and need to be the first to raise prices and send a signal to our competitors	30
3	Because we need to cool demand	20

In addition to listing interests, assigning weights to them—the cumulative total of which adds up to 100, for example—can help you reason in percentages. This weighted list enables you to evaluate and compare different options more efficiently and quickly.

When presenting multiple equivalent simultaneous offers, it is useful to offer several options simultaneously rather than submitting one request at a time. By making trade-offs between elements in the offers, both parties can extract greater value from factors that matter most to them.

I recall a particularly satisfying case in May 2017, when I helped entrepreneur Piero Reggiani renegotiate his divorce agreement. Piero had separated years earlier, and just five days before the court hearing, an opportunity arose to revise the agreement following a groundbreaking ruling by the Corte di Cassazione.[36] The court had redefined the "right to maintenance in divorce," shifting its basis from the continuation of the marital standard of living to the economic self-sufficiency of the financially weaker spouse.[37] This change allowed Piero to reduce his financial burden significantly.

The timing was critical, and the situation intense. Piero, calm and action-oriented, seized the opportunity with a sense of responsibility and commitment. Despite setbacks and obstacles, he remained focused, adapting and finding alternative solutions as needed.

I did not attend the meetings between the parties, but based on the feedback I received and the progress made in closed sessions, it was clear that Piero followed the guidelines we had developed together. He understood the importance of prioritizing his interests and focusing attention and time on the most critical points of the agreement.

---

36   This is the highest court of appeal in Italy. Its primary responsibility is to ensure that the law is correctly applied throughout the country.

37   Prior to this ruling, alimony was often granted to guarantee the economically weaker spouse a standard of living similar to that enjoyed during the marriage. With judgment 11504/2017, the Supreme Court ruled that the main criterion for determining entitlement to the maintenance allowance is no longer the maintenance of the marital standard of living, but the economic independence of the requesting spouse. This means that the maintenance allowance should only be granted if the applicant spouse is unable to support himself or herself, taking into account their working capacity and the economic resources at their disposal, and represents a significant change in the Italian legal approach to the recognition of maintenance allowances in divorce cases.

Before negotiating the draft agreement, we had worked hard to identify his interests and those of his ex-wife. Piero grasped the significance of asking open-ended questions such as "Why?" and "For what reason?" He also used targeted inquiries like "What might be objectionable with what I propose?" to uncover the motivations behind his ex-wife's resistance.

This approach allowed him to make proposals based on a deeper understanding of both his and his ex-wife's needs, leading to a more effective and satisfying negotiation process.

It is difficult to determine whether the agreement reached was the best possible outcome. It is even more challenging to assess whether the relationship between the two parties deteriorated due to the intense negotiations preceding the judge's ruling. The absence of children—and the myriad issues that arise in association with children in a divorce—simplified matters, as there was no need to preserve a good relationship for their sake. Ultimately, it was a good deal because, with the support of a competent matrimonial lawyer, numerous options were proposed and carefully evaluated.

Once again, the parties' interests—the real purpose of negotiation—were satisfied. This happens when the skills and resources of both parties are effectively utilized, and the potential for combining those resources is thoroughly explored.

Collaboration and Risk, Trust and Time

Collaboration

Two eight-brick Lego joints can be stacked in twenty-four different ways. If you stack three eight-stud bricks together, the possible combinations increase to 1,060. With six eight-stud bricks, you can create as many as 915,103,765 combinations!

For me, Legos are an endless source of inspiration.

Have you ever observed a group of people playing with Legos?

A group of people, regardless of age, engaged with Legos creates a captivating scene. Their creativity comes alive as they experiment with countless combinations, collaborating to build something unique or competing to create the most imaginative design. It's a vivid reminder of how limitless possibilities emerge when ideas and perspectives come together. The way they approach the task—some following instructions methodically, others improvising boldly—mirrors the diversity of problem-solving and collaboration in real life.

When I was six, my father, Giovanni, was promoted to the position of bank manager. Shortly before Christmas, my family moved from Cremona to Milan. For us, it was yet another change of city.

The Sfligiotti family (parents, two boys, and two girls) lived on the same floor as us on Ceradini Street. We spent many afternoons together, and one of our favorite games was Lego, a classic and always-welcome Christmas gift at the time. We always played together, pooling all our bricks into a large cylindrical drum[38] (usually a repurposed washing powder con-

---

38   In the 1970s, laundry soap, typically in unconcentrated powder form, was sold in large, sturdy cardboard drums. These bulk containers were in keeping with the era's preference for purchasing household products in larger quantities, and offered convenience and economy for families who laundered frequently. After use, the barrels were often recycled for various purposes around the home.

tainer, back when detergents came in large, heavy cardboard cylinders). We had similar skills and an equivalent collection of colorful bricks. By combining everything, we could create expansive and beautiful constructions that none of us could have built individually. Through collaboration, we enhanced the value of our creations.

Some afternoons were spent at the oratory, where we played soccer with a ball my grandmother had given us. Here, the resources and abilities were different, and although we all aspired to score goals, we always managed to agree on the ideal lineup to beat the opposing team. Finally, all six of us pooled our small savings to subscribe to *Topolino* (a digest-sized weekly comic featuring Mickey Mouse). Although each of us contributed different amounts, no one could have afforded the subscription alone.

These experiences taught me that collaboration is not just about pooling resources or skills—it's about trust, shared vision, and the willingness to combine efforts for a greater outcome. Whether building with Legos, forming a soccer team, or saving for something special, the essence of success lies in recognizing the power of unity. These lessons resonate far beyond childhood games; they are principles that apply to solving complex challenges and achieving shared goals in any endeavor.

As we grow and face new opportunities, understanding how to balance collaboration with individual accountability becomes critical. And that's where the concept of risk begins to enter the picture.

Risk

The ability to create value arises from the different perceptions of value that each person holds. If there were no differences in valuation, there'd be no buying and selling, as no one would have an incentive to part with the more valuable commodity for the less valuable one (and any given commodity would have the same value for all people). Factors like risk tolerance, available time, and marginal value shape these perceptions. I personally enjoy risk, but my partner does not. Risk, after all, is simply the probability of an undesirable outcome occurring.

In negotiations, outcomes are rarely certain. Conceding to a negotiating partner in the hope of later claiming equal or greater value carries inherent risks, especially when considering the principle of reciprocity we discussed earlier. There is no guarantee that the partner will reciprocate once their interest has been satisfied. In fact, negotiating in exchange for a "favor" or expecting something in return can backfire, as it may make you appear ungrateful or lead to the other party feeling obligated, creating an unhealthy dynamic.

Risk in negotiations is not limited to making concessions. It might also involve other factors, such as disclosing information that could weaken your position or relying on a partner who might fail to honor their commitments.

Once you acknowledge that risk is part of any structured negotiation, you can better assess your willingness to accept the possibility of negative outcomes or results that don't align with your interests. Understanding your risk tolerance helps you define and set up your best alternative to a negotiated agreement (BATNA).

There are risks associated with the effectiveness of the strategies and tactics negotiators use. A poorly chosen strategy might lead to worse outcomes than if a different approach had been employed. Additionally, risks arise in connection with the certainty and quality of the BATNA.

Even after reaching an agreement, inherent risks remain, such as the possibility that the terms fail to address all relevant interests, the parties fail to uphold their commitments, or the agreement's terms prove unenforceable. While risk can be considered an objective probability of an outcome, it is perceived differently by different individuals, influencing their actions.

Trust

Trust is closely related to risk, as it shapes an individual's perception of outcomes. When trust is present, one feels reasonably confident in a favorable outcome. Conversely, a lack of trust amplifies the perceived likelihood of unfavorable results.

Counterfactual thinking, in which an individual focuses on hypothetical scenarios and how they might affect negotiations, can impact trust. Insecurity and lack of confidence foster negative attitudes, leading to constant rumination about how things might have gone differently. On the other hand, overconfidence can lead negotiators to underestimate the likelihood of unfavorable outcomes.

Unfortunately, outcome uncertainty can fuel either confidence or mistrust. A confident negotiator can effectively advocate for their position, persuading the other party to make concessions and achieving more favorable results. However, I find it more intriguing to channel positivity, confidence, and self-esteem into constructive actions. These qualities can enhance a negotiator's ability to create value by building rapport with the other party and exploring diverse options.

Through careful observation, I have learned that people subjectively define the level of risk they are willing to accept. They consciously avoid scenarios in which the perceived risk exceeds their personal threshold, ensuring they remain within their comfort zone.

Risk aversion exists on a spectrum, representing varying levels of acceptable risk. A completely risk-averse person would rather stick with a sure thing than take a chance on something that might turn out better, worse, or the same, even when the risk of worse outcomes is low, and there's a chance of a much better outcome.

Time
The time factor and timing are critical components of any negotiation. Ensure that time is on your side, as it allows you to pursue your goals, test strategies, explore alternatives, update plans, and refine objectives. Sometimes, the passage of time can align circumstances in your favor, making your goals the only—or best—possible outcome for your negotiating partner. At that point, negotiation becomes almost redundant, as the agreement is practically assured. Other times, however, you must consciously create the time necessary to achieve your goals.

I have two wonderful daughters: Giulia, born in 1998, and Alessia, who arrived two years later. They have differing personalities, but both have been a source of immense joy and satisfaction for me. They constantly remind me of the importance of time in negotiation. When they were little, I didn't get to spend much time with them, which I regret to some extent, but that's how life was. They always knew when I was in a hurry, and they capitalized on it, turning every activity necessary to leave the house—getting dressed, brushing their teeth, putting on coats and shoes—into prolonged and frustrating negotiations.

Last week, I spoke with a client who shared her thoughts on the impact of time during negotiations. She said:

"When time is on my side, I stay calm. When I'm short on time, however, I struggle to relax and not get nervous. The less time I have, the harder it is to take a deep breath and avoid capitulating or losing control. Ironically, when this happens, I know I'm negotiating against myself, which only adds to my anxiety and frustration. I'm usually less emotional at work than at home, but when I'm rushed and don't get what I want immediately, it's equally exasperating."

Her words resonated with me and brought back fond memories of my daughters. Alessia, in particular, taught me the value of time in negotiation. I recall a day when I was in a rush to get her to kindergarten, after which I needed to drive to Bologna airport and catch a flight to Sydney, Australia. Alessia was throwing a tantrum. I knew from experience that it would be futile to yell. Instead, I firmly stated my position, hugged her, and took five deep breaths. Then I waited. Sure enough, Alessia eventually put on her boots, grabbed her down jacket, and even brought me my scarf.

While I've never tested this tactic in a professional negotiation, I don't believe hugging an opposing lawyer—or your boss—would yield quite the same results. The example illustrates, however, that using time to your advantage is invaluable, particularly under pressure, which often arises toward the end of negotiations. Staying calm and composed can be a powerful tool.

It is essential to have stamina, resilience, and familiarity with techniques to maintain composure when your negotiating partner raises the stakes. If they act forcefully or irrationally, don't panic—it often gives you time to think. In some cases, they might even feel embarrassed by their reaction.

The takeaway: Don't let time become your enemy, even when it seems to be working against you. Learn to make time your ally. Aim to manage timing effectively, and if possible, shift critical issues to your negotiating partner's side of the table. While timing can sometimes be a matter of happenstance, with preparation and strategy, you'll find that it is often consciously shaped, more so than you might expect.

BATNA:
Best Alternative to the Negotiated Agreement

Not reaching an agreement is perfectly fine, especially in situations where the costs outweigh the benefits or when there's a better deal elsewhere that meets your needs. You can satisfy your interests in two ways: by negotiating an agreement or by pursuing an alternative with someone else. Having a solid alternative to a negotiated agreement strengthens your position—and the better your alternative, the stronger your position will be.

Take Chef Giuseppe as an example. If he had alternative job offers with different roles, locations, and salaries, he could evaluate them based on his priorities and rank them in order.

ALTERNATIVES

ISSUES	A	B	C
RESPONSABILITIES	Equivalent	More	Equivalent
LOCATION	Milan	Milan and Portofino	Paris
SALARY	+10%	+15%	+30%

Only Giuseppe can determine which of these options is his **best alternative to** a **negotiated agreement (BATNA)**, a term coined by negotiation experts Roger Fisher, William Ury, and Bruce Patton.

My encounters with Ury and Patton have forged a personal connection to this concept. Whenever BATNA comes up, I am reminded of their invaluable insights, which have left a lasting impact on my approach to negotiation.

Giuseppe's BATNA doesn't require negotiation; it's a fallback he can pursue if an agreement isn't reached.

A more relatable example. Imagine you're applying for a new job while currently employed. If you don't have any other job offers, you're more likely to feel pressure to accept whatever terms are presented. But now picture that you've already received competing offers from two other companies, both of which align with your career goals and financial expectations. Suddenly, you're in a much stronger position to negotiate—your alternatives give you the freedom to walk away if the terms aren't favorable. This is the essence of a BATNA: having a clear and viable alternative provides leverage and confidence during negotiations.

One reason people fear negotiation is the possibility of losing the deal. A strong BATNA gives you confidence and reduces this fear. It also provides clarity on when to stay at the table and when to walk away. The quality of your BATNA depends on the options you've identified and the effort you've put into finding them.

Mistakes in preparing and evaluating your BATNA are common. Sitting at the table without a plan for what to do if an agreement isn't reached can lead to insecurity and doubts about whether to continue or walk away. I'm sure you've experienced this before. If someone tells you, "Take it or leave it," you're left with two choices: surrender or call their bluff, risking the possibility they're not bluffing. Without a well-thought-out BATNA, the negotiation can devolve into a standoff, with one party walking away with an unearned advantage.

Even worse is assuming you know your BATNA without investing time to explore all possible options creatively. Even if you don't ultimately use your BATNA, simply having it strengthens your position. It puts creative pressure on the other party and helps you focus on what you want and how to achieve it without settling for unsatisfactory terms. Developing your BATNA follows the same logic as identifying your interests.

Let's return to Francesco and Giorgia and their Porsche purchase. After carefully developing their alternatives, they worked to make them more practical, aligned with their interests, and achievable. When negotiating with their chosen dealer, they were ready to accept an offer only if it was better than their BATNA. The more they refined their BATNA, the stronger it became, creating a virtuous cycle: as their BATNA improved, their confidence grew, and so did their chances of securing a better deal.

Keep in mind that every negotiator likely comes to the table with their own BATNA. While it's nearly impossible to determine their BATNA with certainty, you can make educated guesses about what it might be and how they might act if no agreement is reached. By analyzing their interests, you can find ways to make their BATNA less appealing—whether by complicating its execution, reducing its value, or influencing their perception of how unwise or costly it might be.

The goal of negotiation is to achieve better results than you could without negotiating.

The stronger your BATNA, the greater your negotiating power. Many assume that power comes from resources like money, connections, or influence. In reality, negotiating power often depends on how attractive each party's alternative to an agreement is. The better your alternative, the more confident and powerful you'll feel at the table.

If your negotiating partner believes you lack a good alternative when you actually have one, it's often wise to let them know. However, if your BATNA is weaker than they assume, revealing it could harm your position rather than strengthen it.

The analysis during the preparatory stage should go beyond simply defining your BATNA and assessing your negotiating partner's. Both will be critical if no deal is reached. You'll also need to come to the table with two additional tools: the zone of possible agreement (ZOPA) and the reserve value.

Zone of Possible Agreement and Reserve Price

Zone of Possible Agreement

The zone of possible agreement (ZOPA) is constituted by the overlap between the expectations of the respective parties to the negotiation. It represents the common ground on which negotiators can agree given their demands and concessions. To reach an agreement, the parties must understand each other's needs, interests, and options.

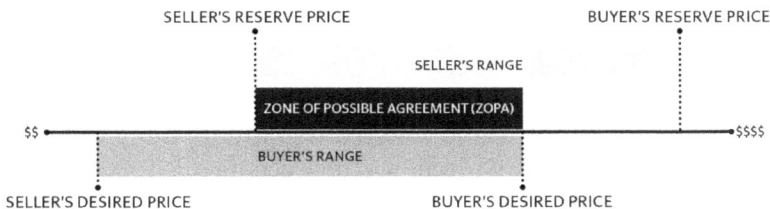

For example, let's say the seller wants to make €2,000 and will never sell for less than €1,600 because, below that price, their best alternative to the negotiated deal is preferable. The buyer would like to pay €1,400, and will only buy at a maximum of €1,850 because, above that price, their best alternative to the negotiated deal is preferable. The ZOPA thus consists of the range between €1,600 (the minimum value acceptable to the seller) and €1,850 (the maximum value acceptable to the buyer).

"Pietro, I've been preparing to sell my Corso Como studio apartment in Milan, just as you advised: assessing interests, options, BATNA, and everything else. I also researched properties similar to mine in that area, and hoped to sell for €575,000. The buyer made an initial offer of €520,000—much lower than I expected—which reduced the chances of a deal and affected the entire negotiation. In the end, we closed at €530,000. What did I do wrong?"

"Carlo, you did well to prepare. Completing this exercise before a negotiation was essential. Unfortunately, it wasn't enough because, in this case, the other party influenced you by setting a powerful anchor price."

"Could you explain that in a little more detail? What do you mean by anchoring? And how should one behave in this situation at the negotiating table?"

"Pay attention and try to follow along. Anchoring is a cognitive bias that leads people to give too much importance to the first number put on the table, which conditions the entire negotiation to such an extent that the final values of the agreement often remain close to the starting point. Cognitive bias refers to a deviation from rational thinking, resulting in a distortion of reality, inaccurate judgments, and illogical interpretations of the facts under consideration. These biases often arise from the need to quickly take a position in response to certain stimuli, even without having all the necessary information. While cognitive biases enable fast decision-making, they typically sacrifice accuracy."

This concept dates back to 1974, when psychologists Amos Tversky and Daniel Kahneman published the results of their experiments in *Judgment under Uncertainty: Heuristics and Biases.* Their research demonstrated that individuals often make decisions using a limited number of mental shortcuts, relying on these heuristics instead of the sophisticated rational processes we assume we employ.

My partner, Caterina, has extensive experience in real estate—a field she's also passionate about. Jokingly, we say we have properties everywhere because we frequently visit houses, land, and villas that we ultimately decide not to buy. We call it dream-home excursion—a fun way to explore the market without committing to a purchase. When we discuss the opening proposal, she is always right. At first, I found her offers almost outrageous, because they seemed far removed from the value I had mentally calculated. However, her proposals became convincing when she backed them up with sound principles and solid arguments.

Caterina excels in preparation—studying, researching, analyzing, and asking questions—and she's also outstanding in using anchoring effectively. She always makes the first offer, which she tailors to her role: slightly lower when buying and slightly higher when selling. It's like an anchored ship: the wind may shift, and the tide may rise, but the anchor holds steady.

Negotiators often gain an advantage by making and anchoring the first offer. Here again, preparation is key. Whether to make the first offer depends on your understanding of the ZOPA and your assessment of the other party's knowledge of it.

If you feel your negotiating partner knows more than you do, anchoring effectively will be difficult. In such cases, you must gather as much information as possible. If both parties have a clear understanding of the potential agreement range, anchors are unlikely to be effective. However, if neither party has a clear idea of the possible agreement range, making an initial offer could risk being either too lenient or too aggressive. When you know more about the ZOPA than the other party—for example, when buying or selling an asset like real estate or a car, where you have extensive knowledge—you should make an aggressive first offer. Conversely, if the other party anchors you, respond promptly with a counteroffer to avoid weakening your position.

Let's revisit Carlo's example. With the opening offer at €520,000, the temptation might be to counter with €600,000. However, before doing so, it is essential to make it clear that €520,000 is simply an unacceptable offer.

Always be prepared for situations like this and respond clearly and firmly: "I'm not trying to play games with you, but we are miles apart on price." Avoid arguing the counterparty's offer, even if you have evidence from the preparation of the search for similar properties.

If you don't remove your counterparty's anchor first, you send the message that the €520,000 is within the bargaining zone. Instead, you must make it clear to your negotiating partner right away that their offer is below the ZOPA. Once you've done that, be prepared to make a counteroffer without mentioning the negotiating partner's initial offer. Simply repeating it would validate it to some extent. When making your counteroffer, explain why you believe it is fair and justifiable.

One of the most common mistakes in negotiation is misjudging the ZOPA and failing to reassess it during the process. The ZOPA can expand, shrink, or even disappear as the parties refine their priorities and reevaluate their options. What you initially considered to be the ZOPA might need correction, and you must adjust it in the process of negotiation by asking questions and using active listening. Setting criteria for evaluation will also help in this process.

When preparing for a negotiation, always remember that circumstances can change, and your ability to adapt to these changes—sometimes sudden ones—is a critical factor for success as a negotiator.

In some cases, there may not be a ZOPA at all. If you are well prepared, you might uncover the other party's underlying interests and create value, even in these situations. Always consider whether you can identify something that holds high value for your negotiating partner but low value for you.

Reserve Price

Let's revisit the example of buying and selling real estate, where you are the seller: you clinch the deal by throwing in some furniture, such as a custom-made kitchen designed specifically for the house. That kitchen has marginal value to you, as disassembling it, moving it, and finding a buyer who needs precisely that size kitchen would be cumbersome. For your negotiating partner, however, the kitchen has high value, as they would need to purchase one regardless.

For many years, I participated in significant negotiations, often believing that if I didn't renew specific contracts, the company would fail or that losing a key customer would be catastrophic. In those days, my business was highly concentrated, with the top three customers accounting for more than 50 percent of sales. Losing just one of them would have meant finding at least ten or fifteen smaller customers to compensate for the loss. However, as my client portfolio became more diverse, my approach shifted. I rediscovered a sense of power because I knew I could walk away from negotiations. Having a viable alternative in case an acceptable agreement couldn't be reached gave me confidence. I became more assertive, and this shift was palpable to the other party, who, in turn, became more cautious about pushing too hard.

That said, walking away from a negotiation is never easy, especially after you've invested time and effort in it. Emotionally, you want to close the deal, and this feeling is even stronger when you sense the agreement is within reach but elusive. Not closing a deal can feel like a defeat, a loss that weighs heavily.

During the preparation phase, I always think about ways to avoid reaching that critical point in the negotiation where leaving the table becomes too painful—typically, when it's too late to walk away easily. To mitigate this, I try to define potential deal-breakers in advance, saving both parties time, energy, and the stress of a potentially doomed negotiation. In many cases, negotiations fail to conclude because the parties hold irreconcilable positions. Proper preparation involves defining a reserve price—your minimum acceptable value—and a firm limit beyond which you cannot go.

I have witnessed numerous negotiations in which negotiators reached their reserve price, determined during the preparation phase, yet continued negotiating and making concessions. In such instances, the so-called minimum value wasn't treated as such. It's important to remember that your reserve price can change if you acquire new information during negotiations that justifies adjusting it.

Years ago, I sold several items on eBay. My friend Grazia, a collector of French and English silverware, now uses Catawiki. Both platforms feature a "reserve price," which is the minimum amount below which the seller won't accept an offer. If the reserve price isn't met, the item won't be sold. An experienced negotiator acts much like sellers on Catawiki or eBay, holding firm to the reserve price. In contrast, less experienced negotiators often give in, dynamically lowering their reserve price and gradually aligning it with their negotiating partner's offer—driven by the fear of losing the deal.

In 2020, a client of mine fell in love with a small two-story house located in Borgo San Giuliano, Rimini—a highly sought-after, charming neighborhood. He believed he had anchored the seller by making an initial offer of €180,000. However, after a few exchanges, he ended up accepting a counteroffer of €252,000.

He contacted me, desperate. "Alberto," I reminded him, "we had defined a reserve price of €200,000, and we prepared it thoroughly. That should have given you the confidence you needed to negotiate effectively. You shouldn't feel scared, agitated, or frustrated about walking away from a negotiation—especially when you've prepared well! That's when things got out of hand. That house is beautiful—I like it too. It's tough, especially since your architect estimated €195,000 maximum, and Alessandra bought the twin house for €200,000. But remember, walking away demonstrates strength, confidence, courage, and integrity. Even if you don't close the deal, people will see you as honorable. You'll be able to hold your head high, and your wisdom will earn respect."

Sometimes, we feel trapped. You can't systematically walk away from every negotiation, but it's empowering to know that you can walk away from those you really need to. The reserve price is one of the most critical elements to prepare before sitting at the table. When we walk away from an opportunity, we might initially feel regret for not closing the deal. However, that feeling often fades, replaced by the realization that we did the right thing. Walking away allows us to maintain self-respect and often earns the respect of our negotiating partner as well.

If you need to walk away, do so civilly and courteously. It's always wise to maintain good relations with the other party—you never know what the future might bring. Few sentences are as wise as: "If you reconsider, call me." And walking away may convince the person to call you back with a better proposal!

Data Retrieval, Engagement, and Arbitration

Finding Information

Nowadays, much of the information useful for negotiations is easily accessible, reducing the impact of information asymmetry, when one party has more information than the other and can exploit it to their advantage.

This imbalance can sometimes reach extremes. In Chile, for example, every economic operator can access the import database, allowing them to check the prices and quantities imported by all other operators, including direct competitors. When I first went to Santiago to close a contract with a new client, I was unprepared for this dynamic. At the negotiating table, my demands turned out to be misplaced. The price I paid for this ignorance was steep: my interlocutor presented evidence of the prices I charged their direct competitors and those set by my German competitors.

This example is undoubtedly a borderline case, but today, accessing information has become relatively easy. Years ago, in Italy, the bible for buying new and used cars was the monthly *Quattroruote* (in the US, the equivalent is *Kelley Blue Book*, while in France, it's *L'Argus*). Now, all this information is available online. Technology allows us to verify facts in moments, enabling us to research competitors' products, pricing, performance, reviews, regulatory requirements, market trends, and other factors that have a bearing on the negotiation.

Research tools can be employed both before and during negotiations, and in some cases, they can even be used in real-time to adapt strategies and responses as discussions unfold. Being well prepared is more critical—and easier—than ever; it has become the new normal. Useful sources include websites, press releases, financial statements, and stock assessments, which can reveal details about products, services, customers, suppliers, growth plans, facilities, and financial health. When researching a

negotiating partner, it is also prudent to investigate their customers, suppliers, and competitors.

The parties to a negotiation often enter it with inherent
respective structural advantages. For example, the seller or
manufacturer might have detailed knowledge of costs, while the
buyer likely has insight into the seller's strengths, weaknesses, and
their own consumption needs.

If I am to convince the other party of the legitimacy and fairness of my proposal, I must first convince myself. Then, I must
support my claims with external standards or objective criteria
to substantiate their fairness. Once again, preparation is crucial.
Preparing to persuade takes time, effort, and access to the right
information. This preparation enables you to demonstrate convincingly to your negotiating partner that the criteria, standards, and
references you present are appropriate to the context. Arriving
unprepared to discuss objective criteria can be costly.

In the past, I used to think it wasn't my responsibility to
ensure the other party fully understood the legitimacy of my
proposal. This approach often led to a failure either to reach
agreements or for the agreements to be respected when they were
reached. When my negotiating partner did not fully understand
the basis of the agreement—or when I couldn't clearly explain
its fairness—they were less likely to uphold it. I eventually realized that it was my responsibility to provide all the necessary
information to facilitate a fair agreement and, crucially, to put
my counterpart in a position to explain the agreement to third
parties. These could be their superiors, family members, or
members of their organization.

At the end of a negotiation (or any phase of it), we all have
someone to whom we must explain the outcome. This could be a
boss, a client, or, in personal contexts, a partner or family member.
Regardless, our image and credibility are on the line.

When negotiating, it's easy to assume that explaining the
agreement is our counterpart's problem, not ours. This is a critical
mistake. If they fail to communicate the agreement effectively to
those to whom they are accountable, their problem will return
to us like a boomerang, striking us squarely. If they can't provide

convincing arguments for the agreement, it will be difficult for others to accept—or respect—it.

At that point, their problem has undoubtedly become our problem.

Commitment

The engagement theme became much more apparent to me after studying and analyzing preparation from the perspective of **communication** and **relationship**.

Relying on a single (albeit objective) rationale for a possible agreement may be not just insufficient but also dangerous. Approaching the negotiating table with the conviction that your solution is the only correct one is a surefire way to find yourself in a tense, confrontational, zero-sum negotiation where there's a clear winner and loser. It's far better to have a range of data, principles, or criteria ready with which to propose a variety of solutions.

Taking the time to prepare options that align with the interests of both parties is essential. Equally important is having a broad selection of objective criteria that can help both sides understand which solutions are most appropriate given the circumstances. Preparing plausible and persuasive standards or criteria will not only strengthen your position but also increase your awareness of how the other side views the negotiation. By thoroughly preparing several different criteria, you will be more effective in proposing the most beneficial ones—both for yourself and for the progress of the negotiation. In some contexts, finding a criterion that helps both parties reach an agreement can be relatively straightforward.

A few years ago, I met with a long-standing client in Shanghai after he decided to exercise his option to purchase an industrial property in Pudong, as stipulated in the lease agreement. Each year, they paid the American landlord the equivalent of about €2.8 million, a sum revalued annually according to a contract signed twenty-five years earlier—an amount significantly higher than the current market value of the property.

To prepare for the negotiation, I advised my Chinese clients to engage an experienced consultant. They chose Cushman &

Wakefield, who conducted an appraisal of the property, analyzed comparable properties for sale in neighboring areas, reviewed actual transactions, and assessed rents for equivalent properties using income ratios. They arrived at an estimate of €9–€10 million, depending on the criteria used. I sought arguments that had inherent appeal, hoping the owners would find them reasonable. Unfortunately, despite several meetings, none of the arguments resonated, and no agreement was reached. The positions of the two parties were simply too far apart.

Initially, the matter was referred to an assessor, which conducted its own appraisal. However, both sides challenged the expert's findings. After three years of litigation, the court issued a ruling in favor of my client, aligning with the estimates provided by the consultant engaged by my client. Although we won, the legal process enriched the law firms involved while delaying substantial investments the Chinese company had planned, which depended on full ownership of the property.

Regrettably, neither the initial experts nor the Shanghai court were able to resolve the dispute quickly, underscoring the complexities and costs of prolonged negotiation and litigation.

While we ultimately achieved a favorable resolution, the drawn-out process highlighted the costs of inflexibility and strained relationships. True commitment in negotiation means not only advocating for your position but also seeking pathways to mutual understanding, even when the stakes are high. Balancing thorough preparation with a willingness to adapt can help avoid prolonged disputes and preserve both relationships and reputations for the future.

Negotiation is a long-term process in which you play with reputation and relationship. The reputation is yours. The relationship is that with your negotiating partner, because you will have to negotiate with them again at some point in the future.

Arbitration
I often accept or propose including arbitration clauses in contracts, as they expedite dispute resolution and help safeguard the relationship between the parties. In simpler contexts, agreeing

to involve a third party is a solution I appreciate. The arbitrator should be chosen based on trust, competence, and impartiality, with the agreement of both parties.

However, as the case of my Chinese client illustrated, involving third-party assessments doesn't always guarantee a resolution. In that instance, the parties appointed an assessor to evaluate the property, but neither side found the results satisfactory, and the disagreement persisted. This prolonged the dispute and ultimately led to years of costly litigation. The experience underscores that while third-party interventions like arbitration or expert assessments can provide valuable insights, their success depends on the parties' willingness to respect and accept the findings.

An arbitrator—or any impartial third party—can assist in bridging the final gap between positions that are supported by arguments but lack sufficient persuasiveness. However, when trust in the process falters or the stakes are exceptionally high, these interventions may merely serve as a stepping stone to further conflict. This dynamic mirrors what we often experienced as children when faced with disagreements. If two siblings quarreled over who should get the last piece of cake or take the first turn in a game, they would often appeal to an authority figure—typically a parent—who was trusted to make a fair decision. The parent's role was to listen, mediate, and deliver a judgment that both sides could accept, ideally maintaining harmony.

But what happened when such authority wasn't available? Children often devised their own methods of resolving disputes, relying on rules and systems that both parties recognized as fair. Games of chance, like Odd and Even or Heads or Tails, introduced an element of impartiality, allowing fate to decide when reasoning failed. In matters of division, such as splitting a treat, the rule of I Cut, You Choose cleverly ensured equity: one person divided the item, knowing the other had the right to pick first.

The simple childhood strategies resonate with the core principles of arbitration and negotiation. They emphasize the need for impartiality, mutual agreement on the process, and an outcome that both parties perceive as fair—even if it doesn't leave everyone entirely satisfied. They also underscore the importance of trust: just as children trust a parent or a game's fairness, parties in negotiation must trust the process and the person or mechanism tasked with resolution.

Communication and Relationship
with the Negotiating Partner

Verbal, Nonverbal, and Para-verbal Communication

Negotiation is a discussion between two or more individuals aimed at finding a solution that satisfies everyone. But how can such a discussion be effective? Only through communication. The effectiveness of a negotiation is therefore directly proportional to the effectiveness of the communication on which it is based. Always remember: the better the communication, the better the negotiation.

A discussion is not about arguing or raising your voice—it is about exchanging ideas, thoughts, and opinions. It goes without saying that if you have good (or even excellent) communication skills, you will be able to conduct effective discussions, which will, in turn, lead to effective negotiations. To excel in any type of negotiation, it is essential to master communication. Like negotiation, communication is both an art and a skill. Fortunately, it is something that can be learned. Your negotiating partner can only access your thoughts and ideas if you share them, and since they cannot see inside your mind, much depends on how you speak and act.

The study conducted in 1972 by Albert Mehrabian, *Nonverbal Communication*, remains highly relevant even after more than fifty years. Mehrabian demonstrated that the message we convey through communication is only 7 percent attributable to verbal language.

The effectiveness of a message depends, therefore, only to a small degree on the literal meaning of what is said. How this message is perceived is heavily influenced by **para-verbal**[39] and

---

39   Para-verbal communication refers to the way something is said, not the words themselves. It includes tone, pitch, volume, speed, and pauses. These ele-

nonverbal[40] communication, especially in cases where there is unfamiliarity between the interlocutors. Hence, the importance of preparation extends to more than just numbers, timing, performance, and counter-performance. It is a complex process that serves the parties involved to communicate in the best way possible to meet their interests.

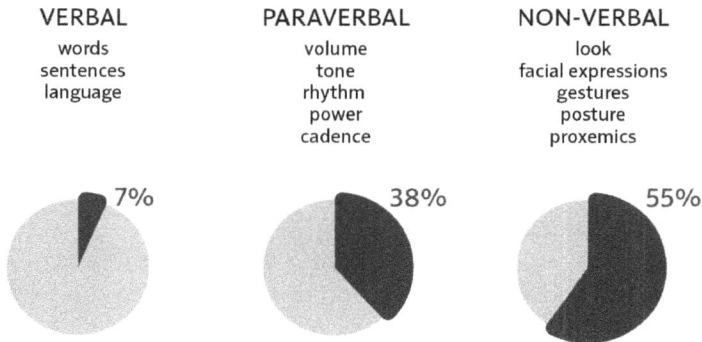

VERBAL	PARAVERBAL	NON-VERBAL
words	volume	look
sentences	tone	facial expressions
language	rhythm	gestures
	power	posture
	cadence	proxemics
7%	38%	55%

Active Listening

My brother Paolo was an extraordinary person and my best friend. Unfortunately, he passed away when I was in my thirties, and I still miss him deeply. One of the many fond memories I have of him is that he would always prepare a script for speeches. So many negotiators spend most of their energy thinking about and preparing what they will say to the other side. This is fine, of course, but by itself, it's not enough—it can't be enough. Many people make this mistake because it provides a sense of confidence. However, no matter how reassuring it may be to prepare a detailed speech, it limits your ability to focus on what truly matters: listening to and understanding the other person. Even

---

ments can change the meaning of verbal communication by conveying emotion or emphasis.

40   Nonverbal communication refers to communication without words, such as facial expressions, gestures, posture, eye contact, and body language. It helps to convey feelings or reactions that cannot be expressed verbally.

better, practicing active listening—paying attention not only to what is said but also to the speaker's para-verbal and nonverbal cues—yields far better results.

The issue isn't just about rigidity, such as sticking to the prepared text or script even when it's irrelevant or outdated. It's about perspective, specifically the attention given during the negotiation. Let me explain: if you prepare by focusing solely on what you plan to say, you will likely be unprepared to listen effectively to what your negotiating partner has to say. As a result, you'll also be unprepared to respond adequately or to understand how your words might be interpreted.

Even the most skilled negotiator, while being aware of their own intentions and perceptions, might fail to grasp how the other party perceives their words or actions and the impact they have on the negotiation. Similarly, as we listen or observe, even if we are fully aware of what our negotiating partner says and does, we often lack insight into their intentions or perceptions about our words and actions. Traditional advice emphasizes the importance of active listening—intentionally striving to understand the other person's perspective. The aim is to gain a deep understanding of their views, motivations, thoughts, and expectations while suspending judgment.

Active listening differs from simply hearing in silence. It involves adopting an open, impartial, and nonjudgmental attitude while adding curiosity and a genuine desire to understand the other person's perspective and motivations.

This skill is essential to successful communication, but it can be difficult to develop. One of the hardest aspects of active listening is resisting the urge to rush to conclusions or judge the speaker's words before they've finished. To cultivate active listening, the first key step is to practice presence. This means eliminating distractions, such as checking your phone or thinking about your next response, and instead focusing entirely on the speaker. By being fully present in the moment, you show respect for the other person's words and can truly absorb their message. Suspending judgment is another important aspect of active listening.

Often, we tend to judge information based on our own experiences or biases. However, to truly listen, we need to withhold our conclusions until we've heard the full perspective. This doesn't mean we agree with everything the other person says, but rather that we take the time to understand their point of view, free from preconceived ideas.

As you listen, it's helpful to ask clarifying or open-ended questions, rather than immediately jumping into your own thoughts or opinions. For example, asking questions like, "Can you explain that further?" or "What led you to that conclusion?" encourages the speaker to elaborate and provides you with more context, which will help you engage deeply with the conversation.

Empathy and validation also play a crucial role in active listening. Even if you don't agree with someone, acknowledging their feelings or point of view can prevent misunderstandings and create a sense of rapport. For instance, saying, "I see where you're coming from" or "That must have been difficult for you" allows you to connect on a deeper level and fosters an atmosphere of mutual respect.

Another important component of active listening is focusing on the underlying message, rather than just the literal words. Sometimes, what's more important than the words themselves is the emotion or intention behind them. Paying attention to tone, body language, and what's being left unsaid can provide valuable insight into the speaker's true feelings or motivations.

One of the most challenging aspects of active listening is allowing for silence. In many conversations, we feel the need to fill silence with our own thoughts or responses. However, allowing a pause gives the speaker time to gather their thoughts and continue expressing themselves, often leading to a more insightful discussion.

Finally, active listening requires regular practice. Like any skill, the more you practice, the better you'll become at it. Make an effort to apply these techniques in everyday conversations—whether with colleagues, friends, or even strangers—and gradually, you'll find that you're able to listen more attentively and with greater understanding, especially during high-stakes negotiations.

Overcoming the instinct to rush to conclusions is another key challenge. It's easy to jump ahead when you feel confident about your position or when you're eager to find a solution. But the key to successful negotiation often lies in slowing down and fully understanding the other party's perspective. In fact, by remaining curious and patient, you'll not only avoid making hasty decisions but also uncover deeper insights that could lead to more mutually beneficial outcomes.

Awareness of your own biases is another step in overcoming this tendency. Simply recognizing when you're about to make a snap judgment can help you return to a state of active listening. By doing so, you make space for the other person's perspective, which can significantly enhance your ability to negotiate effectively and maintain positive, productive relationships.

In addition to listening actively, it's also essential to engage in dialogue. Attentive silence should be alternated with questions, rephrasing, and other interactions that keep the negotiation flowing and allow you to empathize with your negotiating partner in various ways.

One common oversight is failing to prepare to listen. If we don't invest time in the listening process (both before and during the negotiation), we tend to hear only what we want or expect to hear rather than what the other party is actually communicating. This element of preparation is often neglected, either because it's undervalued or due to time constraints.

To effectively prepare for active listening, the first step is to clear your mind and set aside any preconceived notions or assumptions about the other party. Before entering the negotiation, remind yourself that the goal is to fully understand the other person's point of view. This might involve taking a few moments to reflect on your own biases and how they could influence your perception of what's being said.

Another technique is to do some research on the other party's interests, needs, and possible pain points. This will help you tune in to the relevant aspects of the conversation and prevent your mind from wandering to your own interests. Additionally, practicing mindfulness or relaxation exercises can help you stay focused during the negotiation. By being fully present, you'll be better able to absorb the information the other party is sharing.

During the negotiation, active listening requires you to pause and reflect before responding. One simple but effective technique is to take a brief pause after the other party speaks, allowing yourself time to process the information before jumping to conclusions or formulating a response. If necessary, repeat or paraphrase what the other person has said to ensure you've understood them correctly. This also signals to them that you value their perspective and encourages more open communication.

Conversely, however, it's vital to anticipate what your negotiating partner might say and to be ready to recognize messages that differ from your expectations. Without this openness, your assumptions could prevent you from hearing something unexpected.

Of course, the same applies in reverse. To be effective during a negotiation, you should also prepare to send messages and signals that can be understood and received correctly by the other party.

Achieving this isn't easy—it requires thought and reflection on how your statements might be interpreted (or misinterpreted) by your negotiating partner due to their filters, biases, and assumptions. You may need to rephrase your statements to ensure they accurately convey your intended meaning while minimizing the risk of misunderstanding. One effective strategy is to ask your interlocutor to state their understanding of your points, which can help identify any potential misunderstandings. When done properly, your communication serves a higher purpose.

Effective communication not only helps you meet your needs by clearly expressing your thoughts and experiences, but also strengthens your connection with the other party, enabling you to better manage your relationship with them.

The Relationship with the Counterpart

If, for example, there is a poor working relationship between two parties, a potential agreement may fail—even when, on paper, the two sides could easily have reached an understanding. In such cases, a **bad relationship** can derail an otherwise promising **negotiation**.

It is not always necessary for the two parties to like each other, nor is it essential to share values or interests. However, when we find ourselves negotiating, we must focus on using a productive process to handle disagreements effectively, reach an agreement, and set the stage for smoother future negotiations.

The quality of a relationship directly depends on how we interact to foster mutual understanding, build trust and respect, encourage persuasion over coercion, and maintain a balance between reason and emotion. It also correlates with our ability to improve information flow and communication.

We often confuse relationship issues (such as disagreements, hurt feelings, grudges, or remorse) with issues of substance (such as numbers, dates, terms, or conditions). If we fail to distinguish between these two aspects, we may attempt to fix a relationship by making substantive concessions. However, this approach doesn't work.

If there is a relationship problem—such as a lack of trust or respect—we may feel tempted to lower the price or accept our negotiating partner's terms on substantive matters, in an effort to resolve the relational issue. But such a decision could in fact worsen the situation. There is a real risk that our negotiating partner might conclude that, to extract more concessions, they should exploit the poor relationship by worsening it further! Remember: relational issues "are not for sale."

Therefore, during the preparation phase of the negotiation, it is crucial to distinguish between substantive and relational issues without conflating them. Once both are clearly identified—perhaps by preparing two separate lists—consider how to address and manage them independently. For substantive issues, ensure you are well prepared on interests, options, legitimacy, alternatives, and commitments. For relationship issues, plan constructive steps to improve the relationship, regardless of the other party's behavior.

Any steps you take should be positive and aimed at fostering a better relationship, regardless of whether the other party reciprocates. Any action in this regard is aimed at building the relationship on a solid foundation, always considering your interests and steering the ties in the desired direction, but never resorting to concessions that fall within the realm of a "substantive relationship."

Terms Sheet and Agenda of the Meeting and Unilateral Draft of the Final Agreement

The Terms Sheet

Given that it is crucial to consider the evolution of a relationship, it is equally essential to prepare for defining the endpoint of a negotiation (i.e., the conclusion, the finish line) and to chart the course to get there.

Maurizio Nichetti, the Italian Woody Allen, characterizes a good film thus: "*A good ending with a good beginning is useful. A good start without a reasonable conclusion is disappointing. It is a pity when a good start and a good end are separated by a tedious development.*" The same principle applies to negotiation.

Close your eyes and imagine what the final deal will look like once it's done. Then, mentally walk back through the negotiation process—move forward and back, reflect on the give-and-take, and review the facts and information you'll bring into the discussion. While you can't predict every detail, having a clear vision will help you organize your thoughts and better handle disagreements or unforeseen challenges when they arise.

As a rule, negotiators focus on where and how to start. However, the parties ultimately commit to each other at the conclusion of a negotiation. For a negotiation to be successful, commitments should be clear, well planned, robust, and durable.

Understanding what you want to achieve means defining the end goal. Thinking clearly about your objectives, rather than relying solely on instinct, is crucial. A broad perspective and a well-defined vision instill calmness and clarity. A skillful negotiator, for instance, can envision prices, delivery terms, payment schedules, order-handling processes, bonuses, and penalties. When negotiating a property purchase, a skilled negotiator anticipates the price, down payment amount, payment timelines, terms, dates for agreements and deeds, inclusions (such as furniture), inspections, repairs, special clauses, and expense allocations. They know how to manage processes to control quality and address inevitable disagreements. With proper preparation, you can approach the agreement discussion having already considered and addressed key terms.

In 2016, I assisted a client in negotiations with Neil Pryde Ltd., a Hong Kong-based sporting goods group operating across three key business platforms: manufacturing, distribution, and brand management. The company focuses on high-performance products, premium quality, style, and a winning attitude. Pryde Group is a wholly owned subsidiary of the Shriro Group. With over 2,500 employees, operations in more than forty countries, and nearly fifty years of experience, it is one of the world's most significant players in the water and adventure sports market. Neil Pryde aimed to secure an exclusive license to produce, market, and sell the fastest version of the Kite Race Foil and to position itself as a preferred Olympic supplier.

I suggested that my client use a Terms Sheet in a more evolved and comprehensive format, such as a Memorandum of Understanding (MOU) or Letter of Interest (LOI, or Letter of Intent). I have been using this method for over twenty years, refining and improving it along the way, and it has become an indispensable tool in my contract negotiations. A Terms Sheet is a non-binding document that outlines the substantive terms and conditions of a potential business agreement, establishing the foundation for future negotiations between seller and buyer.

My version is divided into four columns: Topic, Requirement, Proposal, and Final Agreement. At the outset, in addition to identifying the signatory parties, the purpose of the agreement is clearly stated, as this drives the entire document. In Neil Pryde's case, the Terms Sheet covered essential elements such as territory, future project developments, exclusivity, royalties, pricing, confidentiality, joint marketing, and fifteen other critical points. When negotiations are more complex and detailed, the Terms Sheet becomes even more substantial, incorporating additional specifics as needed.

ISSUE	REQUIREMENT	PROPOSAL	FINAL AGREEMENT
Signing Fee	Based on WorldSailing's approval as a nominated supplier for the Olympic Games, NPL will pay a one-time signing fee	Based on WorldSailing's approval as a Nominated Supplier for the Olympic Games, NPL will pay a one-time design fee of US $100,000	NPL will pay US $100,000 as a signing fee and, subject to approval by WorldSailing as a Nominated Supplier for the Olympic Games, NPL will pay a one-off design fee of US $200,000
Non Disclosure	Neither party shall disclose confidential information of the other party	Confidential information shall be provided to Licensee only for the purposes set forth in this Agreement and may be disclosed by Licensee only to persons whose access is necessary to perform their duties	Confidential Information may be disclosed to Licensee only for the purposes set forth in this Agreement, and such Confidential Information may be disclosed by Licensee only to those persons for whom such disclosure is necessary to carry out their duties

I always prepare the Terms Sheet in advance. When I face major negotiations, particularly those with significant legal repercussions, I also submit it to a law firm, asking them to analyze it solely from a technical perspective without delving into the terms of the agreement (to avoid the substance being distorted). Typically, if my Terms Sheet is strategically sound, I share it with the negotiating partner before the meeting, along with the agenda, making it clear that I am open to modifying it during the negotiation. A well-defined Terms Sheet facilitates discussion by clearly identifying areas of agreement and disagreement early in the negotiation, reducing the likelihood of escalation into more costly, risky, and stringent negotiations.

Once the Terms Sheet is completed in collaboration with the negotiating partner (by filling in the fourth, right-hand column by mutual agreement), it serves as a valuable guide for attorneys in preparing a proposed final agreement.

The Meeting Agenda

I also find it helpful to prepare an agenda for the meeting, as those who draft it gain the advantage of defining the topics, the sequence of their discussion, and, in some cases, the framing of each issue. By setting the structure of the meeting, you can subtly prioritize your key points, ensure sufficient time is allocated to topics of greater importance, and guide the flow of the conversation in a way that supports your objectives.

However, this practice is not without its disadvantages. Sharing the agenda with the negotiating partner in advance makes your position more explicit, offering a clearer picture of your priorities, strategies, and concerns. This transparency provides the other party with the opportunity to anticipate your arguments, prepare counterpoints, and potentially develop strategies that undermine your objectives. Moreover, the act of defining topics may inadvertently limit flexibility, as the discussion can become overly focused on pre-established points, leaving little room for dynamic responses to new opportunities or challenges that arise during the negotiation.

In short, while an agenda can be a powerful tool for structuring discussions and asserting control, it comes at the cost of reducing your element of surprise and increasing the risk of your position being scrutinized in advance.

The Unilateral Draft of the Final Agreement

When preparing for a negotiation, I recommend that you prepare a unilateral draft of the final agreement. This draft will serve as a preliminary outline of the commitments, terms and conditions you hope to achieve. While it's unlikely to be complete and may be subject to significant revision, it will provide a structured framework to guide discussions and clarify your objectives. By outlining key elements in advance, you can identify potential gaps, conflicts or ambiguities that may arise during negotiations.

Pay close attention to the specific commitments that need to be included to ensure that the agreement is both sustainable and workable. Think about the practical implications of these commitments: Who will be responsible for each action? How will the conditions be monitored or enforced? What mechanisms will be in place to deal with potential disputes or changes in circumstances? Structuring the commitments with these questions in mind can increase the durability and effectiveness of the agreement.

It is also important to establish a realistic timetable. Break down the various activities, deliverables and milestones that will result from the agreement. Whenever possible, use a graphical visualization—such as a Gantt chart or flowchart—to show these elements. Not only will this help you anticipate and manage complexity, but it will also serve as a valuable communication tool, enabling you to manage the negotiation process in a more constructive and collaborative way.

By approaching the negotiation with a well-thought-out design and clear visual planning, you can stay ahead of potential challenges, streamline the process and work towards an agreement that is both practical and mutually beneficial.

Who Will Be Sitting at the Negotiating Table?

Information makes all the difference, so gather as much information as possible about your negotiating partner before meeting with them. Who will be sitting at the table? Look for details about their personality, background, hobbies, and interests—social media platforms such as Facebook, Instagram, and LinkedIn can be valuable resources. It may also be helpful to seek out insights from friends, colleagues, or business partners who have previously negotiated with this person, regardless of whether those negotiations were successful.

One of the key elements to consider is your negotiating partner's style, so it's important to gather basic information such as their values, ethnicity, culture, age, and any other factors relevant to the negotiation. These elements, however, are not absolutes. Avoid relying on simplistic cognitive mechanisms in an effort to create order and predictability; in short, steer clear of stereotypes. Remember, we live in a world of differences and complex social relations, and the richness of subtle nuances often plays a crucial role in understanding and evaluating situations. By focusing on these nuances, you can retain useful details that might otherwise be overlooked.

Negotiators are diverse, with infinite variations in personality, background, and style. Some may be professional negotiators, some may negotiate professionally but as part of other roles, and others may not approach negotiation with much structure or strategy. They may be similar to you, or (as is often the case) completely different.

Over the years, I have negotiated with a wide variety of people. However, I dislike categorizing individuals using "dimensional reduction" (i.e., oversimplifying through stereotypes, as mentioned earlier). Instead, I strive to balance some helpful reduction of complexity with a preservation of the meaningful aspects of the **original data**. This approach allows me to identify key behavioral traits without losing sight of the individual's unique characteristics. My work often begins with many observations and variables, so I've found it useful to distill common behavioral traits into seven **basic profiles**. These profiles help me manage relationships effectively, though I don't see them as rigid patterns.

A person may not always behave in a single, consistent way or fit neatly into just one profile. Instead, they might exhibit a dominant behavioral component alongside characteristics of other profiles, which manifest with varying intensity. What's important is to use this framework as a guide to recognize (even broadly) the behavioral tendencies of the person in front of you. The sooner you can do this, the better.

Identifying your interlocutor's behavioral characteristics allows you to understand their preferences and anticipate their needs. This, in turn, enables you to manage the relationship more effectively: you can adapt your behavior to put your negotiating partner at ease and expand the comfort zone for both parties.

Ideally, a point-by-point analysis of the other party is best, although this is not always practical in casual business relationships. Nevertheless, it's worth striving to pick up clues and gradually narrow the field by exclusion until you can approximate the profile of the person you're dealing with. I've distilled the following seven types from the variety of negotiators I've encountered.

The seven types of negotiators are:
1. The Intimidator
2. The Flatterer
3. The Seducer
4. The Complainer
5. The Arguer
6. The Bullshitter
7. The Logical Thinker

1: The Intimidator

Intimidators play with emotions. They aim to throw you off balance, prevent you from thinking clearly, and blame you for everything. If something goes wrong in the negotiation, it's suddenly your fault. Their goal is to put you on the defensive and separate you from your rational self, hoping your wounded ego will keep you from objectively observing and steering the negotiation. They attack your vulnerabilities because they don't want you to regain balance—they want you to give in to their demands. Why do they do this? Always remember: a deal made under stress is likely to be inadequate.

Is your negotiating partner yelling, flailing, or pounding their fists on the table? Then you're dealing with an intimidator. Typically, intimidators speak loudly, talk frantically, move aggressively, and often use gratuitous vulgarity to emphasize their points. They also tend to interrupt constantly, refusing to let you finish your thoughts.

Intimidators make demands but rarely offer constructive suggestions. If you propose something that could benefit both parties, they may claim offense, adopting histrionic tones. They might threaten to cancel the negotiation altogether or escalate the situation by involving your boss. More often than not, these behaviors are bluffs, and you'll need to address them accordingly.

There is another type of intimidator: the silent one. This individual cunningly manipulates you with subtle but penetrating insolence. Their behavior is typically expressed more through body language than verbal antagonism.

The best way to defend yourself against any intimidator is to refuse to sink to their level. Stay calm, focused, and in control. Avoid emotional involvement and redirect the conversation back to the issues at hand, perhaps by asking open-ended questions about the purpose of the negotiation. This approach can help the intimidator calm down and recognize that you're not engaging in their game.

If an intimidator threatens to walk away from the negotiation, assess whether they're bluffing and how serious the threat is. You might concede something of little value to you or ask directly what they plan to do if they follow through. Your goal should be to call their bluff. If they leave the table as an intimidation tactic and your initial position is solid, they will likely return. When they do, your position will be even stronger because you've exposed the bluff.

2: The Flatterer

Like the intimidator, the flatterer focuses more on your emotions than on facts and logic. However, the flatterer relies on overly optimistic and insincere remarks to manipulate the negotiation. The goal, once again, is to provoke an emotional reaction, distract you from the facts, and cloud your judgment. The flatterer assumes (often correctly) that everyone enjoys receiving compliments, and they will try to appeal to your ego. They may compliment anything: your e-commerce platform, your latest product launch, your customer service team, or even your appearance. The flatterer's objective is to make you feel like you are winning the negotiation, lulling you into a false sense of security to induce a truce and extract concessions.

The first red flag of a flatterer is an excessive number of smiles and compliments early in the negotiation. They may even go so far as to praise your negotiating style to make you more compliant and erode the advantage you've gained. It's difficult not to get caught up in this vortex of compliments, especially when delivered with soft, non-confrontational language. After all, who doesn't enjoy hearing nice things about themselves?

But no matter how flattering the compliments or how affable their tone, you must always stay focused on the purpose of the negotiation: achieving your goals. Your approach with the flatterer should be similar to the one recommended for dealing with the intimidator: concentrate solely on the substantive elements of the negotiation, show due attention to your negotiating partner, remain calm, and ignore the flattery.

Sometimes, it's helpful to demonstrate that their flattering tactics are ineffective. You can do this by showing indifference, avoiding inflections in your voice, and maintaining a professional coolness in your responses. Introducing a diversion involving a third party may also help, as it shifts attention away from you and redirects the negotiation to facts and objectives.

One crucial tip: avoid reciprocating flattery! Doing so will likely invite more flattery, entangling you in an unserious and potentially hazardous negotiation.

3: The Seducer

You have likely encountered at least one seducer in your life. The seducer paints a perfect picture, describing everything exactly as you want to hear it. But if you dig into the enticing details, the illusion quickly fades. Imagine you're negotiating a partnership agreement, and your counterpart enthusiastically agrees to all your key demands: profit-sharing, deadlines, and even exclusivity. It seems too good to be true—and it is. When you review the draft agreement, you discover that the fine print includes vague language, exceptions, and conditions that undermine the very commitments they seemed to concede during the discussion. The negotiator used the promise of agreement as a tool to lull you into a false sense of security. Too late—you've been seduced.

The seducer is clever, often toeing the line of moral propriety. They propose tempting offers and concessions, and once you've taken the bait, they captivate you by telling you exactly what you want to hear. Unfortunately, these offers and concessions are often riddled with half-truths (and half-lies) that will slowly come to light. At that point, the seducer will rely on excuses tied to policies, company regulations, or higher authorities to justify their actions.

The seducer is skilled at controlling the pace of negotiation to achieve their goal. Pay close attention to the rhythm of the negotiation: a skilled seducer might speed things up to finalize the deal before you uncover their illusion, or they might intentionally slow things down to distract you, perhaps with a sudden phone call or an unexpected need.

Protecting yourself from a seducer is straightforward: don't engage in negotiation. Refusing to negotiate dismantles their seduction tactics, rendering them irrelevant. For instance, you might say, "I was going to pay cash." If there's still time, try to revise the agreement, involve a higher authority, or explore alternatives.

Preparation and research are critical when dealing with a seducer. The more informed you are, the better your chances of identifying a potential seducer in advance and avoiding negotiation altogether. If you decide to proceed, arm yourself with detailed information and ask question after question. The more you confront the seducer with concrete facts and reality, the more their influence diminishes. If helpful, take notes and maintain a skeptical attitude—this is always a valuable tool in any negotiation.

4: The Complainer
The complainer is the least dangerous, deceptive, and unethical of the seven profiles. This profile represents an insecure negotiator: a strategy-driven individual who primarily wants to be heard and understood. When this happens, the complainer becomes more reasonable, and dealing with them becomes more pleasant.

Complainers are successful if they can make you feel bad about their grievances. You can recognize them by their tendency to try every possible way to guilt you into softening your demands. Sometimes, they may come across as positional negotiators because they are focused solely on their immediate needs. Even when they seem unwilling to move from their position, they often secretly hope that you will find a way to work out an agreement to end their stream of complaints.

How can you defend yourself against a complainer? By using empathy, patience, understanding, and active listening. Encourage them to share more, even if you don't necessarily need the information. Show genuine interest, make eye contact, and provide verbal acknowledgments. If this approach works, the complainer will relax, creating an opportunity to steer the discussion back to the negotiation details. At this stage, ask open-ended questions to gain clarity, offer a small concession, and work toward reaching an agreement.

5: The Arguer

The arguer thrives on conflict and creating disagreement. If conflict and disagreement don't exist, they will generate them because they feel most comfortable in such contexts. With an arguer, negotiation becomes a continuous and relentless argument over both significant and trivial points. Some arguers may appear calm in the early stages of the negotiation, only to switch to their preferred combative mode when you least expect it. They are often finicky and struggle to distinguish between what is essential and what is not. It is easy to spot an arguer because they engage in intense, often unnecessary discussions in response to every request. Additionally, they attack your every move to complicate the negotiation.

To defend yourself against arguers, rely on a shared agenda, which helps keep the discussion focused on the agreed program. Ignore unnecessary debates and react only to the important issues. Focus on finding solutions and concentrate on the most critical points of the agreement, leaving minor disputes for your negotiating partner to "win." Since perpetual argumentation is often a distraction tactic, arguers hope to wear you down or lead you into making errors.

Some arguers behave this way to accumulate as many victories as possible, no matter how small. In many cases, it's crucial to decide whether you want to be "right" or close a successful negotiation. While it is sometimes possible to achieve both, if you have to choose, it's usually better to prioritize closing the deal over being right. As with other negotiation styles, stick to the facts. If the negotiation becomes unproductive, calmly inform your negotiating partner that you may have to step away. Above all, avoid becoming an arguer yourself, because that would be a dead-end negotiation!

6: The Bullshitter

The bullshitter relies on a mix of outright falsehoods, half-truths, omissions, exaggerations, broken promises, and distortions of anything from relationships with mutual acquaintances to their authority in the company they represent. It makes little difference whether these are white lies (e.g., lies meant to please or avoid offending someone's sensibilities) or black ones (falsehoods told to gain an advantage): the bullshitter feels entitled to embellish the truth to make their product, service, or offering seem more appealing.

The bullshitter thrives in the absence of hard evidence, relying on the fact that there's no counterevidence either. If you pay attention, you might notice their shifty eyes or a faltering voice—perhaps you'll get the nagging feeling that something doesn't quite add up. With experience, your inner voice will start to warn you: "Too good to be true." This is your signal that you're dealing with a bullshitter.

Sometimes, a bullshitter's exaggerations or hyperbole may not technically be *lies*, as they fall within the realm of subjectivity. Nevertheless, you should be cautious if such statements occur frequently. Once again, the best defense is to rely on facts and objective criteria, presenting them confidently and without hesitation. Address falsehoods (or even exaggerations) from the outset and strive to remain as honest as possible yourself.

While *The Two Liars* might make an excellent title for a collection of short stories by Isaac Bashevis Singer, a similar dynamic transposed to the negotiating table would result in absolute failure!

7: The Logical Thinker

The logical thinker is the most reasonable of the profiles you may encounter in a negotiation. However, some tend to overanalyze problems, spend excessive time on them, and get overly nitpicky about minor issues.

Logical thinkers can be challenging because if you disagree with them, they will want to understand your reasoning; if you agree, they will want to understand even more! Unless you are averse to delving into details, negotiating with logical thinkers is usually manageable. They are perceptive and refrain from using emotional mind games to throw you off course. However, their continual focus on detailed analysis can be risky for you, as it may cause you to lose sight of the ultimate goal. It's important to note that this behavior stems from their natural way of thinking rather than a deliberate negotiating tactic.

What should you do? Indulge them. Negotiating with logical thinkers becomes easier if you have patience and can satisfy their thirst for details. Remember that logical thinkers thrive on facts and figures. By nature, they are skeptical, precise, detail-oriented, and prone to asking many questions.

Beware of false logical thinkers who ask questions or request analysis not out of genuine interest but to throw you off balance or block an agreement they don't want. You can recognize them by the superficial nature of their questions. Pay attention to the persistence of their inquiries, the level of detail required, and how they react to your answers. With this type of negotiator, it is essential to be well prepared, ensuring that every statement you make is clear and supported by facts.

In general, you should engage with logical thinkers by satisfying their need for information. Asking them questions in return can help you establish rapport and get in tune with their thought process. Be cautious not to overdo it, however, as this could prolong the negotiation unnecessarily. Keep the pace brisk and focus primarily on substantive topics.

Mix of Styles

The negotiation style adopted and developed by an individual is a function of their personality, which is innate and typically unchanging. If, during the preparation phase, you can identify a negotiating style, you'll be better equipped to handle it at the negotiating table. Additionally, this process can help you identify and assess your counterpart's personality (and gain a deeper understanding of your own).

I've always been fascinated by the DISC behavior model, proposed in 1928 by William Moulton Marston, a Harvard physiological psychologist, in his book *Emotions of Normal People* (1928). Marston deliberately focused only on psychological phenomena that were directly observable and measurable through objective means. He studied the differentiated behaviors and interactions between people by evaluating them in various contexts and environments. Experience has led me to conclude that there are multiple shades of personalities, and your negotiating partner will often be a blend of these personalities—though one may predominate.

1: The Dominant / Aggressive

The dominant / aggressive negotiator is motivated by a desire for influence, power, and control, asserting themselves over others. You can recognize this type because they talk and act quickly: dominant / aggressive negotiators are frantic, hurried, impatient, and easily bored. When preparing to negotiate with them, ensure you have all the necessary elements in advance and be ready for a fast-paced discussion.

Only two things matter to this type: winning and getting as much as possible while conceding as little as possible. If this doesn't happen, they may become agitated and even more difficult to deal with. To manage such a negotiator, slow the pace of the discussion by remaining calm, avoiding emotional responses, and sticking to a well-structured agenda and facts.

2: The Passive / Submissive

At the opposite end of the spectrum is the passive / submissive negotiator. Shy, introverted, a good listener, quiet, insecure, and eager to please, this type focuses on satisfying their negotiating partner. They are uncomfortable with conflict and disorder, speak little, and only express their thoughts and opinions when prompted. They rarely take control of the negotiation, preferring to follow rather than lead.

When dealing with a passive / submissive negotiator, it's not necessary to defend yourself. Instead, there is a risk of taking advantage of their position. Resist this temptation to preserve the relationship and maintain future opportunities.

3: The Logical / Analytical

The logical / analytical negotiator is organized, prepared, critical, thoughtful, skeptical, and apprehensive. This type likes to delve into the facts, details, and information of the negotiation.

They arrive well prepared and, even if they are not in a hurry, will always be on time or early.

Logical / analytical negotiators are creative problem-solvers who gain power through knowledge. However, they may make you feel scrutinized, as they will closely examine your proposal for errors and inconsistencies. To negotiate effectively with them, come thoroughly prepared and bring supporting materials like charts, diagrams, and reports. If necessary, you'll need to respond quickly and confidently.

Never bluff with a logical / analytical negotiator. Avoid taking risks with lies, distortions, or half-truths, as they will likely catch you. Be mentally prepared for what may feel like being "on trial."

Sometimes, logical / analytical negotiators lack confidence in their data and seek reassurance in details. Try to offer this reassurance, as they may otherwise stall the negotiation indefinitely in search of the certainty they need to move forward.

4: The Friendly / Collaborative

The friendly / collaborative negotiator is often viewed positively, as they work patiently, honestly, and creatively to achieve results quickly. They build trust through agreements and develop solid relationships for the future. Courteous and empathetic, they aim to learn as much as possible about their negotiating partner. You can recognize this type by their warm smile and friendly demeanor.

However, don't be fooled: friendly / collaborative negotiators have a sharp business sense and are true professionals. Always remain vigilant—verify the genuineness of their behavior and watch closely for their reactions when you respond to their unreasonable requests. If a conflict arises, you may have exposed their underlying strategy.

5: The Uncooperative Evader

Evasive / uncooperative negotiators often seem reluctant or resistant to negotiate, sometimes giving the impression of being almost absent from the negotiating table. In reality, they deal with problems (and people) by avoiding them altogether. They are typically insecure, fearful, and introverted. These negotiators avoid cooperation because they don't feel prepared or knowledgeable about the topic being negotiated. This insecurity leads them to behave in a cold, pessimistic, and indifferent manner. They often remain silent to avoid saying anything uncomfortable or that could weaken their position.

Their secrecy, combined with their introversion, often generates frustration as discussions are postponed, critical information is withheld, or decisions are procrastinated. Many problems remain unresolved when dealing with such individuals. Managing these personalities is challenging, and it is essential to diagnose the causes of their insecurity and help them overcome their fears. However, be cautious not to fall into the temptation of withholding information in retaliation.

6. The Expressive / Communicative

Expressive / communicative negotiators are generally talkative, spontaneous, and energetic. They approach their work with enthusiasm and a positive attitude. Sociable by nature, they enjoy conveying a sense of humor and amusement in most situations.

However, they require significant attention as they are easily distracted, partly because they are not strong listeners. Their primary focus is on closing the deal, feeling instrumental to the result, and entertaining you along the way. When you attempt to build a relationship with them, they may become suspicious, so it can be helpful to let them take the lead initially to establish rapport. Once this foundation is built, guide the conversation back to the agenda and avoid unnecessary chatter.

Remember that the behavioral styles analyzed here do not represent rigid, fixed categories—they are broad examples. By understanding these behavioral types, you can identify common traits in your negotiating partners and manage them accordingly.

The Five Core Concerns

I have said this several times before, but I want to repeat it: in any negotiation, preparation is essential to achieving a good result. Unfortunately, we often don't find the time or manage to prepare properly (or at least not as well as we would like). In such cases, it helps to know that there are five elements common to all negotiations. Understanding these in depth enables you to make quick and effective decisions.

These five elements form an additional and crucial link in negotiation preparation. I am referring to the five core concerns, initially expounded by Roger Fisher and Daniel Shapiro (2016) in *Beyond Reason: Using Emotions as You Negotiate.* I have had the privilege of being in the classroom with Professor Shapiro several times in Cambridge. He has a rare ability to captivate his audience, combining contagious passion with an extraordinary talent for stimulating critical thinking. Every topic he addressed became a fascinating journey, and each lesson was an opportunity to broaden horizons and see the world from new perspectives. I've always appreciated his innovative approach to negotiation and conflict management, which integrates principles of psychology, communication, and interpersonal dynamics. Attending his classes gave me a deeper understanding and recognition of these concepts and has greatly improved my negotiation skills and perception of negotiation.

The personalities of those involved in a negotiation significantly influence how they behave and react during the process. For example, individuals with dominant personalities may be more inclined to seek control and exert pressure, whereas those with cooperative personalities are often more willing to pursue compromise solutions.

Personality also affects the emotions that emerge during negotiation, such as aggression or a predisposition to seek harmony. Emotions play a crucial role in negotiation, influencing both behaviors and outcomes. Feelings like anger, frustration, fear, or excitement can shape the decisions and strategies of the parties involved. Effectively understanding and managing emotions contributes to more constructive negotiations and greater satisfaction for both parties.

The behaviors adopted during negotiation are often shaped by the emotions and key interests identified by Shapiro. For instance, individuals who prioritize status or belonging may adopt assertive or competitive behaviors to defend their interests. Conversely, those who value appreciation or relationships may lean toward collaborative behaviors and seek solutions that benefit both parties.

Emotions are experiences. When someone says or does something personally meaningful to you, your emotions respond. You may feel a physical sensation, have a thought, notice a physiological change, or experience an urge to act. Emotions can be positive or negative—positive emotions are comforting, while negative emotions can be unsettling.

Working closely with Daniel Shapiro has deepened my passion for studying emotions and his **framework**. When applied correctly, his model yields extraordinary results. I am currently working on a project related to analyzing these dynamics, but I am still at an early stage and unable to describe it in detail.

Negotiations often fail because they are sabotaged by emotions, which are contagious and viral. Anger breeds anger, stress generates stress, and heated discussions that escalate into confrontation alienate the parties, causing them to lose sight of the negotiation's goal. The common tendency is to prepare a strategy by focusing on talking points, offers, and counteroffers, rarely planning for the emotional aspect. When we think about it, core concerns are nothing more than fundamental **human desires.** These needs are crucial to nearly everyone and are present in virtually every negotiation. While often not explicitly stated, they are just as important as tangible interests.

In nearly every negotiation or dispute, one or more core concerns are at stake. Understanding these needs allows you to recognize and analyze your negotiating partner's emotions while leveraging your positive emotions. However, failing to address these core concerns can jeopardize the negotiation. Although strong negative emotions can incur high costs at the negotiating table, not all emotions are detrimental. Positive emotions can facilitate favorable outcomes, and even feelings like anxiety or nervousness can be channeled effectively to contribute to success.

For over fifteen years, I have included the five core concerns in my preparation checklist. These are "sensitive areas" that must always be considered in negotiation. The five main concerns are:

Appreciation: Do you feel heard, understood, and appreciated? Does your negotiating partner feel heard, understood, and appreciated?

Affiliation: Is there an emotional connection between you and your negotiating partner? Do you feel close to him or think you are being treated as an adversary?

Autonomy: Do you feel free to make decisions, or is someone guiding them? What about your negotiating partner: can they make decisions independently, without someone else imposing choices on them?

Status: Who is important? Who is not? Who feels respected because of their status? Who feels disrespected?

Role: Do the people who sit at the negotiating table play a meaningful role? Are they fulfilled?

The following table provides an example of how the five core concerns framework can be applied in preparing for a negotiation with an individual named Marc Goldberg. By systematically analyzing and addressing these concerns, it becomes possible to better understand the underlying emotional needs of the counterpart, fostering a more constructive and collaborative dialogue.

The table illustrates how these categories can serve as a practical tool for preparation. Each row highlights a specific core concern, explores how it might manifest in the context of the negotiation, and outlines the negotiating strategy to be applied. This approach can be tailored to any negotiation scenario, helping to anticipate potential challenges, identify areas of alignment, and develop strategies that enhance mutual understanding and trust.

Concern	About Marc Goldberg	Negotiation strategy
Appreciation	Son of Robert. Industrial family for four generations. He graduated in Economics from Stanford in 1991 and received a master's degree from Harvard. After four years at BCG, he worked for ten years for several US private equity firms. For the next twelve years, he was at Blackstone, climbing the ranks, and then founded his own private equity firm, MSE, with Alexander Bolt in 2017.	He is certainly a leading authority in economics, but he does not disdain entering technical discussions; therefore, first and foremost, actively listen and understand his expectations before proposing our ideas and solutions; value everything he is willing to share. He has extensive expertise in all financial aspects, so be highly attentive to both what he says and how we communicate our message.
Affiliation	Plays golf (4 handicap). He is an oriental cuisine enthusiast and wine connoisseur; in his youth he was a bartender in Newport for two summer seasons. He met his wife at Stanford. He met partner Alexander Bolt at Harvard. Outside of MSE, he likes to invest directly in startups in the world of AI (Open AI), quantum computing (ColdQuanta), and biotechnology (Ginkgo Bioworks).	Focus the opening conversation on common interests, taking advantage of affinities and acquaintances (such as golfing friends). Mention that you took cooking classes at the Blue Elephant in Bangkok, and that you know Cambridge pretty well: you and your wife visit often because your daughter is studying law at Harvard. Also, mention that you are considering investments in innovative companies.
Autonomy	His coworkers say he would make even coffee nervous. He has a deeply inquisitive mind and a strong creative flair. He aspires to be the best in his family. He suffers from comparison with his father, a highly successful man.	Respect his autonomy and, since he wants to make his mark, leave him free to make his own proposals without imposing yours; alternatively, involve him and ask him to contribute to decisions.

Status	His status is determined by his professional achieve-ments, leadership positions in recognized companies and organizations, his role in the family and his philanthropic activities.	Emphasize his social status, academic background, and professional experience, and ask him to apply all his expertise to solving negotia-tion-related problems.
Role	Husband (married since 1997). Father (John, 25, and Jennifer, 23, who has Down syndrome). CEO of MSE. On the board of directors of Open AI, ColdQuanta and Ginkgo Bioworks. Member of the National Golf Links of America. Volunteer at the Down syndrome Connection of Long Island. Supporter of Gigi's Playhouse.	Make it clear that the nego-tiation meetings were orga-nized with consideration of not only professional needs but also personal and family needs. Respect Marc's role as MSE private equity admi-nistrator and recognize his leadership. Interact formally only when necessary and maintain an informal attitude when requesting his interven-tion and skills/experience to solve possible problems.

The five core concerns are universal, and whenever you enter into a negotiation—even when it is your first interaction with someone—you must keep them in mind and know how to use them effectively during the talks. Remember that your interlocutors seek **appreciation**. What can you say to make them feel valued and understood? Prepare by considering how things may look from their perspective. Show appreciation for their reasoning, even when you disagree with them. For example, say, "I understand your reasoning. I see that the price feels too high for you, and I appreciate the candor with which you express that, in your opinion, our margin should be less than 50 percent."

Remember also that your interlocutors value their **autonomy** and do not want it infringed upon. Ensure they have a sense of choice. For instance, instead of saying, "I'll see you tomorrow at 10:30," try, "I'd like to meet you tomorrow at 10:30. Would that work for you?"

Your interlocutors also want to feel a sense of **affiliation**. Explore possible connections between you and your negotiating partner. Make them feel respected for their **status**, and remember that they also want to play a meaningful **role** in the negotiation. Always aim to engage them constructively. If there are differences, invite them to work on resolving them collaboratively.

Even if you have limited time to prepare, take the five core concerns seriously and address them in detail. Doing so will ensure you enter the negotiation much better prepared and empowered.

Where, How, and With Whom

The Field Factor

Competitive negotiation is a bargaining style focused on achieving goals that benefit only one party—resembling sports, where one team wins and the other loses. In sports, the **home field advantage** refers to the edge a team gains when playing in its own stadium. This advantage exists in many sports and arises from various factors, such as fan support, familiarity with the playing field, and the psychological comfort of "playing at home."

Similarly, in business negotiations, choosing the right environment can be equally important, influencing both the process and the outcome. The environment requires careful consideration in negotiation strategy. Most people prefer to negotiate on their own turf because it offers several perceived advantages. Familiarity with the location allows the host to better control the negotiation setting, including selecting the room, arranging the seating, and showcasing the company's resources. Additionally, negotiating at home reduces travel costs, saves time, and allows the host to continue managing other business activities.

Negotiating at home also alleviates the pressure of being away from loved ones, whether family or friends. Over the years, I've observed that negotiators who travel often tend to close deals (or walk away from negotiations) more quickly—sometimes to their detriment. Playing at home provides undeniable advantages—not least the subtle authority communicated by conducting the negotiation at your own office desk.

However, there are situations where negotiating away from home may be more advantageous. The choice of negotiation location carries symbolic meaning. Meeting on your negotiating partner's turf demonstrates serious intent and a strong commitment to reaching an agreement—this gesture can sometimes be critical in securing a deal. More importantly, negotiating on their turf provides a unique opportunity to learn about your partner's activities and organizational context, which can offer valuable insights. Thus, negotiating at home is not always the best option.

There are, of course, scenarios where you have no choice but to negotiate on your partner's turf—such as purchasing a car at a dealership or meeting in a hotel conference room. While many people prefer negotiating at home, this is not always advantageous. For instance, you may not require access to additional information, need to consult colleagues or data, or you might prefer to negotiate in a distraction-free setting away from your office.

In short, whether you are negotiating at home, away, or on neutral ground, the location will matter little if you are thoroughly prepared for the negotiation.

Virtual Negotiations

Before the COVID-19 pandemic, negotiations were usually conducted in person. Since the pandemic, however, things have changed dramatically, with many negotiations now taking place virtually. Only a few years ago, the idea of negotiating and reaching agreements without meeting in person seemed implausible. Today, negotiations can be conducted from anywhere, at any time, and using various tools: work chats, instant messaging, or even email.

The communication revolution has liberated the global business world. However, despite the advantage of being able to communicate with anyone from anywhere, virtual communications often generate less trust. The inability to read body language makes negotiations more challenging and increases the risk of mistrust. This underscores the importance of preparing thoroughly for virtual negotiations and incorporating trust-building elements into your communication strategy.

Trust-building is key. Virtual negotiations tend to produce worse results due to less effective communication and heightened distrust between the parties. While I have successfully worked on many M&A transactions in recent years without in-person meetings, I can confirm that online negotiators, compared to those who negotiate in person, are less likely to reach strong agreements or build rapport, and more likely to lose trust during the process.

People also tend to be less cooperative in virtual settings, as they feel less pressure to be polite. Online negotiations present unique challenges that must be addressed differently than face-to-face meetings. One way to improve virtual communication is to reduce the size of negotiation groups. I've found that video conferences with four or more participants can quickly lose focus. Additionally, using larger, high-definition screens can enhance the quality of online discussions and foster greater interpersonal trust. (It is presumably trivial to point out that video communication is significantly more effective than text-only methods.)

It may take years for us to return to having only face-to-face meetings and negotiations—if we indeed ever do. Recognizing this, I have developed a routine for virtual negotiations that consistently yields good results, and I follow it methodically. At the beginning of a meeting, I start with introductions and dedicate time to small talk to establish personal connections. If the context allows, I also use humor, as sharing jokes can increase trust between the parties. I then set the meeting agenda to ensure that everyone is aligned and that no one leaves early or joins late. This also allows the agenda to be adjusted if necessary.

When I have team members involved in the negotiation, I spend time preparing with them to ensure everyone is aligned. I verify that tasks are clearly understood and that we have contingency plans for surprises or unexpected developments.

In 2019, during a series of ten management presentations to several foreign investors, I created a small tool to assign questions to my team on the fly. My team and I were in the same room, while the investors were attending via video conference. I attached a pencil to the cap of a mineral water bottle, which I kept under the webcam frame so the investors couldn't see it. When a question was asked, I would rotate the bottle so the pencil pointed to the person who should respond. This simple method helped us appear cohesive and aligned as a team. Each question was followed by a timely and natural answer from the appropriate person, eliminating the need for me to say, "This question will be answered by Alessandro." It also subtly conveyed the idea that every team member held a leadership role in the process.

Self-awareness is the secret superpower of any negotiator, especially when the temptation to multitask arises during video calls. To minimize distractions, turn off all notifications on your phone and close unnecessary tabs on your computer, including email and calendar. I've attended meetings where a negotiating partner, while sharing their screen, inadvertently displayed private or sensitive emails or messages. To avoid this, I shut down all non-essential programs, maintaining only a chat channel with colleagues (if needed) for real-time tactical adjustments.

If you feel self-conscious on video, turn off the personal view in your video chat settings to avoid seeing yourself on-screen. Create an environment that allows you to focus entirely on the negotiation and perform at your best, and ask your team to do the same.

Group Negotiations

It is increasingly rare to participate in face-to-face or online negotiations alone, because many negotiations are too complex for a single individual to handle. No one person can be fully informed about every aspect of a negotiation. In such cases, working as part of a group generally guarantees better results, although it requires more internal coordination and effort to ensure a smooth flow of information among team members.

Some negotiations may also require diverse skills (not all of which will necessarily be possessed by one individual) and specialized expertise, such as technical or legal knowledge. If you are managing a team, devote sufficient time to preparation to ensure your team becomes united, cohesive, and reliable. Ensure that all members can participate in strategy discussions as a group before entering into team negotiations.

When it comes to forming a negotiation team, there's a valuable finding from Laura Kray, faculty director of the Center for Equity, Gender, and Leadership at University of California, Berkeley, that's worth keeping in mind. According to her research, it is easier to lie when addressing women. In her study, both men and women lied to female participants more frequently than to male participants. Specifically, 24 percent of men admitted to lying to a female participant during exercises, compared to only 3 percent who admitted lying to a male participant. Similarly, 11 percent of women admitted to deceiving men, while the percentage rose to 17 percent when referring to women (Kray et al., 2014).

Negotiations involving multiple people aren't limited to large business-to-business deals. Imagine negotiating to buy a beach house with your partner, or purchasing a car for your child, where you must balance their focus on aesthetics and performance with your concerns about safety and value for money. This highlights the importance of learning to negotiate as part of a team.

As noted previously, it is increasingly common for negotiations to involve groups rather than individuals. Often, more than one person represents both parties, and multiparty negotiations have become the norm. While a team can be more effective, the best outcomes are not necessarily tied to the number of participants—it's about quality, not quantity.

In *The Wisdom of Crowds*, *New Yorker* columnist James Surowiecki (2005) explores a deceptively simple idea: large groups of people are collectively smarter than individual experts. A group's collective knowledge and diverse opinions often outperform a single individual's decision-making, problem-solving, and innovation, even in predicting future outcomes.

Negotiating as a team has many benefits. A group provides security and power, and sends a strong signal to the other side that you are taking the deal seriously. It also allows for presenting multiple compromises and creative options. However, team negotiation has its challenges. The presence of multiple participants can lead to a lack of focus or the risk of groupthink, where individuals feel pressured to conform to the dominant opinion, stifling dissenting ideas. A false sense of cohesion may arise, creating tension between parties. Genuine attempts at conciliation from the opposing side may be misinterpreted as dishonest tricks and rejected, reducing opportunities to reach an agreement.

Jim Collins's renowned principle, explained in his book *Good to Great* (2001), emphasizes: "First, get the right people on the bus, the wrong people off the bus, and the right people in the right seats." As in sports or travel, selecting the right teammates is critical. Specific criteria such as negotiation experience, technical expertise, and interpersonal skills must be carefully considered. The strength of the group depends on the positive contributions, motivation, and alignment of individuals, all working toward a single purpose. During preparation, select people with complementary skills to build a comprehensive strategy. Individual contributions should be reviewed and challenged by others for greater impartiality and refinement. In group negotiations, aligning all team members to the same strategy is crucial. Everyone must share an understanding of the interests, goals, and constraints involved.

Regardless of the team's size, a strong leader is essential. The leader will steer the negotiation, identify the interests of both sides, and manage the group effectively. Technical experts can support the leader, but they must be managed carefully, as they tend to talk more than they listen. Assign value management to someone skilled with numbers and accustomed to handling financial objectives. This person often works closely with the leader to define the BATNA (best alternative to a negotiated agreement) and establish the minimum deal requirements.

If the negotiation is complex, ensure your attorney is involved—particularly in the final stages of the agreement. I prefer to bring in attorneys only toward the end: my experience with lawyers involved from the early stages has shown them to be slow and sometimes unconstructive. Attorneys are most effective when they step in after the parties have reached an agreement.

Including a team member with a strong, established relationship with the negotiating partner can be invaluable. Their role is to actively listen to the other side's perspectives and interests without intervening directly. Understanding what matters most to your negotiating partner can provide critical insights when presenting offers or counteroffers. Even with thorough preparation, short breaks during negotiations are often necessary. These breaks allow the team to regroup, align strategies, and adjust to new developments.

Multiparty Negotiation

Multiparty negotiations require detailed preparation. Before the negotiation begins, it is crucial for all parties to clarify who the participants will be so they can work on forming coalitions and defining roles. With this in mind, the parties' interests, options, alternatives, external standards, requirements, and contractual commitments arising from the agreement must also be thoroughly prepared and understood.

To ensure the negotiation runs efficiently, it is essential to set an agenda, define a process and appoint a chairperson or moderator. This person will be responsible for ensuring that all parties' perspectives are adequately represented and for handling inevitable conflicts over contracts. For this role, select someone with strong conflict resolution skills who can defuse emotionally charged situations and manage participants' behavior, including tone of voice and disrespectful language. The moderator's primary job is to keep everyone focused on reaching the best possible consensus.

Many negotiations involve agreements among multiple parties, as often happens in business collaborations where each party brings its own positions, interests, and alternatives to the table. This can also occur in simpler contexts, such as within families.

For example, my daughters love to travel, and I try to accommodate them, just as I do Caterina (who has put up with me since 2010!). Giulia enjoys eventful vacations; a relaxing week in the Maldives wouldn't suit her. Alessia, on the other hand, prefers total relaxation—her idea of vacation means, "I won't even bring a book." Neither of them likes cultural trips, so no museums or temples. Caterina, however, would opt for a mix of adventure, relaxation, and a bit of culture. If it were up to me, I'd choose a little bit of everything, provided I don't have to revisit places I've already been—a challenging condition to meet, as I've traveled extensively for both pleasure and business.

Negotiating in contexts like this requires dexterity and an awareness of potential pitfalls, such as coalitions forming between parties. These negotiations demand a broader skill set due to their increased complexity. You must understand, analyze, and build relationships with each participant. Resisting pressure and protecting your interests in the face of a coalition can be particularly challenging. Emotional distress often leads to poor decisions, so preparation is key.

The strategy becomes more complicated with multiple, often conflicting interests. Unlike a two-party negotiation, where each side typically enters with a clear BATNA, in multiparty negotiations, the BATNAs are more dynamic and can change as coalitions form. Therefore, it is not enough to evaluate the participants' initial BATNAs—it is critical to continuously reassess both your own and the other parties' alternatives throughout the negotiation.

The exchange of information and the number of communication channels increase exponentially according to the formula $n(n-1)/2$, where n is the number of participants. For instance, if there are three participants, there will be three communication channels; with four participants, this increases to six; and with five, it becomes ten. This creates a substantial flow of information, which is no longer bi-directional as in two-party negotiations. Instead, it becomes a complex web of multiple exchanges, proposals, and compromises.

This demands significant effort to track and remember all the information being exchanged, which constantly reshapes the relationships between negotiators and affects the atmosphere and mood at the table. Multiparty negotiations require not only preparation but also adaptability and attention to detail to navigate their intricacies effectively.

Equally critical is the process one chooses to follow, which is fraught with pitfalls related to the structure, chosen rules, location, sequence of issues, mode of decision-making, and perception of legitimacy. I have participated in negotiations where the stakes were high, and I recall with satisfaction how wisely the parties opted to use an expert to moderate and facilitate the process. In such negotiations, one of the main goals is to arrive well prepared, thinking in advance about attack strategies (how to build winning coalitions) and defense strategies (how to form a blocking alliance).

Coalitions are like the first two houses in tale of the three little pigs:[41] temporary entities driven by short-term self-interest. However, it is possible to build them solidly and stably if you can get participants to align on the issues at stake and agree on how to address them. During the preparation phase, when building a coalition, start by identifying all stakeholders, including supporters and opponents of your goals. Rank them, considering the influence they can bring to the alliance and their perceived level of trustworthiness. Begin with the most influential individuals, then work to gain allies who are aligned with you but lack significant power—they may gain influence during the negotiation.

Pay less attention to those who are marginal or have little influence, as well as those who are not aligned with you. At the same time, consider ways to block your strongest opponents. For example, you might form an alliance with one of their potential partners, particularly if those partners are motivated by short-term gains.

International Negotiations

Preparing for a multiparty negotiation and reaching an agreement is complex; preparing for an international negotiation is no less challenging. Books have always played an important role in my life, and I've always been an avid buyer. I remember purchasing *Kiss, Bow, or Shake Hands* by Terri Morrison (2006) in 1994, at the start of my business career. The book explores how people from over sixty countries perceive information and negotiate business. I found the sections on cognitive styles, negotiation techniques, and value systems particularly interesting. It offers valuable advice on do's and don'ts, gift-giving, schedules, etiquette, nonverbal language, and much more. When I bought

---

41   The Three Little Pigs is a traditional European fairy tale of uncertain origin. It was first published around 1843 by James Orchard Halliwell-Phillipps in his collection of fairy tales, *Nursery Rhymes and Nursery Tales*. Three pigs build their houses out of different materials. An evil wolf destroys the houses of the first two pigs, which are made of straw and sticks, respectively, but fails to destroy the third pig's house, which is made of bricks.

it, I never imagined I would eventually visit over eighty countries, mainly for work.

After twenty-five years of intensive experience, I have concluded that international negotiations are comparable to multiparty negotiations with differences among groups. While it is a good book and still has a place in my library, the idea that you can standardize negotiations with people from diverse cultures—whether French, Indian, Brazilian, or others—using a "magic formula" is simplistic and may do more harm than good.

Today, the challenge for a manager of a multinational corporation with offices worldwide, or a small entrepreneur with an online business serving customers across five continents, is recognizing and adapting to the different cultures of the people they interact with.

It is impossible to stereotype a professional born in Jaipur who studied in Singapore, lives in Zurich, and works for a publicly traded American multinational. When preparing for international negotiations, many of us fall into the trap of overusing stereotypes and generalizations, which arise from minor differences. This not only limits our understanding but also distracts us from focusing on crucial information.

Over the years, I have found that my international counterparts often defied stereotypes, surprising me with behaviors and strategies I didn't anticipate. I quickly learned to stop relying on stereotypes, as they blinded me to important nuances in their negotiating strategies. I learned the hard way that the other side was not "strange" but simply behaved differently due to cultural differences. I also overcame the fear of embodying negative stereotypes associated with my own culture—a fear that initially made me act unnaturally. In the end, I realized that I could only negotiate effectively by being myself: I am me, Pietro.

While negotiation is often synonymous with communication, in successful cross-cultural negotiation, language and mutual understanding are critical. How often have you felt the other party understood exactly what you were saying, only to later realize they had no idea? When interpreters are involved, it is essential that they are trained in negotiation and that ample time is taken to prepare them for the talks. They should be fully aligned with the context and goals of the negotiation. Minimizing misunderstandings is key to preventing the negotiation from becoming unnecessarily long or laborious.

I recall negotiating with executives from China Banknote Printing & Minting Corp. in 1988 at their opulent headquarters in Xicheng, Beijing. At the time, they were the largest banknote printer in the world by volume. I was assisted by an interpreter who frequently summarized the topics discussed and asked the other side to share key points. Repeating such information multiple times might seem redundant, but ensuring that everyone at the negotiating table is aligned and on the same page is essential.

A negotiation is much like climbing the south slope of Everest: it demands extensive preparation, patience, pauses, and then starting again with renewed energy. Negotiation isn't just about what is said around the table; it's also about how we prepare, reflect and grow from each experience, much like a mountain climber who gains strength and expertise with each summit.

The Coach

When you learn my method, I am confident you will recognize the importance of following it, discarding false myths about
negotiation, and becoming less prone to repeating common
mistakes. Messi, Hamilton, LeBron, Federer—these figures have
been among the greatest performers in their respective sports.
What do these extraordinary athletes have in common? They all
have coaches. The best performers know they need help to reach
their full potential.

A coach can guide and push you to achieve greater success
than you could alone. Simply put, a coach helps you become a
better version of yourself. Together with your coach, you will
work to improve your communication and persuasion skills,
which differ from how you think. The truth is, we don't think the
way we believe we do. If approached correctly, being assertive
and demanding does not make you unpleasant to others—this is
a common preconception.

Zoe Chance, whom I had the pleasure of meeting in Milan in
2019, explains this well in her remarkable book *Influence Is Your
Superpower: The Science of Winning Hearts, Sparking Change,
and Making Good Things Happen* (2022). She emphasizes that
our influence on others depends on confidence and an awareness
of our preferred negotiation strategies, used creatively. After all,
negotiation is simply a conversation between two or more parties
to reach an agreement.

We must believe in our ideas and then ask, negotiate, and per-
sist. Doing so encourages the negotiating partner to make the best
choices (for themselves and for us) by engaging with our enthusiasm. This ethical approach to persuasion and influence not only
improves our abilities but also inspires others to do better. The key
is understanding what drives your decisions and then developing
and training your charisma. Charisma is not an innate gift; with the
support of an excellent coach, it can be cultivated and refined.

A coach teaches you the principles and techniques needed to become a clear and persuasive negotiator, as well as an attentive listener. They also build your confidence through role-playing and practice. I have always relied on coaching in sports, my personal life, and my professional life. Whenever I recognized shortcomings, I sought help. In negotiation, coaching helped me better identify my skills and focus on behaviors needing improvement.

I found the diagnoses from my coaches particularly valuable, as they often pinpointed potential pitfalls in my negotiation style. These diagnoses were consistently followed by practical advice and tools to prevent snags and take proactive steps. After introducing me to new ideas and approaches to negotiation, my coaches supported me with evaluations that helped me learn from mistakes, achievements, and missed opportunities. What I learned could then be applied to future negotiations.

Even as my skills have improved, I continue to seek guidance from high-level coaches. In turn, I've been asked to coach others. I find facilitating learning processes deeply rewarding, whether improving communication skills, broadening perspectives, or fostering creativity. I enjoy giving feedback and encouragement, as it offers opportunities for growth and experimentation. I have also served as a mentor, a role I find fulfilling due to the mutual respect and trust it entails. Over the years, these experiences have allowed me to build long-lasting partnerships based on a shared vision. At times, I've taken on the role of tutor, accompanying clients in learning and applying my knowledge during short-term, focused interventions.

For those like me (and likely you), who share a passion for results and who value coaching, few things are more frustrating than negotiating with a partner who is unprepared—someone who arrives without a clear understanding of their interests or best alternatives. It's a mistake to think that facing an unprepared counterpart is a surefire win. The ideal situation is quite the opposite: both parties should arrive well prepared, aligned on the process, and informed about the negotiation's essential elements (e.g., interests, options, BATNA, legitimacy, and commitments).

While dealing with an unprepared partner may offer a temporary advantage, it does little to foster a good long-term relationship.

Instead, leverage your preparation in a constructive way. If you suspect the other party is not adequately prepared, you can prompt them to prepare better by asking thought-provoking questions (via email or phone) before meeting. This can encourage them to consider the need for preparation.

The optimal scenario is when both parties are knowledgeable and aligned in their approach (preferably using my method). This ensures alignment on the process and crucial negotiation elements, such as interests, options, and BATNA. In some cases, sharing details about legitimacy and commitments can also be advantageous. While this may seem radical, it is far more effective when both sides come to the negotiating table fully prepared. This creates a solid foundation for balanced and constructive negotiations, increasing the likelihood of achieving mutually beneficial outcomes.

Take Time for Yourself and Think Positively

Now that you have devoted time to preparation, it is important to focus on yourself—your body and your mind. First, good sleep is crucial. The quality and quantity of sleep significantly impact negotiation performance. Poor sleep increases the likelihood of distraction, forgetfulness, and poor decision-making.

Negotiating requires both physical and mental stamina. Fatigued people exhibit lower levels of alertness and responsiveness compared to well-rested individuals. If you are tired while your opponent is not, their negotiating power increases significantly. When you are fatigued, you are more likely to make mistakes and struggle with stress. Sometimes, fatigue results from long, intensive work sessions (even late at night) preparing for the negotiation. Other times, it's due to early flights or long meetings. Negotiators should prioritize rest before any negotiation, recognizing the cost of fatigue.

The outcome of a negotiation also depends on your ability to plan, cultivate, maintain, and protect a positive attitude. Most of your conversations happen within yourself, so pay close attention to your inner voice. I have lost count of the number of negotiations that started badly, but I have always maintained a positive attitude, focusing on the ultimate goal. Initial difficulties tend to fade as you move toward your objective, provided you never lose enthusiasm. I've realized that the words I use and how I express myself shape my thoughts and outlook. Therefore, I prepare by using dynamic language, choosing words loaded with meaning, and thinking carefully about their impact on myself and others. I prefer positive action words and thoughts, and I spend my pre-negotiation time with people who care about me, who celebrate my successes, and whose friendship motivates me to celebrate theirs. After all, we often become like the people we spend time with. While we cannot choose our family of origin, we can wisely select our partners and friends.

To develop a winning mindset, you must overcome the natural human tendency to magnify minor, inconsequential problems. I focus on positive thoughts, recalling memories of moments when I felt unstoppable—times when I succeeded at something that seemed impossible. This approach motivates and empowers me, allowing me to access that state of mind when I need it. It's simple. For example, in preparation for an interview, I use anchoring (not to be confused with "offer anchoring," discussed earlier, though there are similarities). A simple stimulus—such as a song, an image, a taste, or a feeling—triggers a coherent, positive response that replaces any unwanted thoughts or emotions with desirable ones. I focus on past successes, my talents, or empowering thoughts to build confidence.

In negotiation, I've found it invaluable to learn how to manage my state of mind and direct my thoughts productively and effectively. I've participated in courses led by extraordinary coaches and trainers, some of whom I later selected for corporate activities. My only regret is not dedicating more time to learning from them. There are practical tools to reshape how we think, interpret past events, and approach future challenges, enabling us to take control of our minds and, consequently, our lives.

There are numerous connections between these techniques and the negotiation process. For instance, using affirmations can reprogram subconscious beliefs, while identifying the thought or representational system someone is using (through analyzing their predictive words and phrases) allows for tailored and effective communication. There's more, too, such as the process of relationship-building through subtle behavioral imitation, which forms the foundation of any meaningful interaction between two or more people.

- You need to spend more time preparing for a negotiation.
- Successful negotiation consists of 80 percent preparation and only 20 percent actual negotiation.
- Always identify your interests and those of your negotiating partner, and remember that an agreement is always possible precisely because interests differ. Interests are the needs, desires, and, unfortunately, fears that drive negotiations.
- You must always have an alternative to the negotiated agreement, and evaluate the commitment resulting from the agreement.
- After determining "the range of the right value," you must develop a strategy to close the deal within that range.
- Remember that position is the means, interest is the end, and you must focus on interests rather than positions.
- Seek cooperation, be aware of risks, trust yourself, and ensure that time is on your side.
- Before you sit down at the negotiating table, ensure you understand the zone of possible agreement and consider your reserve price—the limit beyond which you cannot go.
- Preparing to persuade takes time and thought and requires acquiring the information that allows you to convincingly demonstrate to your negotiating partner that the criteria, standards, and references you share are appropriate to the context.
- Negotiation is a long-term process in which you build your reputation and manage your relationship with your negotiating partner.
- Mastering communication is essential for excelling in all types of negotiations. The message sent through communication is only 7 percent attributable to verbal language, making it critical to know how to listen actively.
- A bad relationship can ruin a potentially good negotiation.
- Always prepare a term sheet, a meeting agenda, and a unilateral draft of a final agreement.

Let us never negotiate out of fear.
But let us never fear to negotiate.

John F. Kennedy

CHAPTER 5

AT THE HEART OF THE NEGOTIATION

No Genie Can Help You
Better Than You Can Help Yourself

No Single Playbook for Every Negotiation

If I were Jinn, the genie of the lamp in *Aladdin and the Marvelous Lamp*, and one of your three wishes was to learn the best way to open a negotiation or the best tactics for successfully handling all negotiations, I would most likely disappoint you. It is more critical and valuable to have a systematic approach to negotiation than to solve a single negotiation successfully.

In my life, I have made mistakes, but I've learned a lot from them. Those mistakes have enabled me to become more effective when facing similar situations or problems. Over time, I have refined my method, making it increasingly systematic and practical. However, the work is never finished and will always continue. If you learn, practice, and gain familiarity with negotiation, then when you encounter a situation similar to one you've analyzed before, it will feel familiar, and you will be better prepared. At that point, even under high pressure, the context will seem manageable because you'll be comfortable and undoubtedly a more effective negotiator. You will become less reliant on intuition and more capable of achieving superior negotiating results through understanding and applying proven tactics. You'll know which tactic is most appropriate, when to use it, and you'll have a range of options for what moves to make during the negotiation.

Remember, even if you successfully conclude negotiations—regardless of their importance—each negotiation is different, and you will have to start from scratch each time.

Negotiating means minimizing your negotiating partner's concerns by presenting your proposal in the context of the value you're offering. Negotiating is instrumental in creating value through agreements that leave both parties better off than they would be without the deal.

Price, Value, and Total Cost of Ownership

Unfortunately, many negotiations focus too heavily on **price**, while one of the primary goals of a good negotiator is to shift the focus to **value**. Value is one of the most overused terms in marketing today.

Earlier, I used the term reserve price, which is interchangeable with reserve value. The determination of value relates to the benefits derived from a product or service. The value of something often goes beyond price alone and can be understood as the perceived benefits (the satisfaction of the interests of those seeking it) minus the perceived cost. As Lord Henry Wotton in the Oscar Wilde's novel *The Picture of Dorian Gray* (1890), famously said, "He knows the price of everything, but the value of nothing." This encapsulates the idea that price is just a number, but value is a more complex and subjective measure.

The calculation of value is deceptively simple. It is based on quantifiable outcomes, but can be divided into two categories: tangible goods (measured with specific units like money) and intangible goods (measured by emotional value scales, like personal satisfaction). Value can therefore be measured in dollars, happiness, or any other relevant unit.

When we refer to happiness as a unit of measurement, we are considering intangible benefits that contribute to emotional and psychological wellbeing, which are often as significant as financial gains in determining value. Happiness can encompass fulfillment, such as the sense of achievement from accomplishing a meaningful goal, or contentment derived from a situation that aligns with personal comfort and preferences. It also includes joy, the immediate pleasure experienced in the moment, as well as the reduction of stress or anxiety, which enhances peace of mind and overall quality of life. These facets of happiness closely align with the five core concerns—appreciation, affiliation, autonomy, status, and role—each addressing fundamental human needs that shape our emotional resonance and satisfaction with any outcome. While not as easily quantified as dollars or physical goods, happiness can be assessed through subjective measures like personal satisfaction, emotional resonance, or the enhancement of quality of life, making it a powerful, if subtle, metric in evaluating outcomes.

Increasingly, I encourage my stakeholders to consider the total cost of ownership of an asset—encompassing the entire lifecycle cost of acquiring, using, operating, and retiring an asset—rather than focusing purely on price. To achieve this, I spend significant time reasoning through numbers and proposals.

Taking the Initiative

If I had to define negotiation algebraically, I would say it is: preparation + discipline. Many fail not because they don't prepare but because they lack a clear, structured method. Preparation involves gathering the right data, identifying priorities, and anticipating the other side's needs and possible objections. Discipline ensures this groundwork is applied methodically during the negotiation, guiding decisions rather than succumbing to impulse or distraction. The situation becomes particularly critical when negotiation time arrives. Years ago, I would sit at the negotiating table feeling awkward as the discussion began, caught in the uncertainty of who should make the first move. Over time, I've realized this hesitation is widespread—most negotiators prefer to wait for the other side to act, hoping to gain insight into their strategy before revealing their own.

Today, I take the initiative. By making the first move, I set the tone and direction of the conversation, avoiding the pitfalls of passivity—such as being led into unproductive discussions, responding reactively to demands, or waiting for the other side to define the agenda. Instead, I actively shape the process, much like the lead in an Argentine tango, where the leader's deliberate movements command and direct the flow.

At the outset, I prioritize two critical elements: communication and relationship. Effective communication establishes clarity, reduces misunderstandings, and builds trust. A strong relationship fosters connection and goodwill, helping both parties collaborate rather than compete. These two elements are especially beneficial at the start of any negotiation, creating a foundation that supports progress and remains vital throughout the process. Together, they are the unseen rhythm that ensures the negotiation flows with purpose and direction.

Discipline in Negotiation

Being disciplined means understanding what to do and doing what is appropriate. Negotiation requires separating behavior from feelings and emotions. **Discipline** involves taking the time to set goals, create a schedule to achieve them, and follow that schedule. It also involves concealing emotions when necessary, like appearing indifferent to an exciting proposal because it's more strategic than showing enthusiasm. The ability to resist displaying the emotions you feel and instead present only those you want the other side to perceive is crucial.

This doesn't mean indifference to all negotiated proposals, but rather discipline in presenting signals that align with your strategy. Think of actors—they know how to deliver a line with deliberate verbal and nonverbal cues, consciously controlling their behavior. The difference is that actors follow a script, whereas experienced negotiators rely on skill, adaptability, and preparation.

Once you have prepared thoroughly, you should have an agenda listing the items to be addressed and the order in which they are to be addressed. A list of participants will allow you to consider who will be sitting at the table, their "power," and their negotiating style, helping to reduce the risk of being caught unprepared. This preparation enables you to maintain control of the topics discussed, even when facing multiple interlocutors. For example, in Germany and China, I have negotiated with more ten people while I was alone—a scenario that required not only thorough preparation but also the ability to anticipate diverse perspectives and maintain composure under the weight of multiple simultaneous challenges.

Always pay close attention to who will be present at the table. Your interlocutor may not necessarily have the power to decide;

they might be agents, lawyers, consultants, or advisors operating under a mandate with rigidly defined boundaries. This rigidity often means that intermediaries are reluctant to take responsibility for exceeding their instructions, resulting in the negotiation being interrupted by requests to expand their authority.

Negotiations involving intermediaries are particularly complex because any message is subject to distortion through deletions (important information is reduced or omitted), generalizations (often influenced by bias rather than logic), and distortions (imagination fills gaps in the absence of sensory stimuli, often influenced by excessive expectations or psychological defenses). Avoid starting with a complex topic, as this could quickly lead to a stalemate. Instead, begin with issues where you can be less flexible, reserving topics for which you are willing to make concessions for the latter part of the negotiation. I have often negotiated favorable deals only to find that a single thorny topic—such as contractual liabilities, penalties, or damages—jeopardized the entire process.

There is no definite rule, but I personally avoid leaving such critical topics for the end, even though contracts typically place them in the concluding sections.

Your Agenda

The agenda should include all items to be discussed. Clearly indicate each item with a verb that evokes an action or activity, and assign responsibility for each to a specific individual. Examples:

1. Discuss options to reduce complaints: Gianna signals an open exchange of ideas, where collaboration is key.
2. Propose initiatives to build customer loyalty: Mark indicates the expectation of presenting well-thought-out plans.
3. Present ideas to increase up-selling: Matthew underscores the need for a detailed and structured contribution.

By explicitly assigning responsibilities to specific individuals, you establish accountability and set clear expectations for participation and preparation. This approach helps ensure that every topic is approached with purpose and that all parties are engaged.

If you want your negotiating partner to complete certain tasks before the meeting, such as gathering data or preparing a presentation, share the agenda a few days in advance. This not only encourages their preparation but also signals your own readiness and professionalism.

In the event that you receive their proposed agenda before sending yours, don't worry. You're undoubtedly prepared. In such cases, review their agenda critically, identifying areas that align with your objectives and those that require adjustment. If necessary, you can revise the sequence of topics or suggest additional items either before the meeting begins or through a written response to their proposal. By doing so, you subtly assert control over the meeting's direction and ensure your priorities are represented without appearing confrontational. Ultimately, a well-prepared agenda, combined with strategic foresight, positions you to manage the negotiation proactively, even before it officially starts.

Active Listening

Active listening requires empathy, focused attention, and significant effort. **Hearing** is involuntary, but **listening** is a fundamental skill that can be practiced and improved. Focusing entirely on the person in front of you and demonstrating genuine interest in what they are saying is an intentional behavior. If you enter a negotiation insufficiently prepared, you may find yourself merely pretending to listen or listening superficially to your counterpart's words, while your mind is preoccupied with planning what to say next.

Selective listening, on the other hand, involves focusing only on what you want to hear. Emotional filters or blinders may cause you to concentrate solely on the variables for which you prepared, while overlooking new information. Selective listening is one of the most critical tools in any negotiation. An effective negotiator listens actively, demonstrates curiosity and empathy, and seeks commonalities rather than differences.

A trained and careful negotiator can accurately process what the other side is saying, uncovering the intentions behind the words. Active listening requires concentration and significant effort to achieve a deep understanding of what is being communicated. It involves interpreting body language, tone, timbre, voice rhythm, vocabulary, and sentence structure. You don't need to be an expert to pick up on obvious clues, but you must be attentive and sensitive to emotional nuances.

Active listening allows you to discover your negotiating partner's needs and goals—information essential to creating win–win outcomes. This is achieved by asking questions, starting broadly and then narrowing in on specifics. While preparation is a critical component of successful negotiation, much of its value lies in the information gathered. Those who possess relevant information have greater control over the negotiation. You can always have more information, so it's wise to define how much of your negotiating partner's data you want to obtain before the negotiation begins.

I advise you to avoid being impetuous, and to let your negotiating partner tell their story first, as this enables you to tailor your proposal to their needs and desires. I have worked hard on myself to avoid interrupting when my negotiating partner is speaking. I now recognize how rude it was when I used to interrupt—a serious mistake, not least because it disrupted a flow of information that could have been valuable later in the negotiation. Let your partner finish, even if they are saying something inaccurate or that you disagree with.

In addition to listening, you must store the data you receive.

"Pietro, two months ago, during the November call, you said that…"

François, whom I've known for at least twenty years, writes everything down, and I strive to emulate him. While I am not yet at his level, I strongly recommend his approach. Every time someone tells you something, jot it down. You don't need to capture every detail—just brief notes that will be useful during the negotiation and especially during the post-negotiation analysis. You'll be surprised at how much valuable and even conflicting information emerges later.

These notes enable you to correct your negotiating partner or refresh their memory with facts and figures shared in a previous session, which enhances your credibility and strengthens your position. Writing requires little time, provides structure to the negotiation, and allows for reflection and deeper processing of what is being said. Though it takes discipline, the benefits far outweigh the effort. This information will also prove invaluable in the final steps of the negotiation: debriefing and filing.

Active listening means paying absolute attention, so create an environment conducive to clear thinking, free of interruptions and distractions. Always maintain eye contact with your negotiating partner to convey attention and engagement. Strike a balance between seeking eye contact and observing their nonverbal cues. This will make you appear trustworthy, honest, and credible.

There Is an Offer for You—Listen to It

When you receive a proposal, take your time to respond. Respond only when you fully understand it. Consider how it aligns with your interests (and those of your negotiating partner), its impact on the relationship, and the commitments it entails. Take as much time as you need to process the consequences.

Pay particular attention to offers where the amounts are so small that the true significance of the sums involved is easily overlooked. For example, the price of gold and saffron is typically quoted per gram, but the perception changes dramatically when viewed per kilogram. Always do your calculations carefully and don't hesitate to ask for clarification.

Borrowing a famous example from Zig Ziglar, how you say something can drastically alter what you intend to communicate.

I did not say that Barbara stole his money.
I *did not* say that Barbara stole his money.
I did not *say* that Barbara stole his money.
I did not say that *Barbara* stole his money.
I did not say that Barbara *stole* his money.
I did not say that Barbara stole *his* money.
I did not say that Barbara stole his *money.*

Are these seven sentences different? If you read the words without catching the change in the inflection of your voice (indicated here by italics), these sentences will sound identical to you, even though they each imply a distinct meaning.

Active listening goes beyond merely hearing words and interpreting intonation. According to Richard Bandler and John Grinder, key figures in psychology, people move their eyes in systematic and specific directions depending on how they process information. Carefully observing a person's eye movements can help you understand how they are processing information. This allows you, for example, to trace their specific thought process, assess its congruence, determine whether the information they are sharing is remembered or constructed, and even elicit their strategy. However, mastering this skill is quite complex and requires significant practice.

In any case, eye contact alone is insufficient. You must also leverage other verbal feedback and observe body language. Summarize and rephrase what you hear and understand, and use pauses and silence strategically before responding. When you do respond, ask relevant follow-up questions to deepen the exchange.

Listening also involves resisting the urge to fill silences. Nodding your head and smiling in approval when something meaningful is said can confirm your attentiveness and demonstrate that you are engaged.

Listening generates deep emotional connections. The more you listen, the more your negotiating partner will feel valued by and connected to you. As this emotional connection deepens, their trust in you will grow, and emotional barriers will fall away. As this process unfolds, your negotiating partner will talk more openly and reveal more information.

Emotional labeling—the act of identifying and acknowledging an emotion—can further enhance this process. When you recognize and name your negotiating partner's emotional state, you help them feel that their reaction is valid, safe, and appropriate. This demonstrates that you are attuned to the emotional aspects of their message, which can significantly enhance rapport.

Emotional labeling is one of the most powerful skills available to negotiators. It helps identify the issues and feelings driving the other person's behavior, fostering trust and a deeper understanding of their motivations.

Emotions and Relationships

The Words I Don't Tell You

Negotiation is not a single event; it is a process that begins long before the meeting (whether physical or remote). At every stage, emotions play a crucial role. Emotions are more important than words because they are ever present—even in silence. They connect all negotiators, including those who consider themselves rational, calculating, and calm.

To recognize and express your emotional state and develop empathy, you must engage in emotional communication with your counterpart. A useful exercise is to write down the emotions you feel (or have felt) during a negotiation. Divide the page into two columns, one for positive emotions and one for negative. You'll likely find that more than one sheet of paper will be needed.

My daughter Giulia has been riding horses since the age of six and specializes in dressage, a discipline in which the rider and horse perform predetermined movements in a rectangular arena. Dressage is a refined and disciplined art. At the stable and during competitions, I've often heard that a horse can sense the rider's hesitation, insecurity, and fear—and tests the rider accordingly. As soon as the horse senses a lack of confidence, it may take advantage of the situation.

Hellen, Giulia's latest horse, is just five years old and weighs about seven hundred kilograms[42]—nearly twelve times my daughter's weight. The young mare's mass and size give her a clear advantage, and if she senses Giulia is not in control, she could unseat her. The same principle applies in negotiation: your emotions influence your negotiating partner's emotions. If they perceive insecurity, lack of confidence, or fear, they will take advantage of it.

---

42   Seven hundred kilograms is approximately 1,543 pounds.

To Hellen's continuous challenges, Giulia responds with non-complementary behavior designed to counter and disrupt the pattern. Similarly, in negotiation, if you lack confidence in yourself, your negotiating partner will have none in you.

You must develop and practice techniques to build emotions that counter your own weaknesses. This is challenging, because it involves mastering both verbal and nonverbal language, requiring you to act contrary to instinct. Positive emotions arise when a negotiator respects their counterpart and the negotiation is progressing well. Negative emotions arise when there is no respect, or the negotiation is not going as planned.

Emotions are contagious, and negotiations are no exception. Negative emotions can significantly impact your ability to analyze situations, resolve conflicts, and avoid impasses. However, positive emotions are not always beneficial. High expectations that lead to unmet results can trigger a sense of defeat. This reinforces the idea that remaining neutral about a submitted proposal can sometimes be more effective than showing enthusiasm or excitement. The goal is not to suppress emotions entirely but to send only the signals you want the other party to perceive.

Antonio, a friend of mine and a professional actor, once explained how he manages his emotions while delivering lines, gestures, and expressions. Actors meticulously organize their characters' behavior to maintain composure and control. Negotiators must adopt a similar approach, with the critical difference being that actors follow a script, whereas negotiators do not. The more aware you are of your emotions, the better you'll be at understanding the emotions and needs of others.

The same logic that applies to interests, BATNA, and communication also applies to emotions: focusing on your counterpart rather than yourself enables you to gather more information. Speech (the literal message) conveys only part of the meaning, while other channels—such as nonverbal cues, tone of voice, facial expressions, and posture—communicate emotional messages. During preparation, you worked to identify the five core concerns that give rise to most emotions, both yours and your negotiating partner's. These emotions are likely to surface during the negotiation and can be leveraged strategically.

Since only 7 percent of communication is attributed to verbal language and 80 percent of negotiation involves preparation, it follows that 98.6 percent of available time should be spent studying, preparing, and applying yourself to elicit positive emotions and mitigate negative ones.

Whatever emotions your counterpart expresses, let them flow uninterrupted. For them to regain cooperation, they must fully articulate their feelings. The more intense their emotions, the less attentive they will be, which creates opportunities to uncover valuable information—for example, that their alternative to the agreement is weaker than it seemed, or that they are constrained by a deadline.

Use the information you've gathered about your negotiating partner at every stage of the negotiation. Beyond leveraging their emotions, you can also use your own strategically. Each emotion has a different effect. For instance, displaying emotional detachment may encourage further concessions, while showing controlled anger could make your proposals more convincing and help you assert control over the negotiation. The possibilities for leveraging emotions in negotiation are vast.

It's essential to understand and manage your emotions while choosing how to communicate effectively, whether through words or nonverbal cues. Recognize and regulate your emotions rather than ignoring them—disregarding emotions is risky. They are ever present and often shape your experiences. While you might attempt to suppress them, emotions will still influence you. Equally important is understanding how your negotiating partner feels. When addressing their emotions, avoid using first-person statements, which may come across as subjective or confrontational. Instead, opt for third-person phrasing to convey neutrality and maintain an objective tone.[43]

---

43   This technique is particularly useful in Latin languages, where formality and neutrality in communication are often conveyed differently than in English. For example, in Italian, the concept of "dare del lei" (using the formal "you") has no direct equivalent in English, highlighting the differences in how formality and neutrality are expressed in different languages.

In negotiation, emotional intelligence enables the strategic use of emotions through compelling messages, facilitating the recognition, discrimination, and management of emotions—both your own and those of others. Statements like, "You think that…" are inappropriate because they assume something you cannot be certain of and can impact the ego of your negotiating partner. It is best to avoid such statements. There is a significant difference between saying, "It looks like the problem is…" and "I think you are…" Both involve speculation, but in the latter, the speaker assumes authorship of the thought, which can feel more personal. In the former, the impersonal phrasing avoids direct reference to the individual. Avoid using the first-person singular when possible, as it may give the impression that you are more focused on yourself than on your negotiating partner. The whole purpose of emotional labeling is to demonstrate interest in the negotiating partner.

When listening, avoid reacting impulsively to what is said with phrases like, "Wow, I never imagined this would be so critical for you," or, "Oh my God, impossible!" Instead, gather the information, use it effectively, and demonstrate interest by responding with phrases such as, "I understand how important timely delivery is to you. We will work to find a solution that meets your interests and aligns with our needs. Are there other factors that you would consider equally important?" Questions like these convey sincere interest to the negotiating partner. In some cases, this interest is aimed at maximizing the outcome of the negotiation; in others, it focuses on maintaining or enhancing **the relationship** with the other party, which may hold equal or greater importance over time.

The Rapport

Relationships can accomplish what knowledge sometimes cannot. Citing precedents can help justify your position, claims, or concessions. Often, parties fall into conflict and begin blaming each other for past adverse events. Just as often, they treat the negotiation as a singular event with no further consequences, forgetting about the continuity of the relationship. Fortunately, this is not always the case, and significant relationships are sometimes established between the parties, who cooperate to maintain them for various reasons.

Relationships often lead not only to the initial agreement but also to follow-up deals, secondary agreements, and renewed partnerships. Relationships are built over time through trust, understanding, respect, and, in some cases, even friendship. A strong relationship can make each new negotiation smoother and more efficient. The desire to feel good about yourself (and to care about how others perceive you) often makes you more responsive to your negotiating partner's interests.

The value placed on the relationship influences your goals and tactics during negotiation. If it is unlikely that you will negotiate with the same person in the future, preserving the relationship may not be a priority, and your goal should focus on maximizing your value. In contrast, when an ongoing relationship is likely or desired, it is crucial to evaluate future benefits and determine the best strategy to create value for both parties. If maintaining a good relationship is your goal, you may be more willing to make concessions on substantive issues to preserve or improve it.

Ask yourself two key questions: "How important is this relationship to me?" and "How important is this relationship to the other person?" The answers will guide you in balancing the concessions needed. Keep the topics related to substantive issues (e.g., prices, quantities, and service levels) separate from those related to the relationship (e.g., shared long-term goals, joint product improvement programs, and future business opportunities). Consider making two distinct lists.

I've often heard phrases like, "If you were a good provider and cared about our relationship, you would…" followed by demands for concessions, discounts, or more favorable conditions. Being prepared to separate substantive issues from relational considerations can help you respond effectively to such tactics without compromising the overall relationship.

In a negotiation, maintaining a strong relationship doesn't require sacrificing value, just as the tracks of San Francisco's cable cars remain parallel—ensuring a smooth journey without ever converging. Both connection and value should rise or fall together, in harmony, reflecting the idea that strengthening one aspect doesn't mean weakening the other. As a skilled tram driver controls the journey along the tracks, a skilled negotiator keeps both the relationship and the deal's substance balanced. The goal is to focus on the merits of the deal, not to make concessions merely to build rapport or keep the relationship intact. The two elements—connection and value—should evolve together, creating a strong foundation for successful negotiation.

When you make concessions, your negotiating partner may feel they have gained control of the negotiation, become satisfied, and be more willing to close the deal. However, the cheapest supplier is not necessarily the one with whom we have the best relationship, and vice versa. You should not feel obligated to barter the relationship to secure a good deal. Instead, focus on exchanging information and generating creative ideas to increase the chances of reaching a mutually beneficial agreement while fostering greater trust that satisfies the primary interests of all parties. Confidence stems from consistency between what you say and what you do.

Recognize and respect your negotiating partner's interests, using the five core concerns of affiliation, appreciation, autonomy, status, and role. As you become more adept at negotiation, you will understand the value of the relationship and identify when a negotiating partner is adopting an aggressive approach. In such cases, you will automatically assign less weight to maintaining the relationship in the long term. Always strive to be judged as honest, upright, trustworthy, and patient—these traits will grant you significant advantages in any negotiation.

Don't just leverage trust when it is already present; work actively to build it when it is absent. The best way to build trust is to be truly worthy of it. In business, this means staying in touch with suppliers you no longer work with, consistently exceeding customer expectations, or even lowering your prices proactively before a customer asks—provided the conditions align or there is a clear benefit to both sides. By doing so, you demonstrate a commitment to fairness and long-term value, showing that your actions are not just about immediate transactions but about fostering lasting relationships. This approach not only strengthens trust but also positions you as a partner who is genuinely invested in mutual success. However, despite all goodwill, trust can sometimes be broken. If you care about restoring it, arrange a meeting in a setting separate from the negotiation to focus on the relationship and its challenges. Address the issues openly, identify points of contention, and explore solutions. If you have made a mistake, be humble—but never submissive—and take responsibility for your actions. Doing so can defuse potential conflict. Admitting a mistake is challenging for many, yet it is simple, effective, and often generates appreciation, esteem, and respect.

Raul Gardini[44] taught me the value of apologizing: a sincere apology is not a weakness but a powerful tool to build trust and foster constructive dialogue. Always take responsibility yourself when you have made a mistake, and especially when the error originated from your organization or a member of your family. This approach reflects confidence and self-esteem. Don't neglect the emotional aspect of the situation; allow the other party to vent or express their discontent with your conduct or beliefs. Avoid defensiveness, and if necessary, ask for clarification and seek a valid remedy.

"Paul, I must admit, this is an area where I have much to learn—I'm relying on your expertise to guide me."

Don't think that admitting your limitations will prompt your negotiating partner to take advantage of you. On the contrary, it often encourages honesty, as it allows them to showcase their expertise. I've confessed my ignorance in multiple situations and, in doing so, was often treated better and more fairly than

---

44   Raul Gardini (1944–1993) was an influential Italian businessman, best known for leading the Montedison Group, one of Italy's largest industrial conglomerates. He expanded the company in the chemical and energy sectors during the 1980s, emphasizing innovation and diversification. A strategic thinker, Gardini worked to modernize Italy's industrial landscape. He was also a passionate sailor, gaining fame as the force behind the Italian yacht *Il Moro di Venezia*, which won the 1992 Louis Vuitton Cup and competed in the America's Cup. In 1993, he was found dead under mysterious circumstances, officially adjudicated to be suicide but still debated.

in many other cases. Admitting ignorance can trigger a rich flow of information as your negotiating partner may feel compelled to explain and teach. It also leverages appreciation, one of the core emotional drivers in negotiation.

You can also ask your negotiating partner for help, though this depends on who you are dealing with and how you make the request. This approach can work because it appeals to their empathy and goodwill. Your interlocutor may respond with a friendly but straightforward "no" or a conditional offer, framing their response as part of the negotiation.

"Suppose I can sign the contract today for 1,230 pieces. Would you be willing to lower the price to €1,050?"

Before accepting such an offer, reevaluate your interests. Perhaps the company urgently needs financial resources, and you could satisfy your CFO with a proposal that combines price reductions with favorable payment terms.

To navigate negotiations effectively, balance relationship-building with achieving substantive value. A skilled negotiator recognizes that fostering trust, admitting limitations, and managing emotions are not just techniques but the foundation of meaningful dialogue and lasting partnerships.

Dad, Will You Tell Us a Story?

If you ask my daughters how good I was at telling them stories when they were little, they will probably lie just because they love me. I would choose a quiet place and create a cozy atmosphere that encouraged them to listen, but I was not particularly good at selecting the right fairy tales. Above all, I failed to involve Giulia and Alessia directly, which is one of the key elements of compelling storytelling.

Stories are one of the most powerful tools for good negotiators. You don't need to be a poet, writer, or someone particularly adept with words. To be a good storyteller, you just need to understand the primary motivations of human beings. You must internalize our innate need to use narrative to make sense of ourselves and the world around us, to comprehend where we come from, and to set a vision for the future. Storytelling is embedded in everyday life, activating parts of the brain that help us interpret the present and imagine the future. Imagination is the key to motivation.

When you negotiate, your job is to help your team and your negotiating partner envision the future you see through your narrative. This involves distilling past events, current successes, and future aspirations into coherent stories. A good story has a beginning, middle, and end, with twists and turns along the way—at least, this is the structure I use when incorporating storytelling into negotiation. This approach is key to motivating those involved, spurring them toward the goals to be achieved, and helping them picture what lies beyond the finish line when the negotiation is successfully concluded.

Some people have a natural ability to imagine possibilities, while others need guidance to see beyond their current perspective. With the latter, I always strive to engage them, excite them, and push them into action. This is the most effective and accessible way to unlock their motivating imagination. Twenty years ago, I relied less on metaphors, analogies, and examples, and I told fewer stories. Now, I use them extensively. Sometimes I wonder if I might be overdoing it—but creativity and imagination have certainly never been lacking. Stories convey lessons and examples that resonate universally, and for millennia, they have been the way humanity has passed on knowledge.

In negotiation, the use of objective, fair standards or criteria is a powerful tool for addressing proposals rooted in positions, emotions or personal desires. Legitimacy plays a crucial role in this process; it is not just about fairness in substance but also about ensuring the other party feels respected and treated equitably. When one party perceives mistreatment—regardless of the objective merits of an offer—they are more likely to reject it, if it could serve their interests and lead to a better deal for them. Establishing legitimacy through fair criteria fosters trust and reduces emotional resistance, paving the way for constructive dialogue.

However, while facts, data, and figures are essential in advocating for ideas, they often lack the emotional resonance needed to persuade effectively. Studies show that combining data with storytelling can significantly enhance the persuasiveness of your arguments. Stories connect emotionally, helping to frame objective criteria in ways that resonate deeply with the other party.

Stanford Professor Jennifer Aaker highlights the transformative power of storytelling in negotiation and beyond. She emphasizes that stories enable us to guide listeners through a journey, aligning their perspective with ours and building confidence in both our vision and ourselves. By weaving fair standards into compelling narratives, negotiators can not only appeal to logic but also foster a shared sense of legitimacy and connection. This dual approach—balancing data with the emotional power of story—creates a foundation for agreements that feel both rational and fair, moving people to action and strengthening relationships. Stories provide space and time for you to stabilize emotionally and then return to your overall negotiating approach. They can also shift the conversation to other topics, effectively "disarming" the other negotiator. They facilitate the transition from a positional to an interest-based approach. Whether you are preparing for a negotiation or in the midst of a contentious process, think carefully about which stories might help you unblock the situation and how they could be used. Employ them thoughtfully and strategically to steer the negotiation toward your desired goals.

Power Games

Another element to consider is power. Power should be understood as the ability not to dominate others but to influence people and situations. The facets of power are many—it can stem from knowledge, skills, role, character, charisma, or even the perception of having nothing to lose.

"We have nothing to lose in this negotiation anyway" may seem like an innocuous statement, but it is full of significance: when you face a negotiating partner with no apparent vested interest, they hold the most power. In the workplace, granting rewards and recognition generates power for those who possess it, just as those with coercive power wield influence.

Power is the driving force behind influence and decision-making in negotiations. It doesn't come from a title or authority alone, but is built on three fundamental pillars that shape the dynamics of any deal.

The first is control of resources. Information, viable alternatives, and financial leverage can tip the balance in any negotiation. Those who control key data and have strong fallback options negotiate from a position of strength.

The second is relationships. Power isn't just about what you have; it's also about who you know and how well you can use your network. Strong alliances and credibility create opportunities and open doors that would otherwise remain closed.

Finally, power is about perception. It's not just about having leverage; it's about making sure the other party recognizes it. Confidence, strategic communication, and positioning can turn even limited resources into significant negotiating power.

Effective negotiators understand that power is fluid. Managing it wisely means balancing these elements, adapting to the situation, and using influence to steer discussions toward the best possible outcome. Some attribute power to gender and the perceived differences between counterparts, a topic that could be discussed at length. In a labor negotiation, other variables influence power, such as access to financial, technological, and human resources, the urgency to close the deal, and a solid BATNA. In most negotiations, one side rarely holds all the power; rather, one side may have more power, creating a balance that leans in its favor.

Open-ended questions can help uncover the values at stake, assess how much of this power is real or merely perceived, and determine the extent to which it is influenced by the weight of the relationship. Finally, perhaps the most essential insight is this: power exists only when it is recognized. Many people possess more power than they realize, but a lack of self-confidence prevents them from recognizing it. With thorough preparation, self-confidence can be exponentially increased. Even when your interlocutor's BATNA is strong, and yours is weak, you still have many opportunities to balance the situation by leveraging your negotiating partner's tendencies and strategically using your tools.

Run Forrest, Run!

Asking Is Half the Battle of Having

Once you have established a channel of communication, built (or rebuilt) the relationship, and measured your power, it's time to enter the negotiation and capitalize on all your groundwork, starting with the negotiating partner's interests. This is the moment to clarify and confirm the interests you identified during the preparatory stage, remove irrelevant ones, add new ones, and adjust their importance. It's also the time to communicate your own interests. There's nothing wrong with being direct and asking: "What are your main goals, objectives, and concerns about the issues we are discussing?" Often, the response will be a position (what your interlocutor subjectively asks for) rather than a rationale (the objective reasoning behind the position).

For example, "Our minimum order is 5,000 pieces" is a position, while "Our minimum order must cover the cost of tooling and setup for the CNC machine" is a rationale.

A response with reasoning provides additional information that can be invaluable in formulating a proposal. Ask well-crafted questions from the start and actively listen to your negotiating partner. Questions inherently carry an emotional impact based on how they're phrased, the context in which they're asked, and the person to whom they're addressed. Their purpose is to unlock a treasure trove of information.

Questions should focus your negotiating partner's attention on issues that matter to you. Closed questions, which can be answered with a simple "yes" or "no," are more about confirming an agreement or securing a concession: "Would you be able to deliver eight million components to us by the end of March?" or "If we supply you with raw materials, would you be willing to contribute your labor?" In contrast, calibrated open-ended questions—starting with **who, what, what else, where, when, why,** or **how**—encourage your interlocutor to delve into determinants of positive aspects and share critical information. This approach shifts the focus from positions to interests.

For example, you might ask: "Is there anything else besides payment terms that is important to you?" or "Is there anything else besides the delivery time guarantee that is of concern to you?" These powerful questions encourage the negotiating partner to reveal more. Repeating what your negotiating partner says, word for word but in interrogative form, can also yield new insights. For instance:

You: "Mr. Wiley, why would you need a buffer stock at our warehouses equivalent to your monthly consumption?"

Mr. Wiley: "Because the stock would be highly valuable to the sales office."

You: "Would that be highly valuable to your sales office?"

Mr. Wiley: "Yes, Pietro. Exactly. The market is extremely volatile and difficult to predict. Although customers provide us with monthly forecasts on which we base our orders, they often need additional volumes. Without stock, we can't meet those needs, resulting in high-margin revenue losses. On the other hand, if we tried to anticipate all possible volumes, we would face financial difficulties."

Repeating and questioning what Mr. Wiley said encouraged him to share crucial additional details. When rejecting a proposal, many negotiators stop at explaining their reasons without exploring the deeper reasons behind their partner's resistance. Avoid this mistake. Always dig deeper to uncover the real motivations. One effective tactic is to use the negotiating partner's first or last name sparingly but purposefully during the conversation.

I also find it particularly effective to ask three calibrated open-ended questions in succession, such as:

"What is the biggest obstacle you face? What do you confront every day? What is the most frequent cause of downtime?"

These questions compel the negotiating partner to think deeply, making their problems multidimensional and yielding more nuanced answers. Equally valuable are guiding, seemingly harmless questions that give the negotiating partner an illusion of choice while guiding their decision. For example:

"Would you prefer a 60-day net payment or a 2 percent discount for prompt payment?"

If the negotiating partner responds, they implicitly accept the assumptions embedded in the question. A common mistake is to avoid asking, assuming the negotiating partner won't answer. While there's no guarantee of a response, correctly phrased questions often lead to the response you're looking for. Good questions inherently contain some answers, but asking is not enough—you must also listen. And as humans, we all love to feel heard.

Some people are accustomed to being asked questions but, by the time they respond, may not feel heard. Therefore, always listen carefully to what is said—and what is left unsaid—then summarize their views. If you have difficulty understanding the other side's interests, suggest possible options and invite their critique. It's often easier for someone to explain why a hypothetical solution won't work than to directly articulate their interests.

In addition to gathering new information, asking questions allows you to clarify and verify existing data and gauge your negotiating partner's level of commitment to specific points in an agreement. The power of questions is unique, as they can even serve to transfer information as in:

"Did you see the forecast for the dollar at 1.10 in the latest UBS report?" Alternatively, questions can spark interest and encourage reflection, such as, "When you think of a great hotel, what do you expect?" Questions like these can also help establish rapport by creating a sense of engagement and understanding between the speaker and the listener.

When sharing information, be strategic and remember that it's a concession with value—one that requires reciprocity. Keep asking questions, but always maintain politeness and ask permission if needed. The more interests you uncover, the easier it will be to develop creative options later. Begin with broad questions, then narrow them down, taking notes as you go. A lot is said during a negotiation, and documenting it ensures you retain valuable insights.

Option A, A1, A2...An

I've watched *Forrest Gump* many times, and I love shrimp! One of my favorite scenes is when Benjamin Buford "Bubba" Blue, while cleaning the floor with Forrest, says, "Anyway, as I was saying, shrimp is the fruit of the sea. You can grill it, boil it, bake it, sauté it," continuing for over a minute about all the ways to cook shrimp.

The same logic applies to negotiation options: there are always more than you initially think. Options represent the creative solutions that can satisfy the interests of both parties, and their importance cannot be overstated. These options are often identified during the preparatory phase of the negotiation, where brainstorming, research, and role-playing help to uncover possibilities. Once discussions begin, additional opportunities may emerge organically, often as a result of listening closely, asking open-ended questions, and exploring mutual interests. By expanding your perspective and avoiding the rigidity of a zero-sum mindset, you can steer the negotiation away from a purely competitive framework toward a collaborative one.

The process of generating and refining options is iterative: think about them, rethink them, and challenge your assumptions to uncover innovative ideas. For example, if price becomes a sticking point, consider other levers such as extended payment terms, bundled services, or shared risk mechanisms. The more varied and well-prepared your options, the better positioned you are to address impasses, demonstrate flexibility, and create value for both sides. Like Bubba's endless shrimp recipes, your ability to identify and present diverse options can turn a challenging negotiation into a fruitful collaboration.

Cheese, Click

Another reason I think of Tom Hanks's brilliant movie is that it makes me smile—and smiling is a powerful tool in negotiation. When you speak and smile, you not only encourage others to respond positively, but your brain, in a positive state, works 30 percent more effectively. This means you can think more clearly, process information faster, and find creative solutions more easily.

Moreover, a smile has a magnetic effect on others. The more your negotiating partner likes you, the more likely they are to cooperate; in fact, you're six times more likely to conclude a deal when there's amicability between the negotiating partners.

Dale Carnegie (2010) devoted many pages to this topic in his timeless book *How to Win Friends and Influence People*, emphasizing the power of a smile to open doors and build bridges. A smile can convey multiple messages, even subtle ones, depending on the situation. A smile of satisfaction, for example, can show genuine appreciation for what the other person has said or done, signaling acknowledgment and mutual respect. On the other hand, a smile of affiliation demonstrates emotional closeness, making the other person feel valued and understood.

Smiling is not just about flashing your teeth; it's about genuine warmth and connection. A forced or insincere smile can do more harm than good, so it's essential to let it flow naturally. If you already know how to smile authentically, use it to your advantage; if not, take the time to learn—your negotiation outcomes may depend on it.

Look at Me

Eye contact is a powerful tool, particularly during initial meetings with your negotiating partner. A direct gaze conveys emotional strength and confidence, signaling that you are attentive and perceptive to their intentions. It subtly communicates that any attempts at manipulation are unlikely to succeed. Eye contact can also be employed strategically to elevate the tone of a negotiation. For instance, when asserting authority or emphasizing a firm stance on a critical issue—such as a deadline or a nonnegotiable term—maintaining eye contact underscores your seriousness and determination.

A steady gaze demonstrates emotional control and leadership, affirming your command of the situation. It can reinforce your position and convey that you are unwavering on specific points. However, balance is crucial. While a confident gaze projects strength, overdoing it can come across as aggressive or intimidating. The key is to use eye contact deliberately and judiciously, reserving it for moments when you need to underline your position or raise the stakes of the discussion effectively.

The Book of 1000 Whys

Your negotiating partner understands the driving force behind your interests, and sharing them can encourage reciprocity. However, be selective about what you disclose at this stage. A well-prepared counterpart may already be aware of some of your interests or might use them strategically. For example, I would never say, "I want to end this contract with you because we lost our main customer." Often, especially at the beginning of a negotiation, it is not appropriate to reveal all your cards. At the same time, if you want to receive something, you must give something in return, showing enough to encourage your negotiating partner to reciprocate. If necessary, explain your reasoning without fully exposing your interests. Sharing interests and illustrating them on a whiteboard or computer for later reference can be helpful. From this initial list of interests—which may evolve as the discussion progresses—you can move on to a joint analysis of options that meet all or most of those interests. I prefer to take control during this stage, running the shared problem-solving and brainstorming session myself. This allows me to introduce multiple options based on the identified interests and encourage my negotiating partner to contribute equally, unlocking creativity from both sides. When both parties collaborate and take ownership of the process, it becomes much easier to reach an agreement.

At this stage, options are merely possibilities. They do not constitute offers or commitments, nor are they typically tied to specific numbers or timeframes. They should be evaluated only against your BATNA or equity criteria. If the process flows smoothly, you may discover new interests that were not initially considered. If any options fail to address the interests of both parties, eliminate them. Together with your negotiating partner, validate the remaining options, narrowing the list to those that meet shared interests.

Absolute Value

During the preparation phase, you worked diligently to identify objective, reasonable, and fair standards, references, and data. As the negotiation evolves, you gain updated insights into your negotiating partner's interests, and together you refine a more focused range of options.

External, unbiased sources, data, references, and even one or more experts can be effective tools for persuasion. However, avoid using references that appear to favor only your position. Instead, choose those that are fair and reasonable from an external, neutral perspective. Presenting such references reinforces your intention to ensure the final decision is equitable and defensible.

If your negotiating partner prefers an option you believe is unfair, use your standards to challenge it. Encourage them to explain why their option is appropriate and defensible while you present how your criteria suggest a different approach. Often, parties arrive at the negotiating table with conflicting data. Together, you must work to determine which standards are most suitable for the context.

In some cases, you may find yourself at an impasse where none of the available standards are sufficient. If goodwill, imagination, and creativity fail to yield a satisfactory outcome, the best course of action is to step back and revisit the process. Define new interests and options that align better with shared and appropriate standards.

The Role of Questions

As noted above, by asking questions beginning with terms like **who**, **what**, **what else**, **where**, **when**, **why**, and **how**, you can gain a deeper understanding of the situation. However, just because an alternative is possible does not mean your negotiating partner is willing to pursue it. Your questions should serve the dual purpose of weakening less desirable alternatives while opening your partner's eyes to other possibilities, guiding them through the process.

Never feel compelled to close a deal simply for the sake of agreement. Failing to reach an agreement is not a failure in itself.

Always prioritize a better option over merely settling. If you cannot identify a solution superior to your BATNA, you should resort to that alternative—but not hastily. The existence of a valid alternative does not mean you should rush to it.

If you can afford to wait, commit to strengthening your alternative and let time erode your negotiating partner's alternative. If, however, you identify several options that surpass your alternative but still fail to reach an agreement, it suggests other important considerations are still not being met —such as commitment or the impact on the relationship. Be patient, take the necessary time before closing the deal, and ensure you have the appropriate authority or proxy for the agreement you are finalizing. Sometimes, as the negotiation evolves, the proxy granted to you may no longer align with the emerging agreement.

Invoking the Policy? How Boring!

In my role as a leader in corporate organizations, I have often relied on documents detailing policies for delegating authority to management. These policies, appropriately structured by level, enable managers to fulfill their tasks effectively. This best practice ensures managers can negotiate with proper representation and authority. However, if such a document is unavailable, it's crucial to carefully consider your actions and avoid being swept away by the euphoria of closing a good deal. Always question whether additional approvals are required.

In 1998, I learned this lesson firsthand while negotiating with Guillaume Carpentier, the commodities purchasing manager of a longtime client. From the start of the negotiation to the agreement stage, I dealt exclusively with him. We were negotiating a one-year contract renewal worth €12 million, covering prices, volumes, and bonuses. The discussions were intense. To close the deal, I avoided price concessions and instead offered an increased volume bonus. At the end of our discussions, Guillaume candidly said, "Great! Pietro, I appreciate your flexibility. Let me talk to Yannick to see what he thinks."

I knew Yannick Carton, the group's CPO, to be a tough negotiator. I anticipated Guillaume might return with requests for further concessions. Remaining calm and firm, I replied, "Of course, Guillaume, I understand. Take your time and talk to Yannick. When you are ready, please send me an email with your decision. I will, in turn, submit it to the board of directors for approval."

With this strategic response, I saved the negotiation. Guillaume did not ask for anything beyond what we had already negotiated. It was a valuable lesson for me. Upon returning from Paris, I shared the experience with my team, emphasizing the importance of negotiating the process first and the substance second.

The **substance** refers to the terms of the final agreement, while the **process** defines how to move from the current position to that agreement. Clarifying your negotiating partner's authority is not just practical; it's legally significant. You may find yourself negotiating with someone who lacks the authority to bind their organization to a contract.

Some negotiations are straightforward, beginning and ending in a single meeting where participants can make all necessary decisions and commitments. Others, especially in business or public policy, are far more complex. These require not only multiple meetings to address various points but also preparatory and follow-up activities to gather critical information, consult key stakeholders, and anticipate potential pitfalls. Managing this sequence of interactions (both internally and externally) demands excellent coordination and communication, achievable only through meticulous preparation.

"I'm sorry, I cannot grant the payment terms you are asking for because we have a policy."

Hearing this phrase often irritates me, as it triggers my rebellious side—I struggle to accept rules dictated by people who neither respect me nor have true authority. This may seem para-doxical, since I set rules in my own work and expect discipline and adherence to them. However, the key difference is that the rules I create are rooted in my own understanding, goals, and values. I set them with the intention of fostering mutual respect and achieving a shared purpose. In contrast, when I encounter rules imposed by others without transparency or respect for my position, they feel arbitrary and unearned. The apparent paradox arises from the contrast between self-imposed rules—where I feel a sense of control and alignment—and externally imposed rules, which can feel like a challenge to my autonomy. In such cases, you should accept what aligns with your goals, negotiate differences if possible, and—if necessary—move on to another provider.

Final Steps

As the negotiation approaches its conclusion, check the timing, terms, conditions, and all implications arising from the agreement. Ensure you've considered every aspect thoroughly. Before committing, confirm whether you can "sell" the agreement to key stakeholders, such as business partners or family members. They might raise concerns or provide ideas you haven't considered.

While much of this analysis should occur during the preparation phase, revisit these elements as new factors arise during the negotiation. Reflecting on these considerations during the discussion—calmly and privately—is essential, but avoid letting them disrupt your concentration and focus.

Feel free to request a break to reflect or consult with others before making a final commitment. If everything has gone well, you should achieve a satisfactory agreement that incorporates all the elements you prepared in advance with methodical care.

Voice, Body Language, and Honesty

Ready, Steady, Go!

Let's go back. Back to the moment you take a seat at the negotiating table. There are no fixed rules on how to start a negotiation. Never negotiate unless you've prepared thoroughly. If your
negotiating partner pushes to begin before you're ready, resist the
pressure and postpone the meeting. If you're comfortable with
small talk, it can help break the ice, reduce interpersonal distance,
and show interest. Otherwise, avoid it and go straight to the
topic at hand. Intentionally look for points of contact with your
interlocutor—shared interests or commonalities. Do something
to establish a connection and affiliation, such as asking about a
vacation, children, studies, or hobbies. These questions often
yield answers that help create rapport and build a relationship.

The initial conversation may also reveal insights about the
other negotiator's style. At this stage, align yourself with their
style. If it's formal, set others at ease by introducing or reintro-
ducing yourself, even to those you've met before, as they may not
recall your name.

"Hi, Marco! Pietro Parmeggiani. We met at the CMA
Congress in Miami, where you were on the fascinating panel
about renewable sources of energy."

Recalling a specific event or place where you previously met
appeals positively to their emotions. Making a round of introductions at the table is also helpful, as you might forget some of
the names of the attendees, and your negotiating partner might
too.

I like to place business cards on the table in front of me,
arranged according to the seating of the people I'm dealing with.
This allows me to quickly reference their names and roles. I jot
down the meeting date and use asterisks to indicate each person's
authority within the group: one asterisk representing the lowest

authority, five the highest. Additionally, I note distinguishing physical features to remember them better in the future.

If there's tension, aim to start on the right foot by expressing appreciation for your counterpart's experience and expertise. Frame the purpose of the meeting, state your commitment to finding mutual solutions, and listen carefully to their concerns to reassure them. You can do this at the beginning of the negotiation, or at any point thereafter, by proposing a more informal and collaborative approach to enhance effectiveness.

Be honest and transparent. Stating the advantages and disadvantages of a negotiation openly fosters strong bonds and builds trust. Your negotiating partner likely won't expect this approach, which gives you an advantage. Imagine you own a car dealership, and a customer is considering a sleek sports car but frequently drives in snowy conditions. While the car is magnificent, honesty would compel you to suggest a model with all-wheel drive and better winter performance, even if it means steering them away from the sports car.

While being open and forthcoming, always keep your goals in mind. It might seem obvious, but as negotiations progress, it's easy to lose sight of them. Avoid the rookie mistake of putting everything into the initial proposal. If you do, you'll have little left to negotiate, and if your offer is rejected, your only option may be to make further concessions.

The more complex your proposal, the harder it will be for the other party to process and decide. Use clear, simple, and explicit language. Be specific about what you want and what you're willing to offer in return. Avoid vague or weak statements, and anchor your variables to make them robust and credible.

When suggesting an option or presenting an offer, always reference a standard or a rationale to back it up. Share your reasoning clearly. Avoid monologues or lengthy speeches; instead, break down complex proposals into smaller, digestible parts. Frequent interaction improves engagement and ensures higher levels of attention.

Give your counterpart time to assimilate your ideas, reflect, and ask questions. Check periodically to ensure you've been understood by asking clarifying questions. Conciseness is crucial. If disagreements or misunderstandings arise, slow down, clarify, and revisit previous points if necessary.

As with many aspects of negotiating, parenting provides valuable examples of the point. When I said, "Alessia, I'll take you to the equestrian center if you put your clothes in the closets in order," she heard only one word: equestrian center. The second part of the sentence went in one ear and out the other. Her perception of order differs greatly from mine, and in talking with other parents, I've realized that this is relatively common among children. Your proposals must always be conditional, and you must not give to get but get to give. Always explain clearly what you expect the other party to do before releasing your claim.

The Artist's Touch in the Voice

For the first proposal, ensure it reflects your preparation and confidence. Choose your words carefully and deliver them in a tone of voice that radiates conviction. The tone should never sound apologetic or submissive; it should be perceived as an assertion, not a question. I always aim for a firm tone. Even though I am clear about what I want, I speak slowly, as if writing, to allow the negotiating partner to process the message and take notes if they wish—all while aligning consistent body language with my words and tone.

In negotiation, tone of voice is the artist's touch. Chris Voss (former FBI hostage negotiator and author of several bestselling books, some of whose lectures I have attended) advocates using a bright, friendly tone. This approach fosters collaboration, mutual gains, common ground, and a positive give-and-take attitude. This tone should be your go-to for at least 80 percent of the negotiation. For the remaining 20 percent, Voss recommends a direct tone with a soothing rhythm. A warm, descending voice is especially useful when seeking to calm your interlocutor.

Here's the technique: to develop a deeper, more soothing voice, breathe through your diaphragm. Stand upright and adopt a positive posture to open the diaphragm, allowing air to flow freely through your body. This will help you create a tone that exudes warmth and reflects your personality—never monotonous but always expressive and engaging. Additionally, using voice mirroring to convey similarity can help build rapport.

Unspoken Words

If voice is essential, nonverbal language is equally critical, though understanding this component can be challenging. You must become aware of your gestures, consciously consider the messages you convey, and sharpen your ability to interpret your negotiating partner's gestures and their meaning.

Nonverbal language reveals people's true feelings. The more fluent you become in this language, the more effectively you can use it. However, avoid drawing hasty conclusions about your negotiating partner's feelings without gathering additional information. For instance, crossed arms do not always signify defensiveness— your negotiating partner might simply be cold or shy. Take the time to analyze the context and look for signs of congruence.

I've delved deeply into this topic and found Erica Dhawan's (2021) *Digital Body Language: How to Build Trust and Connection No Matter the Distance* and Patrick King's (2020) *Read People Like a Book* enlightening, especially regarding the evolution of remote communication. I prefer face-to-face meetings, but recently, circumstances have often made them impossible. Despite this, I have conducted and closed significant transactions, including M&A deals, without ever meeting the counterparties in person. Research suggests that people tend to be more honest in person because they fear being caught in a lie.

Negotiations conducted via email, which are increasingly common, often result in dead-end discussions caused by misunderstandings and the lack of tone or mood management. Telephone negotiations, however, represent a middle ground.

Listen with both your eyes and ears. You can even assign someone on your team to monitor the negotiation closely—tracking how the other side reacts to specific options or their responses to your messages. This technique is particularly useful during the analysis phase of *Incontro* when reviewing the negotiation you've just completed.

Which White Chess Piece Do You Move?

Who should make the first offer? Good question. It's easier to get your friends to agree on the best pizza place in town than to decide who should put the first proposal on the table in a negotiation. Some argue you should never make the first offer and always wait for your negotiating partner's offer. But there's no absolute rule. If you've prepared well and are aiming for a profitable deal, you should boldly submit the first offer. Research consistently shows that the party making the initial proposal often achieves better results. However, avoid starting with numbers, as they are not the only factors that add value to an offer.

By making the first offer, you set an anchor and establish a benchmark that will influence the counteroffer and the negotiation's outcome. As we discussed previously, research shows that people anchor themselves to initial numbers or ideas. By going first, you define the interests to be discussed. Don't fear a one-word response like "No." Rejection is simply the beginning of a negotiation. In fact, hearing "No" is far better than hearing "Maybe."

When faced with rejection, a skilled negotiator probes for reasons. Often, this is the turning point where the negotiating partner (sometimes even feeling a bit guilty) begins to share unspoken interests, doubts, feelings, and other details—solid foundations on which to build an agreement.

"Mr. Cox, would you mind if I explained my idea?"

Most likely, his response will be "No," which essentially means, "Yes, go ahead and explain it to me." This kind of positive no is transformative because it allows you to focus on solutions that meet both parties' needs and interests. In this way, no has great power, and you shouldn't fear it.

Equally useful is the negative yes, which you can elicit by asking well-phrased questions that make "No" effectively mean "Yes."

For example:

"Don't you think this clause is too restrictive?"

"Don't you think we should consider alternatives to this solution?"

After agreeing on critical points, it may even be strategic to stimulate objections and refusals, using no to guide the discussion.

Throughout my career, I've frequently negotiated with clients by arriving prepared and steering the conversation from the start. To prevent clients from initiating negotiations, I would open with discussions about commodity price increases, logistical challenges, force majeure declarations, increased demand in Asia, or hurricanes in the Gulf of Mexico—topics that created favorable ground for my subsequent requests. This approach allowed me to frame the discussion around issues I wanted on the table. I never explicitly stated that I wanted to raise prices; instead, I reframed the conversation to focus on customer needs.

Making the first offer can also positively impact the relationship. When you make the first offer, the relationship often improves, as it allows the negotiating partner to react and share their concerns. Conversely, if they make the first offer, it's up to you to challenge their proposal, which can strain the relationship—starting a negotiation by critiquing your partner's offer is rarely a good idea.

No one likes to be challenged. In a negotiation, a note of criticism can spark mutual accusations, dulling enthusiasm and reducing the willingness to cooperate. Questions should challenge logic, not the person. Avoid phrasing that could be interpreted as accusatory. For example, "*This* argument" is far less confrontational than "*Your* argument." Alternatively, you can pretend you didn't understand, prompting the other person to clarify their position without creating conflict. A misunderstanding that seems to be your fault can encourage your counterpart to explain themselves more thoroughly, easing tension and fostering collaboration.

Positions reflect what the negotiating partner wants, not necessarily what they need. Never accept positions without first asking questions to understand the reasoning behind them. Have the courage to explicitly identify points of contention; if you do so, you will appear as the party with the least to lose, the most diligent and sincere. From a relational standpoint, I prefer to make the first offer and handle the reactions that follow. I also prepare a concession plan in advance, outlining the elements I am willing to yield on. This strategy positions me as diligent, sincere, and willing to take risks, which can work to my advantage.

If you lack complete information about the zone of possible agreement (ZOPA), it may be wiser to delay making the first offer and let your negotiating partner go first. While this means you lose the advantages of anchoring, it also reduces the risk of making an offer that is either too aggressive or too conservative. However, ideally, you should never find yourself in a situation where you lack the information necessary to make the first offer confidently.

"Pietro, I've followed your advice, and the ZOPA is clear. How much should I ask for as a first offer?"

"It depends, Carlo. Your offer should maximize the entire ZOPA. If you make an offer outside the ZOPA, your negotiating partner will likely steer the negotiation back into their range, potentially weakening your position. Conversely, if your first offer is already inside the ZOPA, you've missed an opportunity equal to the difference between your offer and your negotiating partner's reserve price. Your offer must be as aggressive as you can reasonably justify. The higher your ambitions, the more assertive your first offer should be, allowing you to achieve better results."

When you make an aggressive offer, you risk offending your negotiating partner, being perceived as unserious, or creating the impression that there is no scope for agreement. While these risks exist, don't worry too much—they depend heavily on the context and the weight of the relationship. Your offer and supporting arguments should balance your needs with the importance of maintaining a positive relationship. In essence, your proposal should aim for the best possible deal while strengthening the relationship.

Another good tactic is to make an imperfect or exaggerated first offer and then voluntarily withdraw it, acknowledging that it didn't adequately address your negotiating partner's interests.

At this point, submit an improved version of the proposal that aligns better with their interests. This approach demonstrates consideration for their needs and paints you in a positive light. Moreover, presenting an improved proposal without prompting can help break down barriers and foster goodwill, increasing the likelihood of a successful negotiation.

If your negotiating partner makes the first offer, don't worry: nothing is lost, as you still have many opportunities to shape the discussion. First, avoid accepting the first offer hastily, even if it seems advantageous. If the negotiating partner feels they could have gotten more, they may reflect on this in future negotiations and behave differently, potentially damaging the relationship. Instead, appear surprised, puzzled, or skeptical, especially if you believe the offer can be improved (and most offers can be). If you do make the mistake of accepting too quickly, you can still recover by explaining that while the offer is acceptable, you feel it could be improved. It's akin to the classic tactic for dealing with a salesperson: "Sounds like a bargain to me, but I'll need to check with my wife before deciding."

This scenario, however, is extreme. A more practical approach is to either disregard the offer or make an immediate counteroffer to prevent the other party's proposal from setting an anchor. Questioning their proposal or pointing out mistakes can be risky, as it keeps the discussion focused on their offer, reinforcing its anchoring effect.

Alternatively, focus on the positive aspects of their offer and separate them from the less acceptable points. Then, negotiate the problematic elements constructively, suggesting viable alternatives. This approach makes it seem as though you're considering their offer seriously while proposing adjustments. However, this tactic is not universally applicable, especially if the negatives outweigh the positives.

If an offer has no value or interest to you, still express appreciation and remain polite and friendly. This allows your interlocutor to save face and keeps the door open for future communication. Alternatively, remaining silent can prompt your negotiating partner to elaborate, offering additional details and information. Every offer contains a mix of information and influence. Before reacting or responding, learn to separate these components, filtering what is communicated to better guide your perceptions.

Here's a small trick: ask yourself, "What new information have I learned? How does this align with my interests?" If you find nothing valuable, it's likely influence, not information. For example, if someone says, "You should buy this phone because it's the best on the market," this is influence. On the other hand, if they say, "This phone is designed with a durable, water-resistant build and offers a customizable operating system, which makes it great for outdoor use and personalization," they're giving you information that helps you evaluate whether it aligns with your interests.

Get in the habit of mentally rephrasing what you hear. In similar situations, I have responded to offers with a counteroffer encompassing three characteristics: **multiple**, **equivalent**, **and simultaneous** (MESO).

Multiple: Three distinct options (A, B, and C).

Equivalent: They all have a similar total value to you, though the negotiating partner may assign different values to them.

Simultaneous: The three alternatives are presented side by side.

This tactic works because it generates a strong anchoring effect that mitigates the advantage created by the negotiating partner's initial offer. While more complex than presenting a single offer, this approach is effective, as it doesn't corner the negotiating partner or come across as an ultimatum. Instead, it provides the illusion of choice.

Additional benefits include appearing aggressive yet cooperative and flexible, as well as handling bundled interests instead of negotiating each one separately. Addressing issues individually often makes each appear disproportionately critical. When negotiating point by point, it's helpful to remember the principle **Nothing is agreed until everything is agreed**.

Using multiple, equivalent, simultaneous offers in business negotiations is highly beneficial as it projects flexibility, improves relationships, and maximizes results. This principle applies not only in negotiations with clients, suppliers, and M&A, but also within family dynamics. Proposing multiple alternatives is particularly useful when your negotiating partner's interests are unclear; their choices can reveal valuable insights into their priorities and preferences. It's akin to playing Mastermind,[45] the 1970s abstract cryptanalysis game.

For example, imagine a family deciding where to spend the holidays. Instead of just asking, "Where do you want to go?", you could offer three equally balanced proposals, each containing multiple elements: "We could go to the beach with a relaxed schedule, a day trip to a nearby town, and a seafood dinner." Or "We could explore a city with planned visits to museums, a guided tour, and a couple of free days for shopping." Or "We could take a nature retreat with hiking, a cozy cabin, and no tech for a digital detox."

This way, family members can weigh the different components—destination, activities, level of structure, and time for relaxation—and express their preferences. The combination of variables allows you to understand what aspects matter most to them and helps create a solution that works for everyone.

In negotiations, each alternative should include multiple elements: one potentially contrary to your interlocutor's interests, while other aspects vary among options. Providing a choice gives your negotiating partner a sense of control, increasing the likelihood they'll select one of your alternatives. Even if they request a concession on an inflexible element, they are unlikely to forgo aspects that align with their interests. Furthermore, the comparison shifts to your proposed alternatives rather than the initial proposal, reframing the discussion.

---

45   Mastermind is a classic board game invented by Mordecai Meirowitz in 1970. It involves two players: the Codemaker, who creates a secret code using colored pegs, and the Codebreaker, who must guess it within a set number of attempts. After each guess, the Codemaker provides feedback on how many pegs are correct in both color and position, and how many are the right color but misplaced. Using this feedback, the Codebreaker employs logic and deduction to uncover the code. Known for its strategic depth, Mastermind remains a timeless test of reasoning and problem-solving.

Sometimes, the negotiating partner may reject all the alternatives you present. This scenario is an opportunity to ask which option aligns most closely with their preferences, which one is furthest away, and why. Their responses can yield valuable information, enabling you to begin **logrolling**, the mutual exchange of concessions across multiple interests. Some negotiators hesitate to use multiple offers, fearing the negotiating partner will cherry-pick favorable elements from each. While this risk exists, their selections provide critical insights, though it may anchor subsequent discussions. Construct your multiple offers so that each exceeds your goals, leaving room for concessions if necessary.

When presenting multiple offers, plan your concessions carefully. These should appear pre-packaged, with any changes presented as a new proposal—let's call it Proposal D. But note that anchoring doesn't always require multiple offers; a well-constructed single initial offer can serve as the anchor and set the reference point for subsequent negotiations. If you adjust this anchor in response to your negotiating partner's counteroffer, it can lend credibility to your original offer. However, be cautious: seeking excessive clarification and justification for an offer can unintentionally solidify its anchoring effect.

Framing is another powerful tool for achieving significant results. This cognitive shortcut simplifies complex information, enabling both parties to organize and interpret challenges coherently. Effective framing can highlight specific aspects of a problem that align with your goals while de-emphasizing less relevant factors. For instance, I once helped a client convince the ownership of a family business to invest over €10 million in a cogeneration plant. Despite concerns about costs, we framed the proposal around energy savings and sustainability. By emphasizing these aspects, the elderly owner recognized the investment's alignment with environmental stewardship and approved it.

Focus your negotiating partner's attention on critical aspects of the problem while omitting irrelevant details. People are generally more risk-averse when avoiding losses than when seeking new gains. When faced with potential losses, they "play offense"; when pursuing gains, they adopt a more conservative, "play defense" attitude. Framing demands as necessary to avoid losses, and concessions as sacrifices you will endure, taps into this natural risk aversion.

Consider this exchange:

Client: "Sabrina, I don't understand how $42,500 for this kitchen isn't an exaggeration."

Sabrina: "Mr. De Luca, I understand your concern. Other buyers initially felt the same way until they saw the professionalism of our installers and began using it."

Sabrina's response follows the Feel, Felt, and Found structure, demonstrating empathy and persuasion. She validates the client's concerns by acknowledging them, explains that others shared similar doubts, and concludes by highlighting the benefits experienced by past clients in comparable situations. This approach reassures the client while subtly reinforcing the value of her offer.

In the face of an extreme first offer or one far from your reserve price, you can counter-anchor the negotiation by rejecting the proposal outright and making an equally aggressive counteroffer. For instance, if you're selling a car for $20,000 and a buyer offers you $8,000, you might reject the offer and counter with $30,000, even though it's above your ideal price. The extreme application of this strategy can verge on the irrational or bizarre (though creativity is always a given), but it helps set a new reference point and can shift the negotiation in your favor. This approach often yields good results because your negotiating partner may be willing to agree to a deal just to move forward. But what happens if the negotiation reaches a deadlock instead? Regardless of the initial location of the two offers along the axis, these positions define the zone of possible compromise. To move forward, both parties must relinquish some demands to fall within the zone of possible agreement—unless they choose to walk away.

You can mitigate the risks associated with an aggressive counteroffer by expressing a willingness to collaborate on bridging differences and by thoroughly explaining and justifying your proposal.

Another effective strategy is to offer within a narrow range, for example, $120,000–$125,000. The anchor in this case could be any point within the range: S120,000, $125,000, or $122,500. Therefore, it is critical to consider the range values carefully before presenting them. The same logic applies when making concessions: always ensure they are presented conditionally to prevent the negotiating partner from automatically selecting the most favorable value for themselves. For example, in real estate, a property may be listed with a negotiable price, but the final price often deviates only slightly from the initial asking price.

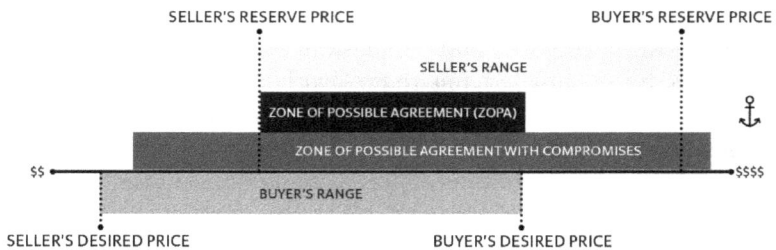

How much to offer? Suppose the goal is to maximize value tactically. In that case, the offer should be close to the buyer's reserve value so that it can be adjusted without triggering a counter-anchor, effectively bringing it back into the zone of possible agreement through negotiation. An extreme but reasonable offer, bordering on credibility, is often effective. If you want something, ask for more, and be prepared to make concessions if necessary. We tend to assume that an aggressive offer will be rejected, but rejection is not inherently harmful.

Of course, an overly aggressive request is not without risks— it may suggest that an agreement is impossible or even offend the negotiating partner, particularly if you have miscalculated the zone of possible agreement. Anchoring is more powerful and effective in situations of significant uncertainty. If you feel anchored by the other party's offer, you can diminish its impact by presenting objective information during the negotiation. If an offer seems inappropriate, redirect the conversation away from numbers and proposals, focusing instead on interests and options, then return to numbers when you have gathered more information.

Another way to handle an aggressive offer is to state clearly that it lacks a basis for negotiation. Provide an explanation of your perspective and ask the other party to reconsider, possibly from a different angle. Keep in mind that the negotiating partner may initially stick to their position to save face, so allowing them time to reflect can be a wise approach. This strategy enables you to subtly anchor their thinking without overtly expressing disappointment.

Asking, "Is this your best offer?" at the right moment can elicit additional concessions or improve the terms without requiring a quid pro quo. Similarly, comparisons to competitors—who are, of course, always better, faster, and cheaper—can create leverage. Downplaying a critical request, such as saying, "After all, I'm only asking for a 2 percent discount," can also prompt favorable adjustments.

The phrase "Take it or leave it!" is a common and intentionally destabilizing tactic. Your own BATNA and your analysis of that of the negotiating partner (which you should have prepared thoroughly) are your primary tools for managing this scenario. You have three options: accept the deal with some concessions, walk away while risking the relationship, or keep the negotiation going. In the latter case, ask questions to determine whether the ultimatum is a bluff and explore the consequences for both parties if the deal falls through, always keeping interests in mind.

If your negotiating partner stops negotiating, delivers an ultimatum, or escalates with dramatic gestures like banging fists on the table, resist the urge to counterattack or concede. Both responses are imperfect: counterattacking can escalate conflict, while conceding can signal weakness and invite further intimidation. These situations often arise from stress, anger, or tension, impairing the negotiating partner's cognitive functions. In such cases, use the tools you've prepared: deflect threats, employ silence, and steer the conversation back to shared interests and goals. Your questions, your BATNA, and a detached analysis of the situation will be invaluable. It can also help to demonstrate empathy and understand the partner's perspective, even if it's challenging after a threat.

A variation of this tactic is the "good cop / bad cop" approach, commonly seen in team negotiations. The "good cop" pretends to be on your side, helping to close the deal, only for the "bad cop" to reenter and renegotiate everything agreed upon. In such cases, you can call out the strategy openly, ignore the "bad cop," or suspend negotiations, stating that the conditions for productive discussion are absent. If you're negotiating with a group, watch for other roles that may emerge, such as the expert, the enthusiast, the intransigent, and the leader. Recognizing these roles can help you navigate the dynamics effectively.

An expert is someone highly skilled and knowledgeable in a specific domain. They are typically highly confident and make decisions rooted in logic and data. However, during a negotiation, they may become overly technical and detailed, risking disengaging others. To manage an expert effectively, it is essential to show respect for their knowledge, elaborate on their arguments, maintain an overview, and emphasize the importance of achieving a balanced solution.

An enthusiast is a creative and solution-oriented negotiator. They excel at finding innovative alternatives and negotiating mutually beneficial agreements. However, they may become overly enthusiastic about their ideas and struggle with compromise. To manage a proactive person, it is important to encourage and enhance their creativity while reminding them of the need for a collaborative and flexible approach. Promoting the proposal of multiple options and establishing criteria for evaluating and selecting the best solution can be particularly helpful.

The intransigent negotiator is rigid and inflexible. They often aim for maximum personal advantage and may resist considering the other party's needs. Managing an intransigent individual requires calm and patience. The key is to identify common points of interest and demonstrate how a mutually beneficial agreement can lead to better outcomes than an inflexible position. Establishing open and respectful communication is crucial, as is involving the intransigent negotiator in identifying acceptable solutions.

The leader is a skilled negotiator who influences and guides others toward a common goal. They demonstrate empathy, clear communication, and strong listening skills. Leaders negotiate collaboratively, encouraging active involvement from all parties. To work effectively with a leader, it is important to recognize and appreciate their leadership abilities, provide space for them to contribute to decisions and strategy development, and maintain an open and transparent dialogue to ensure all parties feel heard and included in the negotiation process.

Each individual is unique and may exhibit characteristics of multiple profiles. The key to successful negotiation is to adapt and take a flexible approach to meet your needs (and those of your negotiating partner) in every case or situation!

Narrowing Roadway

An agreement can only be reached when both parties find an acceptable point between their starting positions. If agreement is lacking, negotiation slows down, becomes tactical, and leaves parties disappointed, increasing the likelihood of power plays. At this point, the negotiation is likely to come to a complete halt. The solution is to temporarily set aside the cause of the impasse, accepting that there is no agreement on a specific issue without making it a focal point.

"Roger, if you agree, let's suspend the discussion regarding penalties in case of late deliveries for now. Can we talk about it later?"

Doing so can preserve the energy of the negotiation while gathering important information instrumental to reaching an agreement. You can revisit the thorny issue later, after addressing other topics. By the time most of the points have been agreed upon, the parties will be more likely to approach the issue thoughtfully, prioritizing the broader agreement over a single point of contention.

There are also common phrases like: "I don't want to accept your proposal because, all things being equal, I have a supplier who offers better payment terms and a less onerous take-or-pay clause." It happens. Even after arriving at an option that meets both parties' interests, one negotiator may indicate that they have a better alternative. This is typically intended to prompt both sides to find an even better option rather than to act as a threat, though misunderstandings can arise.

For example, a response such as " It's not convenient for me to accept either. My plants are already saturated, and I have at least two customers providing reliable monthly forecasts," reflects a similar strategic maneuver. This response subtly communicates that the other party also has attractive alternatives, thereby balancing the scales and encouraging further dialogue.

Getting out of such an impasse requires dexterity. On one hand, both parties have introduced new elements (e.g., payment terms, take-or-pay clause, saturated facilities, forecast orders) that can be worked on to better define interests and options. On the other hand, these revelations give each side a chance to reassess the quality of their alternatives. Once initial offers are made, negotiators often struggle to move from their positions, fearing that doing so signals weakness or surrender.

The focus should remain on the negotiating partner's interests, BATNA, and reserve value, even if an internal voice—representing your own thoughts, emotions, or self-doubt, often driven by impatience, fear of losing the deal, or the desire for a quick resolution—urges you to settle for an outcome that exceeds your reserve value.

To weaken the other party's negotiating position, you can exploit natural human tendencies, such as laziness, the sunk cost fallacy (reluctance to abandon prior investments), and the "bird in the hand" fallacy (preferring a smaller certain gain over a larger but uncertain one). Why should they expend resources and energy searching for new alternatives when a solution is already on the table? By subtly introducing doubt and raising concerns through persuasive yet seemingly sincere and disinterested arguments, you can make them hesitant to explore other options. If neutral and credible third parties can reinforce your points, your case becomes even stronger, as they help magnify the perception that what's already been offered is the best and most feasible solution.

It is also important to avoid overestimating your negotiating partner's position simply because your own alternative seems weak. Their alternatives may not be as strong as they suggest! Do some work to establish the quality of their alternatives (assuming they have any), and remind them of the advantages they would forgo if no agreement were reached. Emphasize what you would prefer to achieve together, but avoid getting into unnecessary detail about your own plans.

During preparation, you likely made several assumptions. Negotiation is the time to validate and challenge them. Try to anticipate your negotiating partner's moves if they were to walk away. Remember that they may exaggerate the quality of their alternatives. If something seems off, ask clarifying questions. Keep in mind that not everything that they claim to be possible genuinely is.

Challenge the viability of their alternative by asking thoughtful, well-reasoned questions and presenting facts that highlight its weaknesses, all while maintaining a respectful and collaborative tone.

Even if you don't convince them, you will prompt reflection.

Imagine the start of a negotiation as a sprint: at first, everyone at the table is eager and energetic. But once offers are laid on the table, participants slow down, becoming cautious in their concessions, often only responding to perceived benefits. This hesitancy is facilitated by an unwritten rule of negotiation: parties understand and expect that concessions must be made to move forward.

In negotiation, reciprocity (exchanging things for mutual benefit) is a powerful and persuasive tool. When you receive a concession from the negotiating partner, it is expected—and natural—to reciprocate. However, it's important to understand the dynamics behind the concessions being made. For example, I once had a conversation with the head of purchasing at Assa Abloy, a world leader in lock systems, who said to me, "Pietro, I'm not breaking the norm; I'm just testing your elasticity." What he meant by this was that, in some negotiations, concessions are made not just to benefit both sides, but to gauge how much flexibility the other party has and whether they are willing to make a reciprocal move. From my experience, some people fail to properly acknowledge the concessions they receive, missing an opportunity to reinforce the obligation to reciprocate. For every concession you make, explicitly point out what it means to you—how much value you are sacrificing and what additional costs you are incurring.

Kathy Aaronson, founder and CEO of Sales Athlete Executive Search, puts it aptly: "No matter how small, concessions should be given very carefully, wrapped in silver, and presented like a monarch's gift."

Convey clearly that every concession represents a cost or sacrifice for you. By doing so, you make it harder for the negotiating partner to ignore the principle of reciprocity. Avoiding ambiguity ensures the negotiating partner understands the value of your concessions and prevents them from taking them lightly.

From my days studying private law at the University of Bologna (the oldest university in the world), two lessons stand out vividly. The first is Article 924 of the Civil Code, which grants the owner of a swarm of bees the right to chase it onto someone else's land. The second is the concept of **sinallagma**, or the nexus of reciprocity.

The term **synallagmatic** (or reciprocal exchange) is far more pertinent. It refers to an implicit element in contracts of mutual consideration, rooted in the Greek etymology of contracting, stipulating, taking, and giving in exchange. This underscores the principle of reciprocal exchange:

If your supplier demands late payment penalties, you should demand penalties for late deliveries.

If your customer asks for a price concession, you should demand additional volumes.

Claim consideration symmetrical to your negotiating partner's logic. If they refuse to grant you a balanced exchange, never agree to give them anything. Be timely, and never concede something now in the hope of obtaining symmetrical consideration later.

Operating on credit doesn't work. If you find yourself in such a situation, ensure you secure an equivalent counterpart to use later as leverage. When faced with a negotiating partner who repeatedly pressures you for small but consistent concessions, resist giving in without a quid pro quo. Even in the case of minor concessions, always seek something in return. When you agree to a concession, signal this clearly, remove the item from the agenda, and summarize the terms.

If you're using a Terms Sheet, document the agreement in the column on the right, or directly on a shared screen visible to all participants (e.g., during a video conference). This practice freezes the progress made, highlights what the negotiating partner has gained (or risks losing if the process fails), maintains control of the agenda, and prevents misunderstandings.

Many conflicts at the negotiating table arise from misunderstandings due to misinterpretation, distortions caused by personal biases, or the lack of accurate and precise information. Never take anything for granted. Always explain why you say certain things, your intentions, and your behavior to eliminate distrust and foster a cooperative spirit.

Recently, a client shared a recurring issue with me: he has a long-term negotiating partner (over ten years) who systematically denies previously agreed-upon points to reopen discussions and gain additional concessions. To preserve the relationship, I advised him to investigate the root of the misunderstandings and document the agreed points during the negotiation, either on paper or a visible blackboard, to prevent denials and ensure clarity for all parties. This approach has already had a positive effect; my client reports that both parties are now more aligned, with fewer misunderstandings, and the documented agreements help keep the negotiations on track.

I grew up watching *Columbo* on TV and loved his seemingly lost and confused demeanor.[46] Lieutenant Columbo, a homicide detective with the Los Angeles Police Department, was brilliant at subtly extracting information from murderers who, step by step, unknowingly revealed everything to him. He never directly asked the suspects for help; instead, his behavior put them at ease, almost obligating them to cooperate. What's fascinating is that this approach entirely dissipated tension and conflict. Columbo cleverly exploited ego, instilling a sense of superiority in the suspects.

---

46   *Columbo* is an American television series that originally aired from 1971 to 2003. The series features Lieutenant Columbo, a shrewd but unassuming homicide detective played by Peter Falk. Columbo is known for his distinctive investigative style, characterized by his disheveled appearance, polite demeanor, and seemingly oblivious nature. Despite his outward simplicity, he employs a clever and persistent approach to solving complex cases, often using subtle psychological tactics to uncover the truth. The character's ability to put suspects at ease while discreetly gathering vital information has made Columbo a popular figure in television crime drama.

Presenting yourself as overly competent with computers, data, or other tools—or flaunting your intelligence—can backfire. How often have I attended meetings without pen and paper, giving the impression that I was almost clueless? How often did I tip over my water or coffee to appear clumsy or distressed? How many times did I ask questions I already knew the answers to, simply to verify the accuracy of information or the honesty of my negotiating partner?

Similarly, some negotiating partners intentionally muddle issues, facts, and figures to derail the discussion and obscure critical elements. This behavior borders on dishonesty. In such cases, the best solution is to politely request a summary from time to time to bring clarity. Speaking of which, what happens if your own honesty is questioned? It could stem from a misunderstanding or be a deliberate tactic by your negotiating partner to undermine you and extract concessions. The best way to resolve this is to clarify immediately by asking pointed questions to uncover why your integrity was doubted. Depending on the answers, you can address the misunderstanding and return to focusing on mutual interests.

"Do you trust me?" Many remember Jack asking Rose this iconic question in *Titanic*, the famous 1997 film about love and adventure aboard the ill-fated ship. I, however, vividly recall when this same question was posed to me twenty-five years ago in Paris by José Flavigny, the CEO of Arjowiggins. Unlike Rose, my answer was a blunt and inappropriate, "No." That question is a trap, and at the time, I was an inexperienced negotiator who fell right into it.

In negotiation, this question puts you in a bind. If you say you trust them, it becomes challenging to reject their statements later. If you say you don't, as I did, it can be taken as an insult, potentially derailing the discussion and jeopardizing any chance of an agreement.

From that significant mistake, I learned a better way to respond to such questions. Today, if faced with José again, I'd say: "José, the problem isn't trust. You know how much I appreciate and value you! The issue lies with [specific point]."

Every negotiation is unique, with differing contexts, processes, and sequences of events, so I cannot offer universally applicable rules. However, people tend to prefer receiving positive news or benefits incrementally rather than all at once. So, to enhance your negotiating partner's satisfaction, deliver gains incrementally. Conversely, to minimize the perception of sacrifice, consolidate losses.

"Caroline, given the commodity situation, I suggest passing all the increases in one go, and when the cycle reverses, lowering prices gradually."

One of the most common mistakes in negotiation is offering a substantial initial concession to demonstrate goodwill. Skilled negotiators, on the other hand, make multiple, smaller concessions of diminishing value, which increases the negotiating partner's satisfaction.

Returning to Francesco, Giorgia, and their Porsche: the couple decided to negotiate with their preferred dealer while keeping alternatives from Stuttgart, Vienna, and Milan in reserve. The Stuttgart option is their BATNA because it's the best alternative, and the Porsche 911 Turbo S Convertible they're eyeing is nearly perfect, with fewer than 3,000 kilometers on the clock. Although well prepared, they make a critical error by not initiating the negotiation.

The savvy dealer starts with an asking price of €259,000. Pressed by the couple, he drops incrementally to €254,000, €252,000, and finally €251,000, concluding with the classic line, "I can't go any lower."

"Pietro, do you think the dealer reached his limit? Was he truthful when he claimed he couldn't go any lower?"

"Giorgia, you should only reveal your lower limit when you have genuinely reached it—or are just about to—and, if you declare it, do so emphatically and firmly. Never waver from that point. Otherwise, you risk not being taken seriously in this and future negotiations, and you'll always face demands for further concessions to finalize the agreement."

In this case, I would suggest asking a few questions to determine whether the dealer truly cannot lower the price further:

Does he have an alternative?

Why hasn't he mentioned it?

What is that alternative?

Has he reached the limit of his autonomy, or could the owner potentially offer better terms?

Sometimes negotiators make "final" concessions but later withdraw them or condition them on receiving a new concession. To avoid this, I recommend establishing a clear rule at the beginning of every negotiation: a concession cannot be withdrawn unless explicitly stated as temporary or conditional.

As negotiations progress, concessions typically become smaller as the reserve value approaches. This is a natural behavior and serves as a signal that the reserve value is near, which can help you refine your initial assumptions about the size of the ZOPA.

When addressing multiple topics, mentally organize them as you would on an Excel spreadsheet, and focus on presenting only two or three of the strongest points at a time. Avoid displaying them in a fixed order, whether ascending or descending.

If you start with the weakest points, you risk being interrupted and attacked right away.

If you begin with the strongest points, your negotiating partner's attention may shift to the weakest ones, which will be freshest in their memory, forcing you to defend less convincing arguments.

Regardless of what you present, always provide a justification to legitimize your request or concession. Whenever you ask for or offer something, include the magic word: because. For your requests, support them with simple, clear, logical, and verifiable details. Do the same when making concessions to ensure they are not perceived as a sign of weakness. Make single concessions and cumulative requests.

The timing of concessions is also critical. If you make a substantial concession too quickly after your initial offer, it can undermine your credibility and weaken your position. However, when making concessions to your negotiating partner, it's important to remember that they will perceive these as gains. To enhance their satisfaction and reinforce the value of each concession, it's often best to deliver them incrementally. This aligns with the principle of spreading out your concessions over time, allowing your partner to feel that each one is significant.

On the other hand, when making requests, which are perceived as losses by the other party, consolidating them is usually a more effective strategy. By grouping your requests together, you create a more impactful ask, and the other party is less likely to perceive each individual request as a separate sacrifice. This approach minimizes the perception of sacrifice and maximizes the impact of your demands.

Silence, Pauses,
and Contingent Agreements

Silence and Pauses

Lately, I have observed many negotiations, more than ever before, and noticed that most people find silence deeply unsettling. Silence creates pressure to fill the empty space, often leading negotiators to speak when they should not. Worse yet, especially in remote negotiations, when you've made an offer and your negotiating partner takes time to respond, instead of waiting in respectful silence, you might become nervous and take the initiative. Without giving your counterpart time to reflect, express doubt, or raise questions, you might repeat your offer as if they didn't understand it or, even more detrimental, make a further concession, mistakenly assuming their silence implies rejection.

Silence—often referred to as "aggressive silence"—is a powerful and destabilizing tool. Over the eight years I lived in Asia, I adapted to silence as a common mode of communication. If you're not accustomed to it, that silence can feel eternal. I recently experienced a similar sensation while walking on Iceland's Vatnajökull glacier, evoking the same feelings I had years ago visiting Taktsang Monastery in Bhutan: absolute silence. In our noisy world, silence is a rarity, and many people feel uneasy in its presence. When I ask my clients to use silence as a strategic tool, they often admit feeling embarrassed—even after just a few seconds.

Learning to manage silence is essential. It allows you time to reflect—thoughts that are inaccessible to your negotiating partner, leaving them feeling more vulnerable. When you remain silent, your offer stays firm, and you avoid concessions. Silence is inherently uncomfortable and can generate unease. Remember that silence often elicits concessions and may be accompanied by nonverbal signals like a sigh, a shake of the head, or subtle mouth or eye movements. Learning to use these cues effectively, where appropriate, can be a valuable skill.

Responding to silence with silence is one of the best techniques, particularly if your negotiating partner initiates the quiet game. Alternatively, you can use tactics like presenting multiple equivalent simultaneous offers, asking open-ended questions, or inquiring, "Do you need more time to think?"

I have encountered negotiators who masterfully wielded silence, and I've made an effort to learn from them. Since it is not an innate skill for most, I've improved through practice and coaching. Silence enhances questioning skills and emotional intelligence. In my experience, over 90 percent of people either avoid silence entirely, unaware of its power, or misuse it in a clumsy manner. While clumsy use may occasionally work against submissive or inexperienced negotiators, it often irritates the other party and leads to a stalemate. Silence must be applied thoughtfully and strategically. With practice, you can use simple signals—a slight nod, an encouraging monosyllable, or a single word—to prompt your interlocutor to speak. Then, you must listen actively and attentively.

Silence should not be confused with a **pause**. A pause is often necessary to replenish energy: grab a snack, drink water, use the restroom, smoke (if you must), relieve tension, consult a colleague, or verify information. Breaks can range from ten minutes to a day or even a weekend.

"I'll sleep on it, and we'll talk tomorrow," is not a sign of weakness. Instead, it allows both parties to step back from the discussion and return with renewed energy and creativity. When proposing a break, do so confidently and without guilt. If you've called for a pause, leave the room so you can decide when to resume the negotiation.

A different situation arises when you need a break but don't want to ask explicitly, or you're concerned about sending the wrong signal. Here, acting skills can be useful—for instance, pretending you need to take an urgent call, attend to a medication schedule, or another plausible reason. If acting isn't your strength, you can always resort to straightforward excuses like needing to send an email or use the restroom. However, be mindful of time constraints and ensure your excuse is credible. This tactic can be particularly helpful when you've just taken a hard blow in the negotiation and need a few moments to step away and regain composure.

When dealing with extensive negotiations, I find it useful at the outset—when the agenda and process are being defined—to establish that everyone has the option to call one or more breaks, like a timeout in sport. This approach normalizes breaks and ensures that requesting one, even after receiving an unfavorable proposal, appears entirely routine.

One tip coming from my experience: if your interlocutor requests a break, and the context allows, ask why they are pausing. They might unintentionally reveal vital information. If they do not specify the length of the pause, take the initiative yourself to set a brief one. Once the break ends and the negotiation resumes, discussions typically continue as before.

As an alternative to reciprocity, you can use conditional offers, where you tie a concession to receiving something in return. For example, "I could reduce the price for an upfront payment." This is a straightforward conditional offer: you're offering a discount in exchange for a specific action. Conditional offers are a safe tactic, but they can sometimes arouse suspicion from the negotiating partner. Be cautious: overusing them could undermine trust and damage the relationship in the long term.

To succeed with this approach, you must clearly understand your interests and those of the other party.

Contingent Agreements

A variation of conditional offers, contingent agreements allow both parties to "bet" on their beliefs about the future. These are particularly common in M&A negotiations to reconcile differing expectations about future performance, such as earnings. However, I've also used them in negotiations involving real estate, horses, cars, artwork, and more. The following provides an example of such a scenario:

Company Alfa has developed an innovative product, begun production, and achieved significant profits. Management expects even higher profits with international sales and values the company at $35 million. However, Alfa lacks the resources for additional production capacity. Company Bravo, interested in acquiring Alfa, has the necessary cash but doubts Alfa's optimistic forecasts. Bravo offers $28 million upfront, proposing contingent agreements based on future turnover within twelve months:

If turnover reaches $10 million, Bravo will pay an additional $7 million.

If turnover reaches at least $8 million, Bravo will pay an additional $3 million.

If turnover falls below $8 million, Bravo will stick to the base price of $28 million.

Contingent agreements are also effective in supply contracts, where uncertainty may arise over raw material prices, purchase volumes, or delivery timelines. These agreements are useful when the parties cannot agree on essential elements but still want to close the deal. They are especially helpful when the ZOPA is negative—meaning there is no overlap between the minimum terms each party is willing to accept. In this situation, the buyer's reservation price (the highest price they are willing to pay) is lower than the seller's reservation price (the lowest price they are willing to accept). Essentially, the parties have incompatible expectations, making it impossible to reach a mutually beneficial agreement. Contingent agreements can also serve as a tactic to test the counterparty's claims or to demonstrate confidence in your offer.

It's important to remember that contingent agreements can be risky when there's significant information asymmetry—as is common when one party has significantly more experience.

If you are the more experienced party, take care to explain the potential effects and consequences of the agreement, especially monetary ones, to the less experienced party. The agreement should remain consistent with the spirit of the negotiation. Otherwise, you risk closing the deal only to face ongoing legal disputes later.

Avoid Unnecessary Concessions

Negotiating and making concessions should not be confused with reaching an agreement through compromise that results in one or both parties accepting less than their reserve value. This mistake often happens when parties fear needing to resort to their BATNA, especially during uncertain times.

Better something than nothing? Absolutely not. If you have thoroughly prepared for the negotiation and realize during discussions that your BATNA is no longer as appealing, take a break to reevaluate the elements that formed the basis of your alternative. If necessary, build a stronger one before returning to the negotiating table.

A good agreement arises from a precise assessment of what it represents to you. Relationships and trust cannot be "bought" by sacrificing your interests as currency. If you accept unfavorable agreements or yield to the pressure of your negotiating partner in the hope of securing a stronger relationship over time, you may find that you've only taught them to expect even greater concessions from you in the future using the same tactic.

"Russell, I offer you $12,000 for the car."

"Jane, I understand you're Elizabeth's best friend, but I want at least $14,000. I'm sorry. To wrap this up, could we meet halfway?"

"You just indicated you'd be willing to accept $13,000. I am willing to pay $12,000. Why don't we split the difference and close at $12,500?"

In this example, Jane's willingness to entertain a "halfway" compromise after already rejecting the original $12,000 offer could be seen as a form of yielding to pressure. By making a concession, even when her original demand was not met, she may inadvertently set the expectation for further concessions in future negotiations. Rather than reinforcing her initial position, she's teaching Russell that her limits are flexible, which could lead to greater demands in the future.

Offers often include intangible elements, such as access to software, trademarks, or know-how that may be essential to your negotiating partner. However, these elements are frequently undervalued precisely because they are intangible. When preparing your offers, always highlight and clearly communicate the unique aspects of what you are offering, even if they seem self-evident. These intangible components often result from significant resource investment, creating a unique value proposition.

When constructing offers—ideally multiple, equivalent ones—always make at least two assumptions. One assumption should exclude intangible elements. This does not mean you are unwilling to grant them but forces your negotiating partner to acknowledge their value.

The Time Factor

In a famous panel discussion with Bill Gates hosted by Charlie Rose on the concept of time, billionaire investor Warren Buffett remarked, "It's the one thing you can't buy. I can buy anything I want, but I can't buy time." This insight applies equally to negotiations: if you're tasked with negotiating an important contract, make sure you allocate enough time to prepare and engage thoughtfully. Avoid rushing, such as by scheduling a same-day round-trip flight to London.

"John, what time is your flight today?"

"Stuart, my flight is tomorrow; we have all the time we need, and if we finish early, I'll take a walk. London is beautiful this season."

Knowing your negotiating partner's deadlines gives you an advantage, especially if they are unaware of yours. The time factor increases pressure, so always assess whether a deadline is real and immovable. While many negotiators set a deadline for concluding the negotiation, nearly all deadlines can be adjusted. Instead of rushing into a bad decision under the pressure of a deadline, consider renegotiating the timeline. If your negotiating partner has invested significant time in the negotiation, they are often more amenable, as the cost of failing to agree becomes a psychological reference point. This is a sunk cost, which logically should not influence decisions, since the expenses are already incurred regardless of the outcome. However, in practice, past investments often condition future decisions.

Negotiations often follow a predictable rhythm: initial momentum slows, then gradually accelerates as the time limit approaches, increasing stress and the likelihood of concessions. Eighty percent of concessions—often unthinkable during initial discussions—occur in the last 20 percent of the negotiation time. Patience pays off, so act when the time is right. When the moment comes, remember that speed and decisiveness are crucial. Seize the opportunity with determination and confidence.

Depending on the situation, time and deadlines can benefit both parties. Knowing how to manage time is essential, as you can press your negotiating partner with openings, promises, and concessions while alternating these with strategic deferrals. However, avoid inducing undue anxiety to conclude, as this can be counterproductive. If your negotiating partner is stalling, consider asking, "What information do you need to be convinced about this transaction?"

Studies indicate that we are more likely to accept offers with a deadline, as they exploit our fear of missing an opportunity. However, not all contexts permit associating a generous offer with a deadline, especially if the deadline is shorter than the time needed to implement an alternative. Allowing too much time, on the other hand, may enable your negotiating partner to strengthen their BATNA.

When the negotiation is going well, there will likely come a time when you feel satisfied with the outcome and decide it's time to conclude. However, your negotiating partner may not share this sentiment. In such cases, it's helpful to signal (without appearing threatening) that there is limited room for further concessions, especially in negotiations with a constant back and forth of offers and counteroffers. This approach is also useful when you know the other party will need to consult internally and is likely to request an additional concession.

Occasionally, you may face a last-minute request for a concession, just when a deal is nearly finalized. Your negotiating partner may introduce an additional condition, banking on your willingness to concede rather than risk undoing the entire agreement after significant time and energy have been invested. This is often a bluff—an unfounded tactic designed to provoke annoyance or embarrassment. Negotiation should be rooted in honesty, so always gather enough information to substantiate what is being claimed. Never agree without securing something in return. If the arrangement was balanced up to that point, introducing a new condition risks upsetting the equilibrium. If your counterpart is acting in good faith, they should be willing to reciprocate.

The book *La Mente di Pinocchio* by Gianfranco Denes (2022) is genuinely incredible. It expertly describes the methods—along with their validity and limitations, both clinical and instrumental—used to identify lies, including the study of the nature and anatomical basis of bona fide lies, confabulations, and false acknowledgments found in language. However, *you* do not lie. Lying is not permissible in negotiation. Ever. There is no need to lie, even when tempted.

The fact that you do not lie, however, does not mean your negotiating partner won't be motivated to do so—perhaps to secure a better deal. But you have prepared well. You have designed a strategy that should discourage your negotiating partner from lying to you. When in doubt, refer to the sources of information you gathered before, during, and after the negotiation. You can ask questions to which you already know the answers or pose cross-referenced questions. Pay close attention to the answers: people who lie often fail to respond in a cohesive, coherent manner. If you suspect a lie, consider using conditional offers. And remember, even if you think your negotiating partner has lied, it's possible they acted in good faith. In such cases, clearly communicate your doubts about what was said. However, if faced with a significant lie that damages trust, you may need to consider ending the negotiation.

In addition to lies, you must be prepared to handle half-truths and omissions. Sometimes, it's more appropriate to offer a willingness to answer alternative questions or politely explain why you do not intend to answer at all. Negotiations are full of peculiarities. After a long discussion, you may feel ready to close, only for your counterpart—perhaps less prepared than they should have been—to want to start negotiations from scratch after acquiring valuable information to improve their position.

By following a sound method, you should be able to avoid such situations. However, if they do arise, redirect the conversation to focus on interests. Make it clear that reopening negotiations risks undoing all the progress made, with no guarantee of reaching a better agreement than the one already on the table. If appropriate, remind them of your strong BATNA.

Sometimes, even when you intend to close a deal, it can be advantageous to give the impression that you're withdrawing. This apparent retreat allows you to maintain control over the negotiation. You can achieve the same effect by withdrawing your offer—especially if you sense the other side is taking advantage of you or pushing for an unprofitable deal.

In some cases, your negotiating partner may intentionally create an issue over a minor detail to distract you, push for a price concession, or use it as leverage to barter for other terms. These interventions are often irrational. Evaluate their claims carefully, and if they lack merit, avoid engaging with them.

If positions remain far apart at the conclusion of a negotiation, you can try leaving the door open by proposing a flexible option. For instance, you might suggest granting your counterpart the right to sell to another buyer if they find one at a lower price. If this arrangement is offered to you, it gives you the opportunity to purchase under better terms without further negotiation, price increases, or concessions.

- Negotiation is instrumental in creating value through agreements that leave both parties better off than they would be without the deal. One of the primary goals of a skilled negotiator is to shift the focus from price to value.

- If negotiation were to be defined algebraically, it could be described as Preparation + Discipline. Discipline involves taking the time to reflect, set goals, establish a schedule to achieve them, and then adhere to that schedule. While preparation is an essential component of successful negotiation, its value lies in the information gathered; those who possess information can control the negotiation. Clear and effective communication is always necessary.

- Emotional labeling is the process of identifying and naming emotions. Recognizing and acknowledging the emotional state of your negotiating partner helps them feel safe, understood, and validated. This approach demonstrates that you are attuned to the emotional aspects of what they are conveying.

- To be effective in negotiation, you must learn to recognize and manage both your own emotions and those of your negotiating partner. Building and maintaining relationships is also critical—not just for the first deal, but for subsequent ones, including new, multiple, renewed, or impromptu agreements.

- Imagination fuels motivation. To be a good storyteller, you must understand the fundamental drivers of human behavior. Stories help engage and motivate others, and they are essential tools in negotiation.

- Always strive to understand power dynamics: Who holds power, and why?

- Shift attention from positions to interests using open-ended, calibrated questions. These questions have emotional impact based on how they are structured, the context in which they are asked, and who is being addressed. Their purpose is to unlock valuable information.

- Options are always abundant and should be analyzed collectively. A good negotiation seeks to satisfy all or most interests. If a better option than your BATNA cannot be found, resort to the alternative—but never rush into it simply due to a lack of alternatives.

- Proposals must always be conditional: you must not give to get, but rather get to give. Always explain clearly what you expect and what actions the other party must take to justify your concessions.

- Pay close attention to smiles, eye contact, tone of voice, and nonverbal language, both your own and your counterpart's.

- If you have prepared well and are targeting a lucrative deal, do not hesitate to submit the first offer. A firm "no," especially when delivered positively, has significant power and should not be feared.

- Learn to handle multiple equivalent and simultaneous offers effectively.

- When faced with an extreme first offer or one far from your reserve price, counter-anchor the negotiation by rejecting the proposal and making an equally assertive counteroffer.

- If your negotiating partner becomes aggressive, rely on your preparation. Deflect threats, utilize silence, and steer the conversation back to shared interests and goals.

- Postpone thorny issues to maintain the flow of negotiations and prevent them from stalling.

- Do not overestimate your negotiating partner's alternatives if your BATNA is strong—it may not be better than yours. Evaluate the quality of their alternatives (if they exist) and remind them of the advantages they would lose if no agreement were reached.

- Reciprocity—the exchange of concessions for mutual benefit—is a powerful and persuasive tool in negotiation. Even small concessions should come with a quid pro quo.

- Concessions typically decrease in size as the reserve value approaches. This pattern signals proximity to the reserve value, offering an essential clue for adjusting your assumptions about the ZOPA.

- Silence is a potent and destabilizing tool; learn to wield it skillfully.
- Contingent agreements—which allow both parties to bet on their beliefs about the future—are a powerful variant of conditional offers.
- Never underestimate the time factor in negotiation. Patience always pays off. Wait to act until the time is right, and when the moment comes, act with speed, skill, determination, and confidence.

Concluding a negotiation, it is like solving a crossword puzzle:
Right words, some wrong, and you'll even come up with some
new ones.

Stephen Colbert

CHAPTER 6

THE AGREEMENT

Closing, Not Closing, Impasse

Do Not Close

Not all negotiations conclude with the outcome intended by the parties: agreement.

Negotiation is full of hurdles, and persistence is crucial. Stay focused on achieving the fateful handshake, even when progress is slow or setbacks arise.

When a negotiation appears to have reached an impasse, negative emotions often arise, especially when it seems the deal may fall apart. These feelings can lead to resentment on both sides. If you do not achieve the desired result, consider reaching an agreement on disagreement. This is not a play on words but a mature and conscious tactic. It can be helpful to openly and transparently clarify the reasons for the negotiation's failure. Despite thorough preparation and a strong start, a deal may not materialize. The goal here is not to assign blame but to investigate the origins of the failure. For example, differing motivations, strong BATNAs on one or both sides, a poor relationship leading to low cooperation, or an ineffective process could have played a role. This clarification can be beneficial should you return to negotiations in the future (leaving the door open when you leave the table) or if preserving the relationship is a priority.

Even if a single negotiation fails, safeguarding the relationship is vital to avoid precluding future opportunities. If the negotiation is not permanently closed, a calm discussion about progress made can lay a solid foundation for resuming talks at a later date. It may even be useful to schedule the next meeting immediately, defining tasks for each party to complete beforehand to ensure a smoother and more productive future discussion.

Impasse

When you have properly prepared and analyzed your five core concerns, you can approach impasses with confidence and mindfulness, avoiding actions that might hurt your negotiating partner's feelings. This awareness is especially critical during the pivotal moments of a stalemate.

If you find yourself at a dead-end, remain calm and trust in your ability to find a way out.

Rely on your preparatory work, stay open-minded, and continue exploring creative solutions.

For instance, consider changing the meeting location—moving to your negotiating partner's office or a neutral space can sometimes shift the dynamics and open new avenues for dialogue. While it might seem counterintuitive, such a strategy has proven effective in certain situations. Additionally, reassess the composition of your negotiating team, including your own role. Involving a trusted mediator—someone respected by both parties—can help navigate particularly challenging obstacles. If needed, take a break to summarize what has been agreed upon so far. This practice not only highlights progress but also reinforces how close you are to reaching an overall agreement, fostering a more positive atmosphere.

Negotiation, especially in high-stakes deals, can be an addictive process where leaving the table feels like admitting defeat. This mindset, however, can undermine your negotiating power. It's essential to acknowledge your emotions and consider the potential regret you might feel if you walk away. When faced with such moments, I find it helpful to ask what an impartial observer—someone detached and unemotional—would do in my position. Answering this question honestly and acting with the same level of detachment and rationality can provide clarity and preserve your confidence.

In negotiations, mindfulness, preparation, and flexibility are your greatest assets. By staying grounded in your core concerns and being willing to adapt your approach, you can overcome even the most challenging impasses and move closer to a mutually beneficial resolution.

Close

Closing a negotiation involves as much science and art as the preparation, initiation, and execution. Reaching this stage indicates that you have successfully navigated complex situations, as many negotiations end up stalled with no resolution.

In the closing phase, results, relationships, and commitments arising from the agreement are closely intertwined. It is crucial to take the time to ensure that no interests have been overlooked, even when time feels scarce. Sometimes, one party must make a concession to finalize the deal. Be cautious not to overextend yourself; instead, carefully choose which variable to concede and ensure it is perceived as deliberate. This approach gives the impression that your concession is thoughtful and strategic, rather than a sign of weakness.

How do you maximize the benefits of a meeting? How do you conclude it efficiently? How do you formalize an agreement? If you use a Terms Sheet, share the final agreement in the right-hand column with the negotiating partner. If not, provide a verbal summary of what was agreed upon. Since you've already done this after every significant step in the negotiation, this final step should be straightforward. However, avoid risking the progress you've made by assuming that what's been said will magically translate into action and concrete results. People's perceptions and memories often differ, and documenting the agreement avoids future disputes and unnecessary delays.

A shared draft agreement is particularly helpful, especially if finalized by an attorney. This draft serves as the bridge between the virtual and real worlds, turning discussions into binding commitments. Attention to relational aspects is critical at this stage to ensure the negotiation concludes amicably and with a foundation for good future relations. A positive indicator is when the conclusion of the agreement brings about such relief and satisfaction that both parties feel inclined to celebrate. However, not all agreements end on such a high note. Tensions may arise, especially if the parties have differing levels of willingness to bring the negotiation to a close or if compromises leave one or both sides feeling less than euphoric about the outcome.

In either case, organizing an informal session to return to a more interpersonal space is essential. This ritual can take many forms: a celebratory toast with champagne, a formal signing ceremony, commemorative photographs, or something more understated, like a casual dinner or drinks. The specific format may vary based on individual preferences, but the overarching goal remains the same: to solidify and strengthen the relationship for the future.

During the negotiation, the relationship likely passed through various stages: exchanges of ideas, moments of tension, and differences of opinion. Ultimately, the parties reached an agreement, perhaps even when it seemed unlikely. It is crucial to reflect on this shared journey, address any lingering disappointments, and, if possible, celebrate a mutual victory over a shared challenge. There have been instances where I achieved a fantastic deal but chose to remain measured in my response because my focus was always on what came next.

Let me share a story from one of the most intricate negotiations I've ever experienced. It was with a long-standing partner—someone I considered not just a business ally, but also a close friend. The stakes were high: we were finalizing a multi-million-dollar agreement with the potential to reshape the future of our industry. Yet, one issue kept surfacing: a seemingly small but contentious point about the timeline for delivery.

We'd reached an impasse. While the details might have seemed trivial to some, they had come to represent the deeper differences in our priorities. My partner wanted to shorten the timeline to maximize short-term cash flow, while I was focused on ensuring uncompromised product quality, which required more time.

This was the moment where the art of closing became critical. I realized it was time to make a strategic concession—not out of weakness, but as a calculated move to break the deadlock. I offered a compromise: agreeing to meet my partner almost half-way on the timeline, but with one key condition—introducing substantial performance incentives for hitting quality milestones.

The room fell silent. My partner leaned back, took a deep breath, and looked at me intently. Then he smiled and said, "You didn't just give me that for free, did you?"

I smiled back and replied, "No, but I'm confident it'll work out for both of us."

That moment was one of tension, but also clarity. The concession wasn't a mere gesture—it was a deliberate, strategic choice that created value for both sides without compromising my primary goal. It solidified not just the deal, but also our relationship moving forward.

We quickly moved to formalize the agreement. Using a Terms Sheet, which had been prepared earlier and reviewed by our respective legal teams, we finalized the details with mutual satisfaction. The final signature wasn't just the end of a transaction; it was a culmination of trust, shared effort, and strategic thinking.

To mark the occasion, we didn't just shake hands and walk away. We hosted a small dinner, surrounded by close team members. The evening was filled with laughter, stories, and reflections on how far we'd come—not just in the negotiation, but in our relationship over the years. That night, we celebrated the agreement, but we also celebrated our partnership, knowing that this was just the beginning of an even more significant collaboration.

The best deals are those where neither party overcommits themselves or others—whether it's incurring an unmanageable loan, producing beyond capacity, or purchasing something unnecessary. Consider the close of a successful negotiation not as the end but as the beginning of a strong partnership. Continue to work with the negotiating partner until the agreement is fully implemented.

In my university days, on cold winter evenings, we often played Risk—a strategy board game of world domination—after a hearty meal of cream and frankfurter macaroni. Stefano won more often than the rest of us—whether because of superior strategy or just sheer luck with the dice, who knows? But in the days that followed, he never missed an opportunity to remind us of his victory. Don't behave like Stefano. Avoid gloating and remain humble, even when closing major contracts. If you're not modest and gracious, your negotiating partners may actively work against you in the future, even at their own expense. Humility goes a long way in fostering trust and goodwill for the next deal.

Multiparty Negotiations
and Post-Settlement Settlement

Multiparty Negotiations

Multiparty negotiations are more common than you might think. They arise not only in the workplace and business settings but also in family dynamics, friendships, and even leisure activities. Dividing an inheritance, deciding where to go on vacation (or even just for dinner), choosing a supplier, or setting annual performance bonuses with unions are just a few examples of multiparty negotiations. These scenarios involve more people, which means more problems, more interests, and more potential solutions. Consequently, communication dynamics become more challenging and complex.

As I explained in Chapter 4, coalitions often form during multiparty negotiations. These coalitions shift as the negotiation progresses, creating conflicts that can hinder the negotiation's development, making it unpredictable and difficult to manage. I have handled quite a few such negotiations, and by following some of my suggestions, you can increase your chances of achieving a positive outcome. The elements to consider during preparation are identical to those in two-party negotiations. However, the task becomes more demanding due to the greater number of parties involved. This requires better organization and careful consideration of potential coalitions. The same applies to the tools employed in the process.

A well-defined agenda is crucial, and the group should appoint a leader to act as a moderator. This person ensures that the diverse perspectives of all parties at the table are adequately represented. Once the framework is established, the group can proceed to the actual negotiation phase, in which participants seek solutions using classic methods. Significant conflicts are typical in these scenarios, and this is where the moderator's role is critical. Their job is to defuse emotionally charged situations and manage participants' behavior, including tone of voice and disrespectful language, to keep everyone focused on achieving the best consensus.

Once the group selects a solution, it develops and implements an action plan. Framing is vital at this stage because individual parties' perceptions strongly influence the choices and outcomes of the negotiation. Attempts at cooperation can easily be misunderstood. Coalition building is inevitable in most multiparty negotiations and often occurs before the negotiation itself during informal meetings. Groups with similar interests are likely to join forces, but these coalitions are inherently unstable because they are based on interests that may change during the negotiation. When interests shift, the atmosphere often becomes competitive and defensive.

Focusing on communication is key. Start by agreeing on clear problem-solving procedures to provide structure to the discussion. Actively listen to each other's perspectives, offering constructive feedback that fosters trust and collaboration. Encourage the exploration of creative, out-of-the-box ideas to uncover innovative solutions. The ultimate goal is to establish a ZOPA (zone of possible agreement), allowing participants to transition from a competitive to a cooperative mindset. By understanding that collaboration facilitates mutual success, participants can work toward solutions that surpass everyone's BATNA, even if a perfect outcome isn't guaranteed.

With the help of a moderator, establishing ground rules is critical to determining how the group will choose the best proposal. To simplify these negotiations, it can be helpful to break them into a series of two-party negotiations, regardless of the number of players involved. This approach helps streamline the process while maintaining focus on the overall goals.

Post-settlement Settlement (PSS)

To think that you went through so much trouble to reach an agreement, only to decide to start a new negotiation—it sounds like a crazy idea. Actually, it's not. In a well-executed negotiation, multiple stages create value through partial outcomes that come together to form a more significant overall deal. If, in the end, there's a chance to improve overall efficiency and enhance the agreement, the idea may be far from wild.

How many times, after leaving the bargaining table, have you thought, *If only I had…*, realizing that some value had been left on the table? You might have reflected that, given another chance to negotiate, you could have achieved a better, different deal. This has happened to me countless times, until I learned how to use post-settlement settlement (PSS) effectively. Daylian Cain, through his insights at the Yale School of Management, opened my eyes and mind to this concept. However, I first grasped the mechanism by reading *The Art and Science of Negotiation: How to Resolve Conflicts and Get the Best Out of Bargaining* by Howard Raiffa (1985). The ultimate goal of negotiation isn't merely to reach an agreement—it's to achieve the best possible deal, the optimal point that increases one party's satisfaction without diminishing the other's.

In day-to-day practice, we often assume that the agreement reached is the best possible solution. Naturally, you want to return to the hotel, take a hot shower, and celebrate. However, the agreement should be seen as a starting point for building even better arrangements. Though it's rare, imagine concluding a negotiation and then, with pen in hand, asking your counterpart, "Is there a way to make this better for both of us?" This can only be done after reaching an initial agreement, because the psychological pressure diminishes at that point, enabling relaxed and creative thinking.

During the negotiation process, multiple forces—chiefly emotions—often prevent you from negotiating at your best or achieving the optimal outcome. Once the parties have secured what they desired, you can approach subsequent discussions with greater confidence. The logic is akin to evaluating the BATNA: you begin by identifying an alternative, then you work to improve it until you reach the limit of what's possible. Similarly, once you've reached a good agreement, it creates a bond between the parties. This bond ensures the initial agreement is secure and won't be questioned.

"Mr. Gabrielsen, I am thoroughly pleased with our work and the results. There were some critical moments that demonstrated how much we both care about this collaboration, but we overcame them, and your contribution, along with your team's, was crucial. I thank you for that. The Terms Sheet we've just finalized will be submitted to our lawyers next Monday for drafting the formal contract. However, before that happens, I have a proposal for you. Without altering what we've agreed upon—which is not in question and cannot be changed—I'd like to consider digging even deeper into our motivations. Let's think outside the box and explore new options to arrive at a deal that's even better for both of us. An optimal arrangement!"

"Thank you for proposing this, Pietro. I had the same idea as you. Let's keep the Terms Sheet on hold. When can we meet? For us, even Thursday or Friday next week would work, if that's okay with you."

It is not necessary to reopen the negotiation immediately after closing it. You can take some time—sleep on it, wait a few days, a week, or whatever period feels appropriate. It is important to recognize that there are options the parties can explore differently and that additional value can still be created and shared. The first agreement provides a sense of security, enabling the parties to build upon what was already agreed. This allows them to negotiate more calmly and productively, uncovering new and creative solutions as they delve deeper into their interests and motivations. At this stage, parties are often more open to sharing information, creating opportunities for better outcomes. The conditions become more favorable for integration and collaboration.

If you think about it, the BATNA for both parties is the agreement they already reached. At worst, they will revert to that original deal; at best, they will achieve an improved outcome for both sides. In the worst-case scenario, the parties implement the initial agreement. In the best case, they reach a super agreement with positive implications for their relationship.

Whenever I discuss this technique, I notice that it is new and unfamiliar to many, and often perceived as unconventional. The most frequent questions I receive are about whether this approach risks renegotiating the original deal or whether it truly delivers tangible benefits.

To the first question, my answer is no—the original negotiation remains frozen and untouched, serving as the BATNA for both parties. To the second, I respond that there can only be real benefits from this technique. If no additional value is discovered, the original agreement is still intact, ensuring that nothing is lost.

I personally love it! The post-settlement settlement (PSS) is a powerful tool that allows negotiators to revisit agreements and identify opportunities for greater value, long after the initial deal has been made. While unconventional, it holds the potential to turn a good deal into a great one. By recognizing the possibility for improvement and fostering a mindset of continuous collaboration, you can create outcomes that benefit everyone involved, strengthening both the deal and the relationship. In the end, the real art of negotiation lies not just in reaching an agreement, but in continuously seeking better solutions—even after the ink has dried.

- Even when you do not close a deal, make a genuine effort to investigate thoroughly and understand the reasons behind the failure.

- If you find yourself at a seeming dead-end, remain calm and confident in your ability to overcome it. Rely on your preparatory work, stay open-minded and flexible, continue researching, and devise creative solutions.

- In the closing phase of a negotiation, results, relationships, and commitments arising from the agreement become closely intertwined.

- When bargaining involves multiple participants, the complexity increases due to more problems, interests, and potential solutions, making communication dynamics more challenging.

- In multiparty negotiations, encourage the participants to shift from a competitive to a cooperative mindset. Help them understand that collaboration makes it easier for everyone to achieve their goals.

- If, after reaching a final agreement, there is an opportunity to improve overall efficiency and enhance the understanding achieved, starting a new negotiation to refine the agreement is a plausible and worthwhile idea.

You didn't win the race, if by winning the race
you have lost the respect of your competitors.

Paul Elvström

CHAPTER 7

DEBRIEFING

Thank You for the Feedback

Boom!

A cannon blast sounds from the race committee boat, confirming that we've won the regatta and the world championship. Onboard, excitement rises as the tension dissipates. The helmsman hugs those nearby, others exchange high-fives, and once the euphoria of victory subsides, some begin lowering the jib. The bow is cleaned, and the mainsail is lowered and folded neatly.

"Well done, Pietro! I was afraid it was a little tight when you called the last layline,[47] but you nailed it," Tiziano, the tactician, tells me. The engine starts as the boat bears away and heads toward the harbor. "Guys, debriefing in five minutes. Then we'll clean the boat, and the chase boat will arrive with food, so anyone who wants can grab a bite to eat," Tiziano adds.

At sea, I learned that not every day is a good one. Some days were marred by avoidable mistakes due to a lack of coordination, leaving us looking like novices. After each regatta—whether successful or not—we would review the critical moments, the maneuvers we executed, and the decisions we made. Together, we'd reflect on what had prompted certain choices and identify ways to improve, especially where things didn't go as planned. Despite my own mistakes, I contributed to the success of several crews. Sailing alongside professional sailors taught me to be methodical and to build proper routines, habits I've applied in everyday life.

47   In sailboat racing, a layline is an imaginary line from a mark that indicates where a boat must tack or gybe to round the mark on the correct side—weather side when upwind, leeward side when downwind—determined by wind direction and sailing angle.

In work, particularly in negotiation, I've tried to be just as systematic. Once a negotiation concludes and the parties meet for one or more PSS sessions, one of the most rewarding aspects of the *Incontro* method begins. A Japanese proverb wisely states, "Sometimes you win, every other time you learn." By paying close attention to every action, you create an opportunity to learn continuously, regardless of the outcome.

In sports and other "finite games" (as Simon Sinek (2019) aptly describes in *The Infinite Game*), the players are known, the rules fixed, the goals clear, and winners and losers easily identified. In contrast, "infinite games"—such as business or life itself—feature ever-changing players, evolving rules, and no definitive short-term goal.

In negotiation, the rules are fluid. There are no definitive winners or losers—concepts like "winning the business" or "winning the negotiation" are illusions. Instead, there are those who advance and those who fall slightly behind, much like a race with no finish line. I've always felt uneasy about instant gratification and participating in finite games, even though I recognize how pervasive this mindset has become globally. I gravitate toward infinite games, which I've come to appreciate and prioritize.

I aim to build and contribute to long-term, sustainable initiatives, valuing lasting impacts over fleeting victories. Unfortunately, I've often faced pressure from analysts and investors driven by quarterly or monthly expectations, demanding short-term results.

Over the years, I've realized that many organizational challenges stem from leaders approaching an infinite game with a finite mindset. This approach often stifles innovation, motivation, and performance. Conversely, I've also met leaders who embrace an infinite vision, building strong, innovative, and inspired businesses.

Ultimately, I've come to see how deeply intertwined leadership and negotiation are. Those who continuously improve these skills foster trust among colleagues and managers, creating resilient organizations capable of thriving in an ever-changing world.

An agreement not reached is not a failure but rather the result of a process—a choice, not a defeat—because you selected the best alternative to the negotiated deal. A good contract is not necessarily an absolute win; it may indicate you could have prepared or negotiated better. Negotiation skills are not acquired overnight; they require continuous refinement. You won't get bored, and you'll never stop learning. Some negotiations yield better outcomes when you develop a method or style, and your learning curve will fluctuate during your evolutionary journey. When the negotiation ends, you have the opportunity to reflect, learn, internalize the experience, and share it with others, applying what you've learned to similar situations, scenarios, and contexts in the future.

Having worked in several multinational companies and participated in many critical negotiations, I've observed that participants often neglect to analyze the talks immediately after they conclude. Groups frequently fail to conduct debriefings after negotiations, which is a significant oversight. By skipping this step, they miss a valuable opportunity to improve future talks. The truth is that not everyone is aware of the immense learning potential available in these moments. There are countless free lessons waiting to be recognized, harnessed, and applied. Once a negotiation concludes, the insights are fresh, clear, and rich. However, they quickly fade unless documented and incorporated into future guidelines.

Personally, whenever I've had the chance—especially when leading organizations—I've worked to cultivate a genuine "culture of negotiation." This included continuously monitoring and evaluating my team's capabilities, providing dedicated training, sharing real experiences (such as case studies), and learning from both positive and negative outcomes. I've consistently found that this approach fosters specific expertise, enriching the group's collective knowledge and experience.

Regardless of the negotiation type, stakes, context, or counterparts, I've made it a routine to dedicate at least thirty minutes (or more, if needed) after each negotiation for reflection. Whether alone or with the team involved, I document everything—lessons learned, skills demonstrated, mistakes made, and new ideas or reflections. These notes are always valuable, including those from an external observer, if present.

Each team member's contribution is crucial because everyone constructs their own "map" of the negotiation, which is not the same as the "territory"—the objective reality of what occurred. Everyone has their perspective, interpretation, and subjective understanding of what they saw, heard, said, and felt. These distinct points of view provide a rich diversity of insights but do not always align with the objective events.

Reflecting on what happened is a critical opportunity that should always be seized. If you can't persuade your colleagues to participate—perhaps due to fear of judgment or criticism—conduct the debriefing yourself. Never skip this step. It should be a thoughtful, articulate, and neutral critique, free of prejudices or superficial judgments. Prejudices often target people, while judgments, though aimed at events or actions, can sometimes be used to undermine individuals indirectly.

Process Analysis

The ultimate goal of analyzing a negotiation is to critique the process, not the people, and to learn. The focus must remain on the facts, decoupling them from individuals. Learning requires meticulously examining every aspect of the negotiation. I find it helpful to analyze the entire process, starting with the choice of location and timing, and ending with the agenda. This includes evaluating how the agenda was constructed, shared, and utilized, whether the parties adhered to it effectively, and how well the various points were managed.

I also examine how timing, pacing, and the use of breaks influenced the negotiation. Were sufficient time and resources allocated to achieve the goals, test different strategies, and explore alternative outcomes? I reflect on what worked well, what didn't, what could have been handled better, and what could have been approached differently. I distinguish between what **could** have been done in hindsight and what **can** be done in the future. From past experiences, we learn to shape future outcomes.

The agenda also ties closely to negotiating styles. I consider what we learned about the opposing negotiator's style and whether they implemented strategies for which we were unprepared or which we failed to anticipate. Developing standardized agendas can help avoid starting from scratch for every negotiation. Additionally, I evaluate how the use of the Terms Sheet contributed to the process and identify areas for improvement.

I begin my analysis by carefully reviewing what my negotiating partner did well. I ask why I perceive certain actions as "good," digging deep to understand the reasoning behind their behavior. This helps identify the best strategies for handling similar situations in future negotiations. Conversely, I consider what the negotiating partner did poorly, what they could have done differently, and the potential consequences of alternative actions. The method remains consistent: always question why things happen and investigate the motivations behind behaviors.

After this phase, I turn to evaluate my own team's performance, including my own. I assess whether the preparation time was adequate and whether additional time would have improved our negotiation. I aim to eliminate regrets and uncertainties, focusing on how preparation could have been enhanced, whether I was sufficiently knowledgeable about each agenda item, and whether the quality of preparation instilled the necessary confidence. As I often say, and will repeat, preparation time is never enough.

Confidence in preparation is critical; it is one of the keys to a successful outcome. Studies show that only 19 percent of negotiators lacking confidence succeed in achieving their goals. Therefore, it's useful—especially during post-negotiation discussions—to gauge the team's actual confidence. Some team members may initially claim that they spent enough time preparing and that additional effort wouldn't have yielded better results. However, deeper probing often reveals that preparation, planning, and strategy development could have been more thorough, which might have affected their confidence.

During this analysis, I assess whether a lack of confidence stems from gaps in specific skills. If so, I note these deficiencies and work to fill them, whether they are mine or those of other team members, to enhance future capabilities. I also evaluate whether the team was well suited to the negotiation, considering the diversity of knowledge, creativity, problem-solving skills, and ability to create value. Additionally, I consider whether better alternatives for team roles existed within the organization.

This stage of critique is sensitive, as it involves evaluating the team's performance. Criticism must be constructive and focused on behaviors, not individuals. For example, avoid saying, "Remember when you responded to John's offer? You were rude." This sounds like a personal attack. Instead, frame it as, "When you responded to John's offer, you interrupted him and didn't let him finish. This is likely to be perceived as rude." This shifts the focus to behavior rather than the person. If criticism doesn't address specific behaviors, it becomes destructive and should not be expressed—nor, indeed, even entertained—as it is neither constructive nor meaningful.

Finally, I assess whether the information gathered about the negotiating partner was accurate and complete. I consider what additional information would have been helpful to improve the outcome. This reflective process ensures continuous improvement and better preparation for future negotiations.

I am always mindful of the impact that biases, generalizations, and premature judgments can have on the negotiation process. Cognitive biases, which often result in mental shortcuts and systematic errors, can significantly influence decision-making and negotiation outcomes. Consequently, I ask myself whether unclear or insufficiently defined situations caused me (or us) to react hastily. I also reflect on whether unconscious biases or premature judgments, based on incomplete arguments or indirect knowledge, may have played a role.

Such situations are more common than one might think. For instance, when relying on intuition to make quick decisions, biases can lead to a lack of objectivity or misjudgments. By conducting a thorough post-negotiation analysis, you can become more aware of these tendencies, enabling smarter and more accurate decision-making in the future. I strive to identify discrepancies between the interests, needs, and options assessed during preparation and those encountered during the negotiation, tracing their evolution and reflecting on areas for improvement. This includes evaluating the effectiveness of questions—both open and closed—that were used to uncover the negotiating partner's interests and brainstorming options. I also ask whether I fully tapped into my creativity and encouraged the same from my negotiating partner.

Often, post-negotiation analysis reveals questions we could have asked during the negotiation, questions that might have yielded critical information about the other party's interests and needs or generated ideas for new options. It's important to reflect on this missed opportunity. Calculate the ratio of time spent speaking to that spent listening—it should ideally be less than one. As Zeno famously said, "Two ears, one mouth." Additionally, consider whether tone of voice, silence, nonverbal language, and smiling were effectively used. Assess if there were any communication barriers, such as language issues, that affected the negotiation.

After examining interests, I evaluate the quality and quantity of information available, the alternatives considered, the fairness of the agreement reached, and the level of commitment involved. I mentally review the negotiation, consult the preparatory materials, and identify areas for improvement. If I made the first offer, I ask whether I was in a strong position to do so, how aggressive the offer was, and how effectively I defended it.

I also assess whether the anchor worked as intended and consider what could have been done to make it stronger or more resilient. If the negotiating partner attempted a counter-anchor, I analyze my response and its effectiveness. Additionally, I review the use of simultaneous equivalent multiple offer proposals, their timing, and the inclusion of non-monetary offers or requests. These reflections often reveal new information or value, leading me to approach the negotiating partner for a post-settlement session. Such insights alone justify the time spent on a debrief. Many completed negotiations, regardless of the agreement reached, still hold untapped value. A thorough thirty-minute analysis, even involving multiple people, is a small investment relative to the potential benefits it can uncover.

I also evaluate the negotiation framework. A common mistake is treating the reserve value (RV) or the zone of possible agreement (ZOPA) defined during preparation as fixed reference points. Both parameters are useful starting points, but they are not static. RV and ZOPA often require revision during the negotiation, especially when new information becomes available. If these values shift (and they often do), it is essential to update them and measure how much additional value could have been captured.

By adopting this reflective and adaptive approach, you can continuously refine your negotiation skills and strategies, ensuring better outcomes in future discussions.

I analyze the work done on the BATNA (both mine and the negotiating partner's) and assess how it evolved, if at all, during the negotiation. This evaluation is particularly fascinating in cases where no agreement is reached, whether due to our own choice (having a better alternative to the negotiated agreement) or the negotiating partner's decision. In both instances, the analysis should determine whether our choice was the correct one and, in light of additional evidence, whether a post-settlement session could be proposed to the negotiating partner. This review should also include elements related to the relationship—comparing trust, esteem, and the overall relationship dynamic before and after the negotiation. Factors such as commitment to joint problem-solving and effective management of differences are also crucial considerations.

Once this has been evaluated, I focus on the equally significant role of emotions. I document the emotions experienced during the negotiation, linking them to specific contexts, situations, and events—similar to analyzing a football game. In team negotiations, I use a double-entry matrix to define key moments collectively. Then, each participant independently lists the emotions they felt, both positive and negative. These lists are subsequently compared within the negotiating group, often yielding fascinating insights due to differing reactions to the same stimulus. To assist this process, I use a comprehensive and continually updated checklist of hundreds of emotions (both positive and negative). Positive emotions often stem from procedural aspects, such as fair negotiation practices or favorable social comparisons, while negative emotions frequently result in adverse negotiation outcomes. I vividly recall creating my first list of emotions—it was astonishing to realize how many distinct emotions could be identified and described with precision.

This emotional analysis is vital because, although strong negative emotions can be costly, not all emotions impact negotiations negatively. Positive emotions can facilitate better outcomes, and even anxiety or nervousness can sometimes be channeled productively. I also examine the core concerns of appreciation, autonomy, affiliation, status, and role, asking targeted questions and comparing the answers to preparatory materials. This helps me evaluate whether the information and strategies employed during the negotiation effectively addressed emotions. If they did not, I identify the causes, update my negotiating partner's profile, and use this information for future negotiations or post-settlement settlement (PSS). Over the years, I have increasingly emphasized the analysis of core concerns, as it provides critical insights into the emotional dynamics at play.

Finally, when an agreement is reached, I review who initiated it, whether it was achieved too early or too late, and the underlying reasons. Over time, I have found that this systematic approach has significantly enhanced my preparation. By focusing on emotional dynamics, I have become more adept at interpreting emotions, which are a crucial component of negotiations. After all, negotiation is a process consisting of individual activities that transform inputs into outputs of greater value. Like any series of events, negotiation can be improved, streamlined, and made more effective. It is no surprise that the logic of continuous improvement can also be applied to negotiations—with extraordinary results.

In my approach, I plan, record, analyze, and act following an improvement cycle widely known as "PDCA" (Plan, Do, Check, Act). Originally developed by Walter A. Shewhart and later refined and popularized by William Edwards Deming—a renowned engineer, lecturer, and consultant—this cycle is a powerful framework for continuous improvement. It aligns perfectly with the goal of consistently striving to be the best version of oneself. I maintain a digital archive that grows increasingly comprehensive, meaningful, and valuable for future negotiations. For many years, all my preparatory materials, notes, and post-negotiation analyses have been consolidated into a single digital repository, meticulously structured for easy reference. This practice constitutes step seven of my method and has proven invaluable in enhancing the effectiveness of my negotiations.

- If you pay close attention to everything you do, you can always learn, regardless of the outcome.

- In many organizations, difficulties often stem from leaders approaching an infinite game with a finite mindset. This approach hinders opportunities for innovation, motivation, and performance.

- Whatever the negotiation's outcome, once it concludes, you have the chance to reflect, learn, and apply those lessons to similar situations, scenarios, and contexts in the future.

- The truth is that few people fully grasp the immense learning potential available to them. Once the negotiation ends, the knowledge gained is fresh, clear, and rich, but it quickly fades if not captured and analyzed.

- At the end of each negotiation, I dedicate at least thirty minutes (or more, if needed) to reflection, either alone or with the entire team involved.

- Make it a habit to debrief independently as well. Never skip this step. And remember that it should always be a time for thoughtful, articulate, and neutral critique.

- The ultimate goal is to critique the process, not the people.

- I strive to distinguish between two perspectives: what I could have done and what I can do; and what we could have done and what we can do. From the past—unchangeable now— you learn lessons to shape and improve the future.

- Confidence in preparation is crucial; it is one of the key factors behind a successful outcome.

- Many completed negotiations, regardless of the agreement reached, still hold untapped value. This alone is a compelling reason to invest time in debriefing.

*Leadership is about three-fourths show-the-way
and about one-fourth follow-up.*

James E. Faust

CHAPTER 8

FOLLOW-UP

It Was Nice, Let's Talk

Closing a negotiation or reaching an agreement is not the end of the negotiation process—it marks the beginning of a series of activities aimed at reinforcing and confirming what has been achieved. Follow-up is a delicate and critical element of the negotiation process. Even after an agreement is reached, you cannot fully relax, as the journey is not yet complete. Prompt follow-up is essential, as it keeps the relationship alive and reduces the risk of second-guessing.

I still recall a significant transaction with Nan-Ya Plastic Corporation (a division of the Formosa Plastics conglomerate) that I witnessed as an observer. An Italian family-owned company had reached an agreement for about €100 million. The Taiwanese group was thrilled about the strategic purchase, which would establish a production site in Europe. Similarly, the seller was satisfied, seeing his life's work secure and ensuring his employees and business were in good hands. However, the agreement unraveled the following day after the owner had reconsidered overnight. Despite the Asians' efforts to persuade him to uphold the deal, they were unsuccessful.

At this stage, the Terms Sheet becomes a crucial tool. Sharing it at the end of the meeting ensures clarity—ideally, it should be read aloud, projected in the meeting room, or shared remotely. Complement this document with your notes and photos of any flipcharts or digital charts used during the discussion. Send these materials via email the same day or, at the latest, the next day, requesting a review and agreement. Trust me, the world is full of "Guillaume Carpentiers" and "Yannick Cartons"—the forgetful and the cunning.

The Terms Sheet is valuable for any negotiation, not just those requiring formal agreements. It outlines the agreed terms and mutual commitments, serving as a reminder and a starting point for assigning tasks, defining timeframes, and delegating responsibilities. When sharing the document, make it clear that it accurately reflects what was discussed and agreed upon. Take this opportunity to thank the negotiating partner and their team. As with the agenda and the first offer, maintaining control is essential—by being the first to send the Terms Sheet, you shape the narrative and establish a foundation for the next steps, ensuring alignment with your objectives.

In complex negotiations, you likely updated colleagues not present at the table, such as shareholders, the board of directors, the CFO, the COO, or legal advisors. Once an agreement is reached, a formal step is necessary to ensure everyone is aligned. Documentation used during the negotiation becomes invaluable for explaining the agreement's terms, interests, and benchmarks. Be prepared to answer questions—sometimes as a formality, but other times to persuade stakeholders and sell the agreement.

I often use the terms "agreement" and "contract" interchangeably. Both represent the coming together of two or more parties agreeing to pursue a common goal or action. However, a contract is typically more formal, written with specific templates and legal language. As a negotiator, my focus is on developing and reaching an agreement, leaving the task of drafting the formal contract to lawyers and specialists.

The sequence is clear to me: negotiation, agreement, and contract. In this progression, the Terms Sheet is an effective tool for any negotiation, particularly for complex, detailed agreements where unpredictability is expected. Such agreements often devote numerous pages to premises and definitions alone. Just as I was writing these pages, I received a forty-six-page contract from a client for a comparable transaction, which closely resembled a sixteen-page contract I had reviewed only days earlier. These documents should be concise, covering the agreement's main points—no more and no less. For instance, my employment agreement with the conglomerate Charoen Pokphand Group spanned just two pages with 1.5 line spacing. Despite its brevity, it served its purpose: making the parties legally bound, clarifying expectations, and ensuring remedies were available if terms were not met.

Many people view contracts with apprehension, seeing them as burdensome, intimidating, overly technical, tedious, and expensive. Consequently, some avoid them altogether, opting instead for informal agreements, like my grandfather Ferrante (born in 1899), who bought plots of farmland with just a handshake and a glass of good Sangiovese.[48] Some entrepreneurs treat contracts as mere formalities, while others believe written agreements matter only if something goes wrong. However, contracts are strategic tools that, when used thoughtfully, can strengthen relationships with customers, employees, contractors, vendors, suppliers, business partners, and service providers.

I view contracts as written relationships forming a legal bond between two or more parties. A good, well-drafted contract establishes the relationship, clarifies expectations, defines obligations, and helps avoid misunderstandings. Everyone appreciates knowing what to expect from a relationship, and a well-written agreement fosters trust from the outset. I am particularly cautious of interlocutors who insist on inserting a clause while reassuring me that it's merely a formality and will never be used. My response is simple: if it's unnecessary and will never be used, why include it?

If you want to succeed in negotiations, maintaining strong relationships is crucial. If even minor agreements require written clarification, it may indicate a weak relationship. In any context—negotiations included—building and nurturing good relationships is the key to success.

"Dr. Parmeggiani, I don't understand what you're asking. This is a standard contract," Marina, a real estate agent, once told me

---

48   Sangiovese is a red grape variety originating from Italy, specifically from the Tuscany region. While it's famous for wines like Chianti and Brunello di Montalcino, it is also widely planted in Romagna, where it is less internationally known. Sangiovese wines are characterized by high acidity, firm tannins, and flavors of cherry and plum, making them great companions to Italian cuisine, especially pasta with tomato-based sauces.

impatiently. Many real estate agents (and other service providers) rely on standard contracts, which outline predefined terms and conditions while leaving blank fields to accommodate specifics. These rigid templates often appear intimidating. In reality, such contracts can be modified by adding or deleting items as needed, provided both parties agree to and accept the changes, typically by initialing the margins.

Regardless of the negotiation, the success of the agreement hinges on the sharing and involvement of all parties as the agreement takes shape. This collaborative approach significantly increases the likelihood of success. However, even after an agreement is reached, the journey is not complete. The next step—implementation—is just as delicate. At this stage, it's essential to define what will be done, by whom, when, and how. This final phase encapsulates the essence of the negotiation and ensures that all the effort invested in reaching the agreement translates into tangible action.

To ensure the success of the agreement, it is crucial to inform everyone involved in its execution about the negotiated terms and the rationale behind the understanding reached. Consider what you have learned about your negotiating partner, particularly their interests. You do not necessarily need to share the entire document, as it may contain sensitive elements or be too complex for some to follow. Instead, a concise explanation in bullet points will suffice and be more effective.

Take the time to clarify the critical aspects of the negotiation process you just completed. This step can provide you and others with valuable insights to highlight and manage potential issues. Be prepared to answer any questions on the topics discussed and remain open to comments and criticisms from others—even to the extent of actively encouraging it. Such feedback is always valuable. For instance, if your request for penalties for late deliveries meets resistance, this may indicate that the supplier fears they might struggle to meet the agreed deadlines.

In such cases, being reasonable and proactive is essential. Analyze the potential risks and challenges, and develop a plan to mitigate them. This approach allows you to address the unexpected and anticipate future problems effectively. Additionally, it can be beneficial to introduce members of your organization who will need to interact with counterparts in the other organization. Scheduling meetings to monitor and analyze the contract's progress will further enhance collaboration and ensure smooth implementation.

- Follow-up is a critical element of the negotiation process.
- It is helpful, if not essential, to promptly follow up on what was achieved during the negotiation.
- The use of the Terms Sheet is beneficial for any negotiation.
- The sequence is clear: negotiation, agreement, and contract. In this, the Terms Sheet proves effective for all types of negotiations.
- If you aim to succeed in negotiations, always maintain good relationships and strive to improve them.
- To ensure the complete success of the agreement, it is crucial to inform everyone involved in its execution about the terms negotiated and the rationale behind the understanding reached.
- You must be prepared to handle the unexpected and anticipate potential future problems.

I rather think that archives exist to keep things safe, but not secret.

Kevin Young

CHAPTER 9

LEARN HOW TO ARCHIVE

Archiving

After the thirty or more minutes devoted to analyzing the negotiation (alone or with your team), it's time to store all the information in a structured database. While this step may feel like the least engaging part of the process—often dismissed as "bureaucratic"—it is an essential practice that will yield immense benefits over time. Properly archiving negotiation data allows for more rigorous preparation for future negotiations while saving considerable time by granting immediate access to a wealth of relevant insights and resources.

Building an archive goes far beyond merely saving meeting notes or filing away agreements. It's about creating a comprehensive repository that captures every aspect of the negotiation journey. Start by including all preparatory materials, such as the agenda, stakeholder analyses, and strategy documents. Add detailed reflections from your post-negotiation analysis, recording lessons learned and noting what worked and what didn't. Incorporate profiles of your negotiating partners, documenting not only their professional details but also their personality traits, communication styles, interests, and previous strategies. If possible, include photos or visual cues to jog your memory during future preparations.

Archiving should also extend to the questions used during the negotiation, both those you posed and those you were asked. Having a record of these allows you to refine your approach and tailor future strategies more effectively. Include tools and frameworks that proved useful, whether for brainstorming, stimulating creativity, or exploring needs and interests. Additionally, make sure all Terms Sheets are carefully stored and categorized, making them searchable and ready to serve as templates for new negotiations.

Imagine having a system where, with just a few clicks, you can recall every detail of a past negotiation: the dynamics of the conversation, the concessions made, and the strategies employed. Such a system eliminates the need to rely on memory, reduces the risk of missteps, and boosts your confidence by providing a strong foundation for every new negotiation.

For maximum efficiency, this archive should be shared with your negotiation team or colleagues, ensuring everyone has access to the same valuable resources. A cloud-based system offers particular advantages in this regard. Not only does it eliminate the need for personal data storage infrastructure, but it also provides scalability and durability while allowing you to access your archive from anywhere in the world. Furthermore, it significantly reduces the time and costs associated with printing and storing physical documents. The flexibility and efficiency of such a system make it an indispensable tool for any serious negotiator.

- Archiving negotiation information may feel tedious, but it is a foundational practice that delivers significant long-term benefits.
- A comprehensive archive should include preparatory materials, post-negotiation analysis, profiles of negotiation partners, key questions, and finalized Terms Sheets.
- A shared and searchable cloud-based system ensures accessibility, scalability, and durability while reducing costs and time spent on manual organization.

There is no such thing as luck, there is only the moment where talent meets opportunity.

Seneca

Chapter 10

NEGOTIATING YOUR SALARY

Are You Brave Enough?

The best gift you can give your negotiating partners is this book. At worst, you will trigger the basic psychological principle underlying negotiation: when you make a concession, your negotiating partner will feel an obligation to reciprocate. At best, you will both adopt the same method. In that case, any negotiation—regardless of what is at stake—will undoubtedly become more efficient, because you will have the same tools at your disposal. The *Incontro* framework exponentially increases the chances of success, enabling you to follow a winning routine that generates ideas for resolving disputes, overcoming deadlocks, and reaching ever-better agreements and understandings. As you may have gathered from this book, I am a firm believer in preparation, mindfulness, and the necessity of focusing on both perspective—yours and your partner's—and emotion. Preparation is an integral part of the negotiation process, where the whole is reflected in the part, and the part retains the essence of the whole, even as it evolves. While every negotiation is unique, they are all methodologically similar.

Take **salary negotiation**, for instance, perhaps the most common type of negotiation—impacting at least 3.5 billion workers worldwide, according to the latest International Labour Organization's data. Salary negotiations are a universal experience, affecting individuals across industries, roles, and levels of experience. They hold significant personal and professional stakes, influencing not only financial wellbeing but also career satisfaction and growth. Yet, discussing one's salary package can be terrifying. As I have shared, I missed at least four opportunities in my career to negotiate my salary. Fear is the primary reason we refrain from negotiating or asking for more. By examining salary negotiations, we address a deeply relatable, high-pressure scenario that highlights the importance of preparation, confidence, and effective communication—skills that are transferable to all forms of negotiation. Negotiating the purchase price of a house or the financial terms of a divorce may not feel as daunting as discussing one's salary. It doesn't matter whether you're on your first job or your fifth—it's time to learn how to negotiate effectively, applying this method.

My intention is not to provide you with a step-by-step recipe for success. As I have reiterated, this book does not offer magic formulas. Instead, it presents a sound, proven method that has guided me over the years and which I now share with anyone eager to learn it. If followed, this method will help you achieve what you deserve.

While I don't believe that being a skilled negotiator necessarily makes you a better employee, the reality today—except for rare cases like Skillshare, Reddit, Jet, Buffer, Magoosh, Tidelift, Ethena and Gravity Payments, which adopt nonnegotiable salary policies—is aptly summed up by Chester L. Karrass's (2013) book title: *In Business as in Life, You Don't Get What You Deserve, You Get What You Negotiate*. Although I believe in meritocratic systems, much of what you achieve today results from negotiation. If you want to get more—and do so in the best possible way—you must learn how to negotiate.

This requires **discipline** at every stage of the negotiation process, starting with preparation and continuing through every step. Never confuse your goal with the means, and separate your behavior from your feelings and emotions. This will enable you to act as the situation demands rather than reacting to satisfy your emotions. You don't need to transform into someone you're not. You simply need to fulfill the requirements of your role at that specific moment.

Experience confirms that in negotiations, there is a definite tendency to wait for someone to make the first move and then respond accordingly. If the rules of chess allowed it, I would suggest starting with a black pawn to illustrate this hesitation. Pawns are the smallest and least powerful pieces on the chessboard, but they play a critical role in the game's strategy and progression. Avoid following your negotiating partner down a path that is not aligned with your goals, and instead, strive to control the situation by leveraging communication and building a strong relationship. Many companies overly focus on the value they can gain immediately, overlooking higher-value opportunities available in the future. This principle applies equally to business dealings and employee management.

A successful **relationship** is built on equality, where offering something to your negotiating partner creates the expectation of receiving something of equivalent or greater value in return. Trust-based relationships reduce the need for extensive monitoring to ensure contract terms are met. A negotiator who neglects the relational aspect often operates from a distributive perspective, aiming to maximize immediate gains. Conversely, those focused on long-term relationships aim to add value to the negotiation.

Let's revisit salary negotiation.

If your goal is to secure the salary you deserve, preparation is crucial. Research the standard salary levels for positions equivalent to yours, considering your industry, local job market, and the size of comparable companies. Without a reasonably accurate figure, you risk being at the mercy of a skilled HR manager. Use online resources and ask workers in your field—gather input from both men and women to avoid being misled by the gender pay gap. While you may not always get a specific number, even a range can lend legitimacy to your claim.

Before requesting a raise, assess whether your request is justifiable. How long have you been with the company? Have you taken on new responsibilities? Have you exceeded expectations, or simply fulfilled your assigned tasks? If the answers to these questions are favorable, you're off to a good start. To strengthen your case, begin tracking your contributions to the company's success at least three months in advance. Document your achievements with supporting data to make your claim compelling. Prepare a list of improvements and successes you've contributed to the organization, supplemented by positive feedback from customers and colleagues. Your ultimate goal is to present solid evidence of your value to your employer.

Avoid basing your request for more money solely on increased personal expenses—that's a **position** rather than a strategic argument. Instead, align your request with the company's **interests** by identifying solutions to its challenges. By demonstrating how you can address these issues, you position yourself as an indispensable resource. Understanding both your priorities and those of your negotiating partner is critical; this ensures you can create proposals that align with their preferences while addressing your key interests.

A remuneration package is often more than just salary—it may include location flexibility, vacation time, bonuses, company vehicles, benefits, and other perks. Understanding the entire remuneration mix allows you to create **multiple equivalent simultaneous offers**, making possible a more dynamic negotiation process. Ask your negotiating partner to share their priorities and explore mutually beneficial compromises. By doing so, both sides can achieve their most critical objectives. Lastly, be proactive and creative—negotiation is as much about problem-solving as it is about persuasion.

When preparing for a negotiation, take time to view the situation from the other person's perspective. When you consider their thoughts and interests, you're more likely to find solutions that benefit both parties. Sometimes, I pretend to negotiate on someone else's behalf, and my performance improves because I approach the situation with a sense of detachment. The same happens when you negotiate for your company rather than for yourself—it feels more straightforward, and psychologically it works because the result impacts the entire corporate structure. While preparing, consider what you'll ask for and how it will affect your interviewer, family, and future. If you are more satisfied with your position and compensation, your hard work is more likely to lead to greater success.

Once you determine your value, you may realize it falls within a range. If so, don't hesitate to aim for the higher end of the pay scale; your employer will likely negotiate, giving you room to maneuver while still ending up with a satisfactory result. To achieve this, ask for more than you want. Doing so accomplishes two things: it increases the value you secure and gives your negotiating partner the satisfaction of feeling they've reached a better deal by negotiating downward. Don't fear asking for too much! Even if your number is initially too high, your negotiating partner will likely counteroffer. The worst outcome of not negotiating is that you get nothing extra, so it's always worth asking.

I recommend that you take the lead in making the first offer, referencing a specific number. For example, instead of asking for €65,000, request €66,000. This precise figure implies you've done extensive research on your market value. Never accept your negotiating partner's first offer outright. Take your time, and use silence strategically. The vacuum created by silence often compels the other person to improve their offer. This principle also applies during moments of stalemate or impasse—stay calm, wait, and avoid rushing. The first mover often concedes without demanding reciprocation.

Negotiation is a virtuous, efficient mechanism for resource allocation and conflict resolution. It can generate incremental value for all parties while maintaining or enhancing relationships. There is always more room for agreement than you might think, and there are creative ways to handle conflict. In addition to silence, **pauses** can be valuable for reflection or consulting with others. Use this tactic whenever necessary before proceeding or making a commitment. There is no standard length for a break—it might last a few minutes, a weekend, or longer. When you receive an offer worth exploring deeply, take your time.

Avoid using ranges during negotiation. For example, never propose a range such as €63,000 to €68,000, as it signals your willingness to accept the lower end. If you initially ask for €66,000 but later drop to €62,000, you've made a **concession**. In such cases, only grant concessions if you receive something of fair value in return. Being generous without reciprocity is a mistake—it risks provoking the other party's greed, jeopardizing your credibility, and setting a dangerous precedent. If you don't value what you're granting, why should others?

In negotiation, there must be an exchange—a beneficial mechanism by which we give to others what is valuable to them and which does not involve a sacrifice for us, and vice versa. Salary is equivalent to the **price the employer** must pay to secure your job performance. A good negotiator is skilled at shifting the focus from price to **value**, which, in this case, is the compensation package. How much is it worth to have a flexible work schedule, a company car, a gym membership, or additional medical insurance?

The next step is to intersect your interests with the company's by listing **options** for a possible deal and abandoning the limiting view that there is only one possible and acceptable agreement. The most innovative and helpful approach in negotiation is to consider all options for both parties and find ways to satisfy everyone's needs. This is achievable precisely because you and your negotiating partner are driven by different interests.

When evaluating your position, take time to build **alternatives** in case the maximum offer falls so far short of your needs that you are forced to reject it. The reasons for rejection may vary, from financial needs to the market value for comparable roles or the need to feel valued with an adequate salary. The result of your analysis should be a prioritized list of alternatives, with the best one becoming your **BATNA**. Walking away from an offer is never easy, but knowing when to do so is essential. It is equally powerful to be in a position to say no. Saying no (or hearing it) is not a failure—it's a normal part of negotiation. In fact, negotiations often truly begin when someone utters this monosyllable.

Another strategy is to "rehearse the part" as if you were on a theater stage until you feel comfortable with the conversation. While this helps, writing a full script is a mistake. Many people do this, wasting energy and time searching for confidence. By focusing too much on what you are going to say, you may limit your **active listening** ability. Active listening involves not just hearing words but observing verbal and nonverbal cues, which together provide a deeper understanding of the situation. Paying attention to the other party is essential because it allows you to interpret their needs and incorporate them into a mutually satisfying solution.

If you plan to ask for a pay raise, timing is critical. Many people wait until the end of the fiscal year, thinking it's the best time because financial statements are being finalized. However, this approach is flawed. By then, companies have often already drafted their budgets for the following year, making it harder to convince anyone to reallocate funds for your raise. To avoid this scenario and the need to wait another year, make your request earlier. Anticipate the conversation before the budget is finalized.

Forget about asking for a raise at the beginning of the fiscal year, such as January or February, and instead consider the company's business year-end, which may coincide with the calendar year for some, especially foreign multinationals. If possible, aim to make your request toward the end of the week, ideally on Thursday or Friday. People tend to be more receptive and flexible as the week winds down, whereas the beginning of the week often brings a more rigid mindset.

Remember to evaluate the **location**—one of the most important aspects of any negotiation. Location can influence space availability, the "psychological climate," time constraints, information flow, stress management, and the selection of communication channels. Salary negotiation is essentially a discussion between individuals to reach a mutually satisfactory agreement. **Communication** is the key tool for making it effective, and the more influential your communication, the more successful the negotiation will be. Engaging in arguments is perfectly fine, as it establishes a flow of information; however, making claims is not acceptable, as it interrupts the exchange of ideas, thoughts, and opinions.

To negotiate successfully, you must develop your communication skills to ensure the discussion remains healthy and effective. If you are negotiating your salary, you undoubtedly have the authority to do so, but your negotiating partner may not have the same authority. For instance, you may be negotiating with your boss, but the executive board might have the final word. Similarly, if you're negotiating with the CEO of the firm, the ultimate authority could lie with the group CEO. This dynamic also applies when arranging your compensation package. It's crucial to understand the process, the number of meetings before a decision is made, and who holds the decision-making authority.

Before entering a negotiation, ensure you are well rested and clear headed, as this will enable you to apply various strategies and maintain a functional state of mind. Boost your confidence and reduce stress by focusing on positive, success-oriented thought patterns. This approach stimulates testosterone (a hormone that enhances confidence), reduces cortisol (the stress hormone), and helps maintain calm, even in tense situations. When negotiating your compensation package, creating a positive atmosphere at the start of the meeting is essential, as it can set the tone for the rest of the interaction.

Pay attention to your **posture** and all aspects of nonverbal language, including your **smile** and **tone of voice.** Once you break the ice, there is no reason to fear the negotiation, especially if you are well- prepared. By keeping the conversation positive, the process becomes much less intimidating. Begin the negotiation by **asking questions**—some closed, but mostly open—to better understand the interests, needs, fears, preferences, and priorities of the person in front of you. Questions are powerful tools that positively influence the outcome of negotiations by helping you understand your negotiating partner's logic and devise solutions to achieve your goals.

Avoid starting the conversation with numbers. Instead, focus on discussing your accomplishments and, more importantly, what you can contribute in the future. Highlight specific instances when you exceeded your role to demonstrate why you deserve a raise. Share your enthusiasm for future activities, such as lightening the workload of colleagues and your boss or proposing newly developed ideas, to reinforce your value and commitment.

Every concluded negotiation involves a mutual **commitment** based on the agreements made, so it is crucial to continuously evaluate what you present, offer, ask for, or are promised. Once the deal is closed, it's time to act on what was agreed upon before the handshake—this underscores the importance of formalization.

When you advance to the final rounds of interviews for a new job and become a potential candidate, it is typical for the company (or recruiting firm) to ask about your current salary. In many US states and some countries, it is illegal to ask this question. However, where it is allowed, the situation can become delicate, especially if your current salary is significantly lower than the market standard or if you're aiming for a substantial increase.

The best approach is to disclose your current salary, including bonuses and benefits, and then skillfully steer the conversation toward more favorable topics. Redirect the discussion to focus on your skills, the value the market places on your expertise, and your professional growth aspirations. Maintaining a positive tone is essential. Never threaten to leave if you don't receive a raise—it rarely achieves the desired outcome. Likewise, avoid mentioning other job offers, recruitment conversations, or (worst of all) discussions with competitors as leverage.

In any negotiation, focus on the future rather than the past. Address new conditions without explicitly referencing your current compensation. Instead, align the conversation with the market value for similar roles and consistently steer the discussion toward the value you bring.

Since you initiated the meeting, you must make the initial proposal, whether requesting a raise or negotiating for a new job. However, avoid putting all your cards on the table in your initial offer. Doing so limits your ability to negotiate further and often leads to a cycle of concessions.

The first proposal carries significant weight—it sets the **anchor** for the negotiation, influencing the subsequent discussions. Anchoring is a cognitive bias that gives undue importance to the first number presented, regardless of its basis. Presenting a higher initial value often results in a better final offer. To maintain control of the negotiation, always aim to be the one making the first proposal.

If your negotiating partner reacts negatively or attempts to counter-anchor, remain composed. Ask open-ended questions to keep the dialogue moving, demonstrating a willingness to collaborate on a mutually beneficial solution. A negative response can provide valuable opportunities if you're prepared to capitalize on them.

Approach the negotiation with a soft, elegant, and kind demeanor toward people, while remaining firm and decisive when addressing problems. This balanced strategy is both strategic and effective, even in challenging or complex situations.

Leverage your problem-solving skills by actively engaging your negotiating partner. Demonstrate relational adaptability and strong communication skills in a strategic, effective, efficient, and elegant manner. This approach highlights your ability to work collaboratively on issues and build alliances to address individual and organizational challenges that require attention. After presenting your advantages, arguing your value, and making your demand, focus on the emotional aspects of the negotiation—a critical thread in any interaction. For example, use flattery to engage the other person, as everyone appreciates feeling valued and heard.

Make use of the **five core concerns** (appreciation, affiliation, autonomy, status, and role). Facing your company's HR manager or boss will then feel much easier. Negotiating with a new company may be more complex but remains entirely feasible. If negotiations hit a standstill, consider introducing new elements to the discussion, such as negotiating for job flexibility, additional vacation time, a better title, or more challenging projects. Conditional **offers** can be particularly effective—these involve a commitment contingent on meeting a specific future condition, such as achieving a business goal, mastering new management software, or implementing a successful project. Conditional offers minimize risk for the company, as salary increases or benefits are tied to the fulfillment of predefined milestones.

For negotiations conducted via email or videoconference, focus on maximizing **empathy** and emulating the dynamics of an in-person conversation. Ensure your message conveys warmth and openness, creating an enjoyable and productive discussion environment. Some negotiations may gradually lose momentum or end without resolution, whether because one or both parties choose not to reach an agreement or fail to identify mutually beneficial terms despite clear advantages. To gracefully exit or reopen such impasses without losing face or bargaining strength, it is crucial to introduce new ideas or creative solutions.

Effective negotiation techniques appeal to the self-interest of all parties, fostering opportunities to continue discussions and explore alternative solutions. However, if an agreement remains elusive, remember that not reaching a deal is not a failure, particularly if you have thoroughly prepared and possess an excellent alternative to the negotiated agreement (such as a better job offer). This principle is more applicable to new roles but can also guide salary improvement requests.

Patience is an essential trait for effective negotiation. While it takes time to develop, it can lead to significantly better outcomes. Patience allows you to reflect, thoroughly evaluate offers, and understand potential risks. Once both you and your negotiating partner are satisfied with the results, it's time to conclude the negotiation. Formalize the agreement in a clear and binding oral or written contract, particularly in labor matters, where roles and responsibilities must be precisely defined.

Although rare, post-settlement settlement (PSS) can be applied to labor negotiations. Rather than adhering rigidly to the initial agreement, PSS offers an opportunity to renegotiate a deal that benefits all parties, especially if new information or insights emerge during the negotiation process.

- What you achieve today is the result of a negotiation process. Therefore, you have no alternative: if you want to achieve more and improve, you must learn how to negotiate.
- Never confuse the goal with the means; keep your behavior separate from your feelings and emotions.
- Relationships built on trust offer countless advantages.
- When negotiating your salary, always present a specific number.
- A good negotiator knows how to shift the focus from price to value—in wage negotiations, this means emphasizing the compensation package.
- Before entering a negotiation, ensure you are well rested and clear-headed.
- Asking questions can positively influence the outcome of negotiations by helping you better understand your negotiating partner's logic and devising solutions to achieve your goal.
- At the end of multiple interviews for a new job, it is common for the company to ask about your current salary; in such cases, it is best to always tell the truth.
- If you want to start or maintain a working relationship, it is essential to keep the conversation positive. No matter what happens, never threaten to leave if you don't get the raise; such threats accomplish nothing.
- In any negotiation, focus on the future, not the past.
- Avoid including too much in your initial proposal. This is a common mistake; remember that by doing so, you reveal all your cards and leave yourself little room to negotiate.
- Be considerate, tactful, and kind with people, but firm and decisive when addressing problems.
- Appeal to emotions and engage the other person by connecting on multiple levels.
- If necessary, use conditional offers.
- To become an effective negotiator, patience may be your most important attribute.

*If you hear a voice within you say "you cannot paint,"
then by all means paint, and that voice will be silenced.*

Vincent Van Gogh

CHAPTER 11

THE ALLURE OF NEGOTIATION

Follow Your Dreams

How many times have you negotiated today? I bet you don't know. Maybe you've just arrived at work and already negotiated several times without even realizing it. Isn't that crazy? We all negotiate multiple times a day, often without noticing. Some people remember special childhood moments, like removing the training wheels from their bicycle, their first day of school, or a powerful emotion tied to a unique experience. Yet, no one recalls their first negotiation—it happened much earlier, before memory could record it.

From childhood, we negotiate to gain more attention from our parents or to receive special treatment. As we grow, life presents us with negotiations for equally important, albeit more complex, desires. Many people believe negotiations are exclusive to significant events involving prominent figures like businesspeople, athletes, politicians, actors, or diplomats. However, their negotiations are no different from the ones we engage in daily. Yours may have less fanfare, but they are just as worthy of attention.

I came to negotiation out of necessity, realizing how crucial it was to understand and master it to achieve my goals in work, family, and social settings. Over time, I became fascinated by it. I was captivated and have never stopped striving to improve. I'm well aware that I'm not Henry A. Kissinger—regarded by many as one of history's most skilled negotiators—whom I had the privilege of hearing speak in Rimini in 1991. While reaching his level may be nearly impossible, I have never abandoned my journey of growth. I encourage you to follow my example. Giving up before starting makes no sense. It's like saying it's pointless to paint because you'll never be Vincent Van Gogh or to play soccer because you'll never match Lionel Messi.

Negotiation is both a science and an art. It is the science of achieving what you want and the art of how you achieve it. While it is neither an exact science nor pure artistic intuition, it is a skillful blend of both. I am constantly searching for new styles and techniques, drawing inspiration from people I observe, authors whose books I devour, and professors at the world's most prestigious universities. These role models inspire me, not to imitate them but to challenge myself. I enjoy stepping out of my comfort zone—it has never frightened me. When you change your mindset, adopt the right strategy, and apply the best tactics, extraordinary things can happen, most of them enjoyable.

It took me a while to realize that my worst enemy in negotiations was myself. Once I overcame my mental barriers and freed myself from misunderstandings, I felt ready to tackle any negotiation.

"Some are born great, some achieve greatness, and some have greatness thrust upon them," said Malvolio in *Twelfth Night* by William Shakespeare.

None of us are born great negotiators. The belief that negotiation is innate can sometimes hinder learning. Everyone knows someone who seems naturally gifted at negotiating—whether it's persuading the boss to give a raise, skipping ahead in a security line to catch a plane, or scoring a hefty discount on a new kitchen. But what about everyone else? Should they resign themselves to letting these naturally talented few take the lead? Absolutely not. Negotiation is a skill that can be learned. While some people may have a natural aptitude for it—after all, negotiation is also an art—anyone can become a better negotiator with the proper training.

Our social context, educational background, and the people we encounter significantly influence how much we can achieve for ourselves and others. Preparing thoroughly, understanding your goals, and listening to different perspectives are essential elements of negotiation. These skills can help you achieve the best outcomes for yourself and the people you work and live with. By reading this book, you've taken a step—perhaps not your first and certainly not your last—toward debunking the myth that good negotiators are born and affirming my thesis that negotiation is a skill that can be developed. You are living proof of this idea, as you represent the foundation upon which you can build and refine this skill with practice.

Scholars have identified more than 20,000 human genes, yet none are specifically linked to negotiation. However, certain traits—such as curiosity, creativity, self-control, patience, resilience, listening skills, acumen, memory, logic, and numerical familiarity—can offer advantages. Among these, the first three attributes are the most critical, but all can be developed to enhance your negotiation abilities: curiosity, creativity, and patience. Curiosity is beneficial only when paired with active listening and keen observation. Creativity requires a solid memory and proficiency in logic and calculation. Patience allows you to tolerate ambiguity and resolve conflict calmly, demonstrating self-control.

The best negotiators tend to achieve success later in their careers, reaching their level through knowledge, perseverance, and countless hours of practice. While good negotiators rely on intuition, it is unwise to depend solely on instinct. Intuition can generate fresh ideas and tactics, but its effectiveness should always be measured against objective data and careful analysis.

Negotiation comprises both mechanical and human components. The mechanical aspect involves preparation and the ability to manage information effectively—structuring offers, counterproposals, and concessions. The human component is more complex, as it is often influenced by bias. A wise and experienced negotiator constantly compares instinctive impressions with objective data, consulting their team and experts before making decisions. Relying solely on intuition or acting impulsively can result in costly mistakes.

Someone with keen insight may seem to possess a superpower—an ability to know something without consciously understanding why. This can be frustrating when they cannot articulate their reasoning, leading others to suspect they are withholding information. Some call this intuition a "gut feeling," but there is nothing mystical or magical about it. It is not pure instinct but rather a blend of accumulated knowledge and experience. Preparation fosters wisdom, while passion and curiosity drive the experience necessary to hone these skills.

"Ultimately, one cannot learn to negotiate from a book. One must deal with reality," writes James C. Freund (1975) in *Anatomy of a Merger.* There is deep truth in this. Books, courses, and teachings serve as valuable guides to improving negotiation, but they can never replace the lessons learned through real-world practice.

I reiterate that negotiation is not a confrontation, and the person on the other side of the table is not an enemy. Symbolically, adopting more round tables and fewer rectangular ones could help foster collaboration and equality in discussions. Negotiation should be viewed as a constructive interaction, where parties with differing interests come together in a cooperative spirit to reach an agreement that satisfies everyone. This may sound impossible, but it's not. You don't need to overpower the other party to get what you want. In fact, you gain much more when both parties take steps toward each other to find a mutually beneficial balance. While the ultimate goal of negotiation is to achieve your desired outcome, the best agreements incorporate conditions, ideas, and proposals from both sides.

A good agreement must be executable. What is the value of an agreement if one party cannot fulfill it because it is too burdensome? Almost nothing. Overreaching and trying to achieve too much can be highly risky.

Every negotiation involves a degree of risk. All too often, negotiators justify risky behavior in challenging contexts, hoping the other party will yield. However, this approach is flawed. Even if the other party gives in—which is far from guaranteed—it risks souring or damaging the relationship in the long run. In such cases, the other party might become overly tenacious or take excessive risks themselves, leading both sides to miss opportunities for mutually beneficial exchanges.

Negotiators should take well-calculated, thoughtful risks only when the benefits clearly and significantly outweigh the costs.

Even small negotiations require preparation and creativity. In today's highly competitive environment, mistakes are less forgivable. Information is readily available, opportunities are fewer, competition is fierce, and profit margins are shrinking. As a result, it is more critical than ever to focus on the right opportunities and make sound decisions.

To succeed in negotiations, you must not only prepare thoroughly and anticipate possible scenarios but also possess the skills and techniques to manage the process effectively. I firmly believe in the importance of rigorous preparation. Once strategies, tactics, and goals are defined, I disregard those who justify emotional reactions—such as anger or frustration—as integral to negotiation. Nothing could be further from the truth. Emotional outbursts, such as yelling, crying, or laughing inappropriately, are misplaced and counterproductive. Just as adding too many ingredients can ruin a good recipe, letting emotions overrun a negotiation is a recipe for failure.

The best approach is to be aware of your emotions and keep them under control. Stay calm, but also show passion when presenting an offer, picking up the pace or making a decision. I always leave emotions for last, because they are the most important. Let's not kid ourselves: who, during a negotiation, has not experienced anxiety, anger, disappointment, and joy? If the answer is yes, it may mean that we are not so willing to respect ourselves, and in this case, we will only learn to listen to our own emotions and those of the other person to gain additional information on managing the negotiating dynamic strategically. We must better understand and control our own and the other person's emotional reactions, because doing so will also improve our negotiating ability.

That is not to say that there is anything wrong with experiencing anxiety, anger, disappointment, and joy. Take my friend Paolo, for example. A life enthusiast, he is always smiling and positive, often celebrating before closing a deal he deems favorable. I've repeatedly told him (with little success, to be honest) that this is one of the worst strategies he could use. Overconfidence can lower his attention threshold, which must remain high at all times. Moreover, this attitude may give the impression that he holds an advantage, prompting retaliatory reactions from the negotiating partner. Paolo struggles to show "strategic disappointment." I've explained to him that he would achieve better results if he tempered his outward enthusiasm. Excessive joy can inadvertently put the other party on the defensive, causing them to counterattack rather than collaborate.

Disappointment, however, prompts others to behave differently, often softening the feelings they believe they have caused. Considering and managing emotions is not a trick or a form of deception, nor does it involve cunning contrivances designed to disguise or distort reality. Unfortunately, tricks are fairly common in negotiation. Over the years, I've encountered individuals I initially thought were credible and trustworthy, only to discover their reliance on unethical tactics. Resorting to such moves is always wrong and can ultimately damage relationships in the long term. My advice is to refrain from using them, and if you ever find yourself in a negotiation where something feels off, remember that you always have the option to walk away. A skillful negotiator doesn't need tricks—they rely on choosing and using the most appropriate tools for the context to reach a fair agreement.

Instead of tricks, I prefer a little secret that has made me more effective in all my negotiations. It comes from a small book, only sixty pages long, with a green cover and a title as curious as it is intriguing: *L'Art de Se Taire.* (Never translated into English, its title could be rendered *The Art of Keeping Silent.*) Written by Abbot Joseph A. Dinouart in 1771, it contains this wisdom: "Silence is necessary on many occasions, but one must always be sincere: it is possible to keep certain thoughts to oneself, but not to feign them. There are ways of keeping silent without closing one's heart, being discreet without being gloomy and taciturn, and concealing certain truths without covering them with lies" (Dinouart 1989, 28).

Silence is powerful. It is one of the most potent weapons a negotiator can bring to the table, yet it is often underused. Long, drawn-out pauses create discomfort and awkwardness—it is human nature to want to fill the void, often without careful thought. Silence is an aggressive technique. How many negotiations have failed due to excessive talking? Far more than those that have failed because of silence.

Silence is invaluable. It creates insecurity and stress for the other party, making them nervous and prone to mistakes. It can convey a sense of mystery and power, hinting at a readiness to walk away rather than settle for less than the desired outcome. Not every statement in a negotiation requires a response or comment. The goal of negotiation is not to win every single point or persuade the other party to abandon their views but to find a solution that satisfies the needs of both sides.

Sometimes, silence leads the other side to reveal critical information—clues about what they are willing to accept or the constraints they face. Learning to master silence is a skill worth developing. Pay attention to when and why the other party chooses to remain silent, as understanding their reasons can provide valuable insight into the dynamics of the negotiation.

- We negotiate from childhood to gain more attention from our parents.
- Negotiation is both a science and an art. It is the science of achieving what you want and the art of achieving it effectively.
- The best negotiators succeed later in their careers, reaching their level through knowledge, perseverance, and thousands of hours of practice.
- Negotiation has both a mechanical component and a human component.
- If we relied solely on intuition and acted purely on instinct, we would risk engaging in actions that could prove very costly.
- It is not necessary to overpower or outmaneuver the other party to get what you want. Much more can be achieved when each person takes a step toward the other to find a new balance that satisfies both sides.
- Every negotiation involves risk. However, negotiators often justify taking risks in challenging situations, hoping the other side will concede.
- Negotiators should take well-calculated, thoughtful risks only when the benefits clearly (and significantly) outweigh the costs.
- It is a sound rule to remain aware of emotions and keep them under control during negotiations.
- A skillful negotiator avoids tricks by selecting and using the tools best suited to the context to reach a fair agreement.
- Silence is powerful. It is one of the most effective weapons an individual can bring to the negotiating table, yet it is often underutilized. Learn to master silence and strive to understand when and why the other side chooses to remain silent.

The devil follows me day and night
because he is afraid to be alone.

Francis Picabia

CHAPTER 12

TO CONCLUDE

Good Habits

We all know that children thrive on routines—they provide structure, discipline, and a sense of security. When I was younger, my mother, Milena, would thoughtfully organize my day: setting times for bedtime, homework, meals, and play. These routines gave my life a steady rhythm. As I grew older, I naturally carried forward some of those habits, like having lunch at 1 p.m. and dinner at 8 p.m. They've become small but meaningful anchors in my busy adult life.

Many people lack a daily routine simply because they have never considered creating one. As a result, they often feel stressed, anxious, and overwhelmed, struggling to achieve their goals and reach their full potential. The same principle applies to negotiations: while following a method can seem tedious, rigid, or even stifling, it is essential for success. I understand that many people prefer to approach negotiations whimsically or creatively, believing that this free-spirited approach grants them freedom. However, they fail to realize that designing, following, and refining a personal method is the most effective path to successful negotiations and fully realizing one's potential.

Incontro is a structured method that works for any negotiation and consists of seven stages: deciding whether to negotiate; preparation and planning; discussion, proposal, and negotiation; agreement; debriefing; follow-up; and filing. There are no shortcuts to preparation—it is the foundation of effective negotiation. Anyone who has tried to prepare knows that it is less complicated than you might imagine, and with practice, everything becomes easy, and the results are always rewarding!

Knowledge Is Power

The goal is not to prepare for every possible situation so that you know exactly what to do, say, and how to react. Instead, it is to spend the necessary time (which often exceeds what is available) strategizing and developing a set of tactics based on **information** that allows you to accurately identify interests, options, alternatives, legitimacy, commitment, and emotions.

People who make decisions possess a certain allure because decision-making is universally recognized as a valuable skill and a challenging task. Today, this ability is considered one of the primary competencies required of a manager. It is fundamental because it carries the responsibility of selecting from countless options, knowing that any choice may lead to unexpected outcomes, including mistakes. Throughout the negotiation process, numerous small decisions must be made, each producing its own effects. Both objective factors, related to the context, and subjective factors, related to the decision maker's logical processes, come into play.

Negotiations are characterized by complexity, uncertainty, variability, limited resources, and high speed. Oversimplifications worsen the situation by causing people to underestimate the true impact of various elements on future scenarios. Objective factors are independent of the parties involved in the negotiation; they are factual pieces of information relevant to determining what should or should not be agreed upon. Information becomes objective when it can be traced back to credible and unbiased sources. Additionally, it must be relevant, easy to process and understand, verifiable immediately or in advance by the negotiating partner, up-to-date, and, most importantly, persuasive to you, the other party, and any third parties.

The strength of objective criteria lies in how they are used. When applied correctly, they provide confidence and support during negotiations. Understanding these criteria and how to leverage them effectively shields you from being exploited by your negotiating partner. Being well prepared with objective facts also gives you the firmness necessary to avoid appearing overly lenient. If you are thoroughly and objectively prepared, you can become an exceptional negotiator, commanding respect from your colleagues, superiors, and negotiating partner. Preparation is one of the clearest hallmarks of a skilled negotiator.

What Do You Want?

The objectivity you employed during the preparatory phase, when exploring your interests, must continue as you define what you want to achieve. Ask yourself honestly: why are you negotiating, what do you aspire to, what would you gain by concluding the negotiation, and how would an agreement impact your satisfaction? The power of questions, even when directed at oneself, is extraordinary.

Negotiations are fascinating, but it's important to acknowledge that you can't always get everything you want. Decide in advance which aspects are most important and where you are willing to make concessions. Great negotiators know what they want before entering discussions, and they are clear about what they will never accept. They also understand the point at which it's best to walk away—their reserve value (RV). If you don't leave the table when staying no longer benefits you, you risk making a poor deal. Walking away from a bad deal is always preferable to closing it.

When you leave the negotiating table, you turn to your best alternative to a negotiated agreement (BATNA). A well-prepared BATNA allows both sides to withdraw from the negotiations and proceed with a different option. This alternative—ideally identified during preparation—may evolve during the negotiation as new information emerges (particularly if you are skilled at using open-ended questions and active listening).

A solid BATNA provides leverage and ensures you have viable alternatives. Before negotiating, spend time developing your BATNA (preferably with your negotiating team, if applicable) and explore various scenarios to identify and improve on your partner's BATNA. Never negotiate without an alternative—it's critical. If no agreement is reached, a strong Plan B allows you to make more substantial demands on the other party. Resorting to your BATNA may involve interacting with third parties who are not at the negotiating table (e.g., continuing to live in a smaller house, buying from another supplier, or accepting a previous job offer). Always consider the consequences of rejecting a proposal and prepare to view the situation from your counterpart's perspective. Understanding their viewpoint enables you to think like them.

When considering others' perspectives, focus on how your decisions will affect their interests. Always weigh the impact your choices will have on the other party. For both sides, potential consequences may include costs, risks, missed opportunities, and relationship damage. While these factors are not external options entirely independent of your counterpart, they remain crucial considerations.

Several years ago, I found myself negotiating the purchase of an equity stake under challenging conditions. At the time, private equity funds were not immediately available to complete the acquisition. My alternative was to consider less costly companies. Advanced divestment negotiations might have improved my financial readiness, allowing the deal to close. So, what did I do? I opted to negotiate strategically by slowing down the process, waiting for sufficient financial resources rather than pursuing less expensive companies. I remained fully aware of my options and successfully delayed the agreement to achieve my goal.

A well-defined BATNA helps you navigate negotiations with confidence, reducing the fear of uncertainty. Without it, you're more likely to make snap decisions based on incomplete information, potentially forcing yourself to accept suboptimal proposals because you feel you have no other options.

Conversely, fear of missing out on a better deal might lead you to prematurely abandon negotiations. However, if you decide to finalize the negotiated agreement, the fear of "what might have been" will quickly dissipate. If you choose to walk away, having a well-defined BATNA ensures you know exactly where you stand and where you aim to go.

I Don't Like to Dance, nor Do I Enjoy Dancing

Too often in negotiations, parties focus on dividing a limited set of resources. This approach can be thought of as haggling: a back-and-forth exchange of offers, typically involving price. The late Harvard professor Howard Raiffa (1985) referred to this process as "The Dance of Negotiation."

Game theory describes such negotiations as zero-sum, where one side's gains directly offset the other's losses: they sum to zero, as any gain by one party is exactly correlated with a correspon-ding loss on the part of the other. If this is the case, it is not a true negotiation. Genuine negotiation occurs when bargaining involves multiple elements simultaneously. For instance, in labor negotiations, the subject of bargaining might be limited to salary alone, or it could include a broader compensation package com-prising variables such as salary, work location, vacation, bonuses, company car, benefits, and more. In the former case, where the focus is solely on salary, the parties are competing, often resorting to forcing or manipulative tactics. In the latter case, however, both parties aim to create mutual advantages through cooperation and the exchange of information. Negotiation becomes truly effective when it addresses a set of elements; for example, a concession like reducing the class of a company car as a benefit might be offset by a larger bonus.

Experienced negotiators prefer these multielement nego-tiations because they enable them to achieve their preparatory goals—and often even more. By working collaboratively with their negotiating partner, they can explore options that increase the total value available to both sides. Skilled negotiators favor this approach because it fosters long-term relationships, facilita-tes future collaborations, and ensures that both parties leave the table feeling they have achieved more than they initially expected.

Always strive to gather as much information as possible about your negotiating partner's interests and goals. Understanding their true needs and strategies allows you to anticipate their positions and respond effectively to their behaviors.

While managing the negotiation agenda is essential, you should also aim to be the first to make an offer. This sets a reference point for all subsequent offers. However, initial offers should not be taken too seriously; they often serve as starting positions and can be extreme or unrealistically optimistic.

When presenting alternatives, focus on the other party's interests, goals, and principles. Use this opportunity to create mutually beneficial situations through an equal exchange of concessions aimed at satisfying shared interests. This approach will significantly increase the value on the table, benefiting both parties.

Be Fair if You Want a Fair Deal

When you start a negotiation, aim to create an open and collaborative atmosphere from the outset, as this is essential to maintain throughout the process. Strive to work creatively with your negotiating partner to develop options that meet both your interests and add value, ultimately reaching a final agreement that benefits both sides. Ensure that any concessions you make are reciprocal. Without reciprocity, an imbalance is created, leading to tension and resentment over time. Often, negotiations break down because one party feels the other is not treating them fairly.

Respect the other side, even if you disagree with their proposals, and always distinguish between the person and the issue. Negotiation should never become personal. As in basketball, the focus should be on the ball, not the player. Avoid lying or misleading your negotiating partner. Negotiate as many clauses as needed but only make commitments you can honor. Otherwise, beyond the legal implications of breach, you risk damaging your dignity, credibility, and the reputation of the company you represent. Remember that time spent on preparation, planning, and strategy analysis is meaningless—or even wasted—if there is no agreement defining mutual commitments.

A negotiation is fair when both parties communicate effectively and work with integrity and balance to find a mutually beneficial solution. If you are ethical and fair, you can always hold your head high and inspire other negotiators. In the real world, negotiations often break down when one party feels the other is acting unfairly or dishonestly. In most cases, this happens because emotions take over. What should you do in such situations? Scream or threaten? Absolutely not. Unmanaged emotions can ruin the negotiation. However, if you are well prepared, you will be better equipped to analyze the context and handle it effectively.

Stay calm, be respectful, and treat others as you would like to be treated. Listening, learning, and adapting will help you navigate obstacles. Even if things don't go exactly as planned, with the right mindset, you can still achieve a win–win outcome. In doing so, you will not only complete the deal but also enhance your reputation as a fair and principled negotiator.

Remember, every negotiation is an opportunity—not just to reach an agreement, but to build relationships, earn respect, and set the foundation for future success.

- Creating a daily routine and adhering to a schedule is essential.
- Designing, following, and refining a personal method is the key to effectively negotiating and fully expressing one's potential.
- Decision-making is considered one of the primary skills required of a manager. Multiple small choices are made throughout the negotiation process, each with distinct consequences and ramifications.
- Negotiation is characterized by complexity, uncertainty, variability, limited resources, and high speed.
- Always remember that preparation is one of the best indicators of a skilled negotiator.
- The power of questions, even when directed at oneself, is extraordinary.
- Walking away from a bad deal is always preferable to closing it.
- Only negotiate if you have an alternative.
- You must learn to change your perspective and view situations through your negotiating partner's eyes—to think like them.
- Negotiation becomes truly effective when it involves multiple elements, as concessions can lead to more significant returns.
- When starting a negotiation, strive to create an open and collaborative atmosphere from the beginning.
- Ensure that any concessions you make are reciprocal. Failure to do so creates an imbalance that generates tension and resentment over time.
- Negotiation must never become personal.
- Always stay calm, be respectful, and treat others as you would like to be treated.

In life, only two things are non-negotiable: dark chocolate and the last word… unless you're a good negotiator.

The Author

Glossary

24/7: Indicates continuous availability and operation twenty-four hours a day, seven days a week. It suggests that a service or activity is accessible or available without interruption.

80/20 rule: See Pareto.

Active listening: Listening carefully to the needs, concerns, and perspectives of the negotiating partner, demonstrating understanding, and responding appropriately to reach a mutually beneficial agreement.

Agenda: A list of topics to be discussed, which should be sent to participants before the meeting. It can include details such as the meeting location and time, helping to focus on critical objectives for more effective meeting management.

Agent: A person who, in a negotiation, acts on behalf of or in place of another person (whether natural or legal) as their representative. An agent has *full* or *limited* authority to act on behalf of the party they represent.

All you can eat: A pricing model offered by some restaurants where customers pay a set price and can eat unlimited quantities of food.

Anchor: An initial proposal made by one of the parties at the negotiating table, designed to set the starting point of the negotiation and influence subsequent discussions. The anchor often conditions the other party to move toward a solution closer to the proposer's expectations.

Arbitration: An alternative method of dispute resolution in which the parties involved submit to the judgment of a third party. A neutral arbitrator, chosen by the parties or appointed by an organization, hears arguments and makes a decision that is binding on the involved parties.

Art director: A professional responsible for implementing the creative aspects of an advertising campaign. They collaborate with the copywriter and supervise graphic designers, illustrators, and photographers to ensure a practical and aesthetically appealing final product.

B2B (business to business): Business relationships involving the sale of goods and services between companies. It refers to a market where businesses act as customers or suppliers to other businesses rather than selling directly to end consumers.

BATNA: Best alternative to a negotiated agreement. This represents the best available alternative a party can pursue if no agreement or an unsatisfactory agreement is reached in the current negotiation.

Bluff: A tactic used to influence the behavior of the counterpart by communicating false or exaggerated information. The purpose is to make the counterpart believe they have less negotiating power, thereby gaining an advantage.

Brainstorming: A creative process for generating ideas and solutions, where participants freely contribute proposals and suggestions. This technique encourages diverse thinking and helps in finding innovative options for resolving disputes or reaching agreements.

Buy-in: The purchase of a stake in a company by an outside investor, such as a private equity fund or a competitor.

Buy-out: The complete acquisition of a company by an outside investor or the existing management team.

Calibrated questions: Strategically phrased questions used in negotiations to obtain useful information and influence the counterpart's behavior. These questions are open-ended and designed to elicit detailed answers while maintaining an open conversation.

Carve-out: The sale or separation of a division or business unit of a company, allowing it to be sold to an interested buyer.

CEO (chief executive officer): The top executive in a company, responsible for corporate strategies and day-to-day operations.

CFO (chief financial officer): The corporate executive responsible for the financial management of a company.

Chef de partie: A specialized cook responsible for a specific area of the kitchen, such as preparing sauces or desserts.

Chef pâtissier: A high-level pastry chef specializing in the preparation of cakes, desserts, and other pastry delicacies.

Chef saucier: A cook specializing in the preparation of basic sauces, stews, and garnishes.

Closed questions: Questions that require a definite answer, such as "yes" or "no." In negotiations, they are used to confirm or reject a specific point.

Coalition: A group of individuals or organizations that join forces in a negotiation with multiple parties to pursue a common goal, enabling them to achieve objectives that would be difficult to accomplish independently.

Cognitive bias: A disruption of our perception and decision-making processes that can lead to errors in evaluation and judgment. Such biases can affect how we interpret information and make decisions during a negotiation.

Comfort zone: A psychological state in which one feels safe, secure, and comfortable, avoiding the anxiety and stress that can impede personal growth and limit opportunities for learning and development.

Concession: An act of granting something to the other party to reach a compromise or agreement.

Conditional offer: An offer dependent on the satisfaction of specific conditions. These conditions may relate to timing, price, quantity, or other variables important to the negotiating parties. The offer is considered binding only if both parties accept the stipulated conditions.

COO (chief operating officer): A corporate executive responsible for supervising and coordinating production activities. The COO works closely with executive management to ensure operational efficiency and the achievement of corporate objectives.

Copywriter: A professional who creates advertising and marketing copy. Their role involves crafting persuasive messages for advertisements, television commercials, online ads, brochures, and other materials to capture the audience's attention and inspire specific actions.

Core concerns: According to Daniel Shapiro, these are basic needs individuals seek to satisfy through negotiation, including appreciation, affiliation, autonomy, status, and role.

Cost of ownership: All expenses associated with acquiring, using, and maintaining an asset or service over its lifecycle. This includes direct and indirect costs, such as the purchase price, operating expenses, maintenance costs, and replacement costs.

Covenant: A formal agreement between two or more parties that establishes specific obligations, restrictions, or conditions. It regulates the rights and duties of the parties concerning services, compliance with terms, or other provisions.

CPO (chief people officer): A corporate executive responsible for managing human resources. This role includes defining and implementing strategies for acquiring, training, and developing personnel to improve organizational performance and productivity.

CPO (chief procurement officer): A corporate executive responsible for strategically managing purchasing and procurement within an organization.

Counter-anchoring: A strategy that shifts the focus of discussions or proposals to a position more favorable to one's side. Counter-anchoring influences the other party's perception by presenting comparisons with less advantageous or desirable alternatives.

Counter-proposal: A response to an original proposal, suggesting changes or alternatives to reach a more favorable agreement for both parties.

Customer service: A set of activities and processes aimed at providing assistance, support, and answers to customer inquiries, ensuring maximum customer satisfaction.

Debrief: A stage following the conclusion of negotiations where parties discuss and evaluate the negotiation process, share feedback, review outcomes, and identify lessons learned for future improvement.

Distributive negotiation: A type of negotiation in which parties seek to maximize their gains at the expense of the other party. This competitive approach focuses on obtaining the most benefit for oneself, using pressure and persuasion tactics. In this type of negotiation, there is no common interest in creating value—only in dividing available resources.

Emotional intelligence: The ability to understand and manage one's own emotions and those of others during the negotiation process. It includes empathy, emotional self-awareness, emotional control, and effectively leveraging emotions to positively influence the negotiation.

Emotions: Psychological and physiological responses to external or internal stimuli.

Empathy: The ability to understand and share the emotions, thoughts, and perspectives of a negotiating partner. Empathy fosters trust and encourages collaboration in pursuing mutually beneficial solutions.

Etiquette: A communication technique that involves assigning a label or definition to a specific behavior or aspect of the negotiation. This helps influence the other party's perception and how the issue is addressed.

Executive: Members of a company's management team responsible for directing and managing the organization. This may include the CEO, CFO, COO, and other executives with specific roles.

Feel, Felt, Found: A communication technique used to address objections or concerns by relating them to shared experiences or perspectives.

Guiding questions: Questions designed to provide specific guidance, obtain detailed information, or stimulate critical thinking. They are manifested through feelings such as joy, sadness, anger, fear, and surprise. They can influence an individual's behavior and decisions. Emotions are often subjective and can vary based on personal and cultural experiences.

Just in time (JIT): An organizational and production management approach aimed at minimizing inventories by ensuring that necessary materials and resources are available exactly when required, thereby avoiding waste and additional costs.

KPI (key performance indicator): A metric used to assess a company's success in achieving its goals. KPIs are quantifiable and enable companies to evaluate performance objectively.

Impasse: A situation in which the negotiating parties cannot reach an agreement due to conflicting views, resulting in a deadlock. An impasse may lead to the breakdown of negotiations if a compromise or mutually satisfactory solution is not found.

Integrative negotiation: A negotiation strategy in which parties aim to reach an agreement that satisfies common interests and creates added value for both, rather than focusing solely on dividing a fixed value. This approach fosters creative and mutually beneficial solutions.

Interests: The needs, concerns, and desires (or goals) of a party involved in negotiation. Understanding these interests is crucial for identifying solutions that satisfy them and for fostering collaboration toward an agreement.

Lead time: The time required to complete a production process, starting from when materials are ordered until the finished product is delivered to the customer. Lead time is a key indicator for supply chain management and production control.

Legal director: A senior executive responsible for managing and coordinating legal activities, assessing risks, defining legal strategies, and supporting clients in complex legal matters.

Legitimacy: The perception that a party's actions, demands, or proposals are authoritative, authentic, and justified according to socially accepted norms, rules, conventions, or written documents such as standard terms, company policies, and price lists.

Letter of Intent (LOI): A written document expressing the parties' intent to move toward a formal agreement. An LOI typically outlines the main negotiated points, preliminary conditions, and terms to be included in the final contract.

Leverage: Power, influence, or advantage a party uses to obtain concessions or favorable outcomes during negotiation. Leverage is derived from resources, knowledge, alternatives, or positions of strength.

Logrolling: A negotiation practice where parties exchange concessions on different issues to reach an overall agreement. This "give-and-take" approach involves offering something highly valuable to the other party in exchange for something equally valuable to oneself.

M&A (Mergers and Acquisitions): Transactions in which two or more companies merge, or one company acquires another, creating a new entity or integrating resources and activities.

Mail delivery failure: An error message indicating that an email was not delivered to the recipient. Common causes include an incorrect email address or a malfunctioning mail server.

Managing partner: The principal partner of a law firm responsible for managing the firm's strategies, supervising staff, overseeing client relationships, and ensuring quality standards for services provided.

Memorandum of Understanding (MOU): A preliminary agreement outlining the principles, objectives, and general terms of a future agreement. While an MOU sets the foundation for collaboration, it is not legally binding like a contract.

MESO (multiple equivalent simultaneous offers): A negotiation technique in which several options are presented simultaneously, encouraging cooperation and enabling the selection of the most mutually beneficial offer.

Multiple simultaneous equivalent offers: See MESO.

Negotiating partner: The counterpart or organization involved in a negotiation, with whom terms are discussed, information is shared, and a mutually beneficial agreement is sought.

Negotiation process: A structured series of steps and interactions between parties aimed at reaching a mutual agreement.

Nonverbal language: Expressive signals such as gestures, facial expressions, posture, and proxemics used to communicate emotions, intentions, attitudes, and moods without words. It is a fundamental aspect of human communication.

Non-zero-sum games: Situations where participants can achieve an outcome greater than the sum of their individual gains, allowing mutual benefit. Game theory often uses such scenarios to study cooperative interactions and winning strategies.

Offer: A suggestion or offer for action or agreement made by one negotiating party to the other during negotiations. The proposal may relate to price, quantity, terms, or any other negotiable matter and represents a critical step in concluding the agreement.

Open questions: Questions that require more detailed and articulate answers than a simple "yes" or "no." In negotiation, open-ended questions are used to gather information; understand the other party's needs, interests, and priorities; and foster greater cooperation and mutual understanding.

Options: Choices available to the parties involved to solve a problem or reach an agreement. Options may include various proposals or alternatives explored during negotiation.

Overlay: A thin protective or decorative layer applied to the surface of a credit card.

Para-verbal language: Vocal characteristics in verbal communication, such as tone, rhythm, volume, intonation, and pauses. These elements influence the meaning of the message and can emphasize or modify the interpretation of verbal content.

Pareto principle (80/20 rule): A concept suggesting that 20 percent of causes generate 80 percent of effects.

Partner: A lawyer or professional who has reached the highest level in a law firm's hierarchy. Partners have managerial responsibilities, guide the work of other lawyers, participate in firm management, and share the firm's profits with other partners.

PDCA (Plan-Do-Check-Act): Also known as the Deming cycle, a cyclical management model used to improve processes and results. It includes planning actions, implementing them, verifying results, and taking corrective actions for continuous improvement. Commonly used in quality management and problem-solving.

PPE (personal protective equipment): Devices designed to protect workers' health and safety in hazardous environments. Examples include masks, goggles, gloves, helmets, and other protective gear suited to specific risks.

Policy: A set of rules, guidelines, or directives established by an organization to regulate members' behavior and actions. Policies may cover various aspects, such as security, ethics, privacy, or operational procedures, ensuring consistency and alignment with organizational goals and values.

Position: A statement outlining what a party wants in a negotiation.

Post-Settlement Settlement (PSS): A process in which parties, after reaching an agreement or signing a contract, identify opportunities to generate additional value.

Price: The monetary value or compensation demanded or offered for a product, service, or good being negotiated. Price is influenced by factors such as demand, supply, competition, and market conditions, and is a common negotiable item.

Private equity: Investments in unlisted companies through the purchase of controlling or minority interests, with the aim of increasing their value and reselling them at a profit. Private equity investors typically include investment companies, pension funds, and other financial institutions.

Probability: In statistics, the numerical measure of uncertainty associated with an event.

Reciprocity: The principle that parties tend to respond positively to favorable behavior by returning equivalent benefits.

Relationship: The interpersonal connection between negotiating parties, characterized by mutual trust, communication, and understanding. A strong relationship fosters cooperation and supports positive negotiation outcomes.

Representation: The ability to act on behalf of another party. This involves working for and making decisions on their behalf, either explicitly or implicitly, as governed by agency laws and rules.

Reserve price: The minimum acceptable price in a negotiation, representing the lower limit below which a party will not agree. This ensures the protection of a party's interests and goals.

Reserve value (RV): The point beyond which a party will not accept an agreement. It represents the minimum value or best alternative available if a satisfactory agreement is not reached.

Risk: The possibility of loss, damage, or undesirable outcomes arising from decisions made during negotiation.

Risk aversion: A preference to avoid high risks or losing control of a situation. This attitude often influences negotiation strategies, leading to more cautious and conservative decision-making.

Selective listening: Focusing only on specific information or topics that confirm one's beliefs or interests while ignoring other perspectives. In negotiation, this can hinder understanding and communication.

Standard: A value or set of values accepted as a reference for evaluating or defining a product, service, or contract.

Stereotype: An oversimplified and rigid generalization about a group of people or a situation. During a negotiation, stereotypes can influence perceptions, expectations, and behaviors, limiting the understanding and flexibility of the parties involved.

Strategy: A plan of action designed to achieve desired objectives during a negotiation. It involves analyzing information, choosing tactics, managing relationships, and adapting to negotiation dynamics to maximize results.

Tactics: Specific actions used by a party to influence the negotiation process or outcome and achieve its goals.

Take-or-pay: A clause requiring the buyer to purchase a defined quantity of goods from a seller on a specific date. If the buyer defaults, they must pay a fixed penalty, which is generally less than the full purchase price of the goods.

Tender: A formal process by which an organization solicits competitive proposals from suppliers interested in providing goods or services. These proposals are evaluated and selected based on specific criteria for awarding contracts.

Term Sheet: A document summarizing the main points and conditions of an agreement. It provides an overview of the negotiated terms, obligations of the parties, and other relevant clauses.

Ultimatum: A final statement or demand made by a party, often establishing a time limit for acceptance or rejection of specific conditions without the possibility of further negotiation or compromise.

Value: The utility or perceived benefit that parties attribute to negotiated items, such as goods, services, or contract terms. Value is subjective and can include aspects like quality, performance, timeliness, support, or cost savings.

Verbal language: The use of spoken language to communicate meaning and information. This includes the words chosen, tone of voice, sentence construction, and structure. Verbal communication is critical in negotiation, where understanding and clarity of terms are essential to achieving outcomes.

Zero-sum games: Situations where one participant's gain is equal to another's loss, resulting in a net outcome of zero. Game theory often uses this type of game to study interactions between participants and to develop winning strategies.

ZOPA (zone of possible agreement): The overlap between the buyer's best offer and the seller's lowest acceptable offer, within which both parties can agree to a deal.

Works Cited

Babcock, Linda and Sara Laschever. 2003. *Women Don't Ask.* Princeton University Press.

Carnegie, Dale. 2010. *How to Win Friends and Influence People.* Simon and Schuster.

Chance, Zoe. 2022. *Influence Is Your Superpower: The Science of Winning Hearts, Sparking Change, and Making Good Things Happen.* Random House Publishing Group.

Cialdini, Robert. 2021. *Influence: The Psychology of Persuasion.* Harper Business.

Ruiz, Don Miguel. 1997. *The Four Agreements: A Practical Guide to Personal Freedom.* Amber-Allen Publishing.

Collins, Jim. 2001. *Good to Great.* Harper Business.

Denes, Gianfranco. 2022. *La Mente di Pinocchio.* Il Pensiero Scientifico.

Dhawan, Erica. 2021. *Digital Body Language: How to Build Trust and Connection, No Matter the Distance.* St. Martin's Press.

Dinouart, Joseph A. 1989. *L'Arte di Tacere.* Sellerio Editore.

Freund, James C. 1975. *Anatomy of A Merger.* Law Journal Press.

Fisher, Roger, and Daniel Shapiro. 2016. *Beyond Reason: Using Emotions as You Negotiate.* Penguin Books.

Karrass, Chester L. 2013. *In Business as in Life, You Don't Get What You Deserve, You Get What You Negotiate*. Stanford Street Press.

King, Patrick. 2020. *Read People Like a Book*. Independent publication.

Kray, Laura J., Jessica A. Kennedy, and Alex B. Van Zant. 2014. "Not competent enough to know the difference? Gender stereotypes about women's ease of being misled predict negotiator deception." *Organizational Behavior and Human Decision Processes* 125 (2): 61–72.

Morrison, Terri. 2006. *Kiss, Bow, or Shake Hands*. Adams Media.

Moulton Marston, William. 2014. *Emotions of Normal People*. Read & Co. Science.

Raiffa, Howard. 1985. *The Art and Science of Negotiation: How to Resolve Conflicts and Get the Best Out of Bargaining*. Belknap Press.

Sinek, Simon. 2019. *The Infinite Game*. Penguin Business.

Surowiecki, James. 2005. *The Wisdom of Crowds*. Abacus.

Tversky, Amos, and Daniel Kahneman. 1982. *Judgment under Uncertainty: Heuristics and Biases*. Cambridge University Press.

Ury, William. 1993. *Getting Past No: Negotiating in Difficult Situations*. Bantam.

Ury, William, and Roger Fisher. 2011. *Getting to Yes: Negotiating Agreement Without Giving In*. Penguin Publishing Group.

About the Author

Pietro Parmeggiani is a renowned Italian manager and business leader who, with more than three decades of industry experience, has built a solid reputation as a skilled and meticulous negotiator.

Born in Rimini in 1966, he earned his master's degree in business management and economics from the University of Bologna. After graduation, he continued to refine his expertise by participating in professional development courses and attending graduate programs in negotiation leadership and mediation, including those at Harvard Law School Executive Education and Yale School of Management.

He began his career as a strategic consultant at Proxima, where he gained extensive knowledge of business dynamics. In 1995, he joined Lucchesi, and after a stellar career, he became managing director at the age of just thirty-two. He spent eight years in Asia as Director of CPPC, a business unit of the Thai conglomerate Charoen Pokphand Group. In this challenging role, he spearheaded efforts to position the company as a proactive and innovative industry leader. He also held leadership roles in plastics companies across Italy, Asia, and North America, successfully managing reorganizations, mergers, acquisitions, and exits.

In 2010, he became CEO of Bilcare Research (now Liveo Research, owned by Lindsay Goldberg), when the company was seeking a professional capable of executing ambitious turnarounds. Thanks to his experience and the efforts of an excellent team, the company was back on track within two years.

Pietro serves as a senior executive and board member across leading global manufacturing firms. In addition, he engages in consulting activities. His skills in situational analysis, persuasive communication, strategic planning, growth opportunity identification, and relationship-building have enabled him to create significant value for the organizations he has worked with.

His pragmatic, results-oriented approach has enabled him to negotiate multimillion-dollar business deals and resolve high-stakes business conflicts. With his academic knowledge, extensive practical experience, and charismatic leadership style, he is considered a genuine paragon in business management and negotiation.

You will find many valuable resources at his website www.negoziazione.academy. Through his platform, he shares a wealth of resources, including strategies and best practices for effective negotiation. The site also features tools, case studies, and insights tailored to empower individuals in mastering the art of negotiation.

Let's Keep in Touch

Dear Reader,

It is with immense joy that I address you, someone who has chosen to immerse yourself in the world of negotiation by navigating through the pages of my book.

First of all, I would like to thank you for your trust in and support of my work. To maintain the relationship established through this book, I have created a website dedicated to negotiation: **www.negoziazione.academy**. Here, you will find a wealth of resources on negotiation to further develop your knowledge of best practices, winning strategies, and emerging challenges. You can access exclusive materials and insights, as well as consult an up-to-date bibliography featuring the latest publications and studies on negotiation.

In addition to these resources, you can also request my professional consulting services through the site. After devoting years to the practice and study of negotiation, I am now a professional dedicated to using my skills and experience to assist those in need. My passion for negotiation drives me to share my knowledge and work with anyone striving to achieve extraordinary results.

I offer tailored programs for those looking to acquire or improve their negotiation skills, which are invaluable in all aspects of life. My services include two primary offerings:

Negotiation 365: I work alongside the client on an ongoing basis, supporting them in all their negotiations to achieve the best possible outcomes while helping them enhance their negotiation skills.

Effective Negotiation: Designed for those facing a critical negotiation, I provide targeted support. This includes analyzing the situation, devising winning strategies, and effectively managing the negotiation alongside the client.

I warmly invite you to visit my website, **www.negoziazione. academy**. It is a space where we can continue to grow together and learn from one another, preparing to face future challenges with determination. Explore the available resources and join the newsletter to stay updated on the latest content and opportunities.

And finally, thank you again for allowing me to be part of your learning journey regarding negotiation. If you wish, I will happily continue this adventure with you!

Acknowledgments

Thank you. Thank you very much!

The extraordinary journey that led to the creation of my first book on negotiation has come to an end, and I would like to express my sincere gratitude to all the people who made this achievement possible.

First, I want to thank Caterina, whose presence and unconditional support sustained me throughout the writing of this book. Her patience, advice, and love were invaluable in helping me move forward.

I also want to thank my daughters, Giulia and Alessia, for providing magical moments and constantly reminding me that no matter how complex a million-dollar negotiation with American and Asian businesspeople may be, it will never rival the ones I have with them.

Thank you, my family—Caterina, Giulia, and Alessia—for your trust, encouragement, and support at every critical stage of this ambitious project. Your love and support gave me the time and energy I needed to complete this work.

Special thanks go to my friends and colleagues Alessandra, Emanuele, Fabrizia, Federico, Francesco, Gianni, Marzia, Mirco, Patrizia, Pierluigi, and Vincenzo. Your invaluable advice, encouragement, and constant support during the writing process shaped the content of this book and made it more comprehensive and relevant.

I also wish to express my gratitude to those who have contributed to my development as a negotiator. A heartfelt thanks to my mentors, Franco, Gianfranco, and Marss, to the professors from Harvard and Yale, and to the industry experts who shared their wisdom and experiences, enabling me to refine my skills and broaden my perspective on negotiation.

Additionally, I extend my thanks to all the authors whose works I have avidly studied. Your texts have enriched my knowledge, inspired me, and guided me along the path of growth. Each author has uniquely contributed to my understanding of the science and art of negotiation, and for that, I am sincerely grateful.

Special thanks also go to my readers, for whom this book was written. I hope these pages provide you with valuable knowledge, inspiration, and new perspectives on negotiation. You are the reason this work has meaning and purpose.

I am deeply grateful to all the professionals and non-professionals who have shared their success stories and lessons learned during negotiations. Thank you for inspiring me with your successes, failures, and unique experiences. I hope your voices resonate through these pages and inspire future negotiators.

Finally, I extend my gratitude to the teams at Agenzia Dedalo and First Editing, who worked tirelessly to ensure this book achieved its goals. Thank you for your dedication, professionalism, and attention to detail. With your efforts, this book has become a reality.

In conclusion, I want to thank everyone who, in one way or another, helped make this book possible.

I hope to inspire all those who wish to begin their journey of learning, refine their negotiation skills, and reach new heights of success.

Thank you for being part of this extraordinary journey.

With gratitude,

Pietro

www.ingramcontent.com/pod-product-compliance
Lightning Source LLC
Chambersburg PA
CBHW071319210326
41597CB00015B/1277

* 9 7 9 8 9 9 3 6 8 6 4 4 8 *